EX LIBRIS

By the same author

What Not to Expect When You're Expecting
The Madness of Modern Parenting

zoe
williams

get it
together

Why We Deserve Better Politics

HUTCHINSON
LONDON

1 3 5 7 9 10 8 6 4 2

Hutchinson
20 Vauxhall Bridge Road
London SW1V 2SA

Hutchinson is part of the Penguin Random House group of
companies whose addresses can be found at
global.penguinrandomhouse.com.

Penguin
Random House
UK

First published in Great Britain by Hutchinson in 2015

www.randomhouse.co.uk

A CIP catalogue record for this book is
available from the British Library.

ISBN 9780091959012

Printed and bound by Clays Ltd, St Ives Plc

MIX
Paper from
responsible sources
FSC® C018179

Penguin Random House is committed to a
sustainable future for our business, our readers
and our planet. This book is made from Forest
Stewardship Council® certified paper.

This book is dedicated to my mother, Gwen

Contents

Contents

Who am I, to think things like this?

If you can do a full-time job and not be sure at the end of it that you can afford shelter, food and warmth, then there is something wrong with your employer, your housing market, your food supply, your utilities' ownership structure or, most likely, all four. This is a fact that is at least as old as the Industrial Revolution. A state in which people cannot afford necessities is not a lean, competitive one; it is a state that is primitive and failing.

(Deep breath.) My name's Zoe and I'm middle-class; through and through, not even upwardly mobile, with a working-class hinterland. I don't worry about heating, because my wages are high and my housing stock is sound, and I don't worry about housing, because I'm 41. Yet the 15-years-younger me cannot afford what I could at the turn of the century. And in 2030 she will not, if we continue in this direction, live as I do. An unequal society that keeps afloat on the hardship of a solid bed of poverty is bad in its own particular way, but that's not what we're looking at here.

There was a way of living that we used to consider normal: we all went to school, some of us went on to university; we tried hard, though we didn't make a big thing of it. We didn't have to justify every second of education, or even every term, by the employable skill it delivered. Then we came out with a degree, got an entry-level job – a job that we got paid money for, by the way, even though we were inexperienced – and hoped to be earning about 30 grand by the time we were around 30. Some people would then peel off, others would stall. The understanding of what it was to be middle-class was that you'd open a pension pot, start saving for a house and buy one, then have kids when you were relatively secure. In fact this was the understanding of what it was to be normal: whether you went to university or not, even the young deserved to be paid; just because you're under 25 doesn't mean you bring no value to the workplace, or that you can live on air. Even non-graduate jobs should have some progression up the ranks, given that you get better at them. The aristocracy is the only place I've ever witnessed unemployment as a lifestyle choice, yet the aristocracy remains fixated on the idea that it's how we would all live, if we could. I must say, it doesn't make them very happy, but they get by.

What else did we all think? That you should be able to retire at 65. You should be able to afford your own house or, if you couldn't, you should be able to rely on the stability of your rented house, be able to afford it, as well as be able to feed your children on the income that you make from working full-time. Even though there have been times in recent history – 1996, 2003 – when these things were no longer a given for everybody, you wouldn't have found any of this promised in a political manifesto. It would have been like promising freedom of religious belief, or clean air. These things were as natural, observable, inevitable and proper as a caterpillar turning into a butterfly.

These expectations, to a graduate, a student or a NEET (Not in Education, Employment or Training) today, must read like the claw-game in an amusement arcade: they know how it's meant to work; they know that, if you put the coin in, concentrate, have a bit of luck and perseverance, you should get the prize; but they also know that it's rigged. Nobody believes in any of these truths any more, for the simple reason that they are no longer true. Wages have stagnated at every point on the pay spine, except for the very top. Jobs are now very insecure; only one in 40 new jobs is full-time.[1] Employers see how long they can keep exploiting graduates by calling them 'volunteers' instead of 'interns'. 21 per cent of people need a cash benefit in order to afford their rent.[2] One million people have used a food bank in the past year.[3] The number of children with rickets has trebled since 2009.[4] Average house prices have risen to ten times average salaries. Exactly how much you could save for a pension, if it took until your forties to pay off your student loan, is a moot point.

It appears that the rules have changed. Some people blame the baby-boomers, some blame immigrants, and everybody, to an extent, blames politicians, but none of it sticks. There is a lot of anger but no agenda and, without it, Westminster forges on unopposed, a wall of suits squabbling with one another, breaking off intermittently to tell us that they're doing things the only way things can be done.

Politics goes through phases – sometimes too fleeting to mean anything, sometimes too trivial to matter, sometimes too tub-thumping, and they just sound over-tired. Since the financial wreck of 2008, politics has veered radically to the right. Mean and suspicious, all brainstem and no frontal lobe, the paranoia of the new rules leads down blind alleys to comically dead-end conclusions. Every day the conversations about things that matter start from a weirder premise: it could be that growth is the only important thing for the country, and the party that returns us to growth is the party of good sense and sound stewardship. But . . . what is the point of growth, if the fruits of it are only delivered to the top, and living standards are still falling?

It could be that businesses are 'wealth creators', and must be lightly regulated, delivered from red tape, enticed with tax breaks and, above all, revered, otherwise they may leave and take all the wealth with them. But go where? Financial services, even though they cause havoc and produce nothing, are 'wealth creators'. But what if the business is paying no tax and ratcheting down wages to their lowest legal degree, for the sake of shareholders who don't care about the business and only care about the return? What then? Still the best we've got, unfortunately.

Or: the economy went bust because the last government was too generous with its social security; unemployed people were lazy; or, sometimes, British people were not objectively lazy, just relatively lazy, when placed next to Polish people ... Either way, the crash was the fault of the poor, indigenous or foreign or, by proxy, the fault of the government for not being tough enough on the poor.

Sometimes: the eurozone crashed because Greek people didn't pay taxes, and French people's employment conditions were too secure, and Spanish people siesta.

Other times: the whole global economy seized up because poor people's debts were sold under false pretences to rich people – so the real problem, underneath the derivatives market, was all those poor Americans, demanding to live in houses they couldn't afford.

Occasionally: we spent so much money on public programmes that the private sector simply gave up. Government spending 'crowded out' good, honest businesses. What does it actually mean? It means that by giving away cancer drugs for free, we stifled all those entrepreneurs who could otherwise have sold them. And that's apparently a bad thing, because everybody knows that everything touched by the state turns into an expensive failure.

All roads lead back to poor people; we caught poverty off poor people, like a common cold. We could solve all this by putting some rich people back in charge.

We know that's not how the debt was created. We know there was a financial crash, and it was caused by activity in the shadow economy, of which almost no poor people (give or take the odd academic) had any inkling. This is all so unjust it takes your breath away, like rubbing the nose of a cat in a mess that, in plain sight with everyone watching, the dog did.

The word 'unsustainable' is bandied about, but rarely used about anything of which we may genuinely run out: fresh water; oil; coltan, the conflict mineral. Rather, healthcare is unsustainable; fire services and adult social care are unsustainable; the Human Rights Act is unsustainable. It is weird, because we built those things with effort, creativity and imagination – qualities as limitlessly replenishable as the species itself. Yet somehow (what a downer!) we have recently managed to exhaust them.

It is frequently given as fact that renewable-energy sources are just an incredibly expensive waste of time that vegetarians like, somewhere between avocados and homeopathy. And that fossil fuels, for all that the mainstream accepts their destructive potential, are just the way of things: the classic mainstream position holds in bizarre equilibrium the belief that climate change is happening, with the acceptance that large corporations will do whatever makes them money, and the Devil take the future. Even though they have grandchildren, too. And apparently that is okay. Because . . . business.

The main obstacle to a decent education, these days, is the regiment of lazy teachers, who went into education to foster mediocrity for reasons . . . I don't know what their reasons are supposed to be. A lot of these ideas are simply stated as common sense, and not developed. Better candidates to run schools would be business folk, because – having made money – they have proven themselves to be proper people.

People – especially immigrants, women and those with a disability, I can't help but notice – are crunched down into the economically productive and the unproductive. A huge amount of discussion is about how to get those in the latter category to rejoin the former: fund their childcare? Send them home? Kick away their fake walking stick? I'm waiting for some UKIP candidate to suggest that we make the unproductive sew on some kind of badge.

Markets are everything; whatever we do, we must not frighten the markets – not with tough talk, not with democratic demands. Maybe banks behave badly, but what do you expect? They're just exhibiting the self-interest that keeps the whole lot of us afloat.

Why doesn't the blindingly obvious cause of the problem – a financial sector that blew all the money, on japes, wheezes, bad calls and their own salaries – trouble the conservatives? Because it gave them the one thing they really needed to win: it gave them a shortage. It doesn't actually matter why, because asking what caused it won't bring the money back. There it is. There is no money left.

Therefore we need austerity.

Therefore generosity is over.

Therefore every decision has to be 'What's the cheapest?' 'We'd love to look at it some other way,' runs 'common sense' in its current incarnation, 'but those conversations, about human beings, about the environment, about social justice, about quality of life . . . those all belong to the days when we still had money.'

Some days I am simply awestruck at the elegance and coordination of this new worldview, the way that it all links up, not just in our politics, but across Europe, all the way to America. Did they spend a decade in a bunker, figuring all this out? It didn't do any harm, of course, that we've lived through 30 years of politics that held money as the highest value, on the basis that we were in a 'post-ideological' landscape and, post-ideology, all there is to believe in is the stuff you can count.

However it's actually not that hard, once you have a set of principles, to make all your arguments work in harmony. Their principles – that self-interest creates good markets, that states get in the way of good markets, that good markets will provide and will make us all richer, and that markets, however raked they look, will ultimately tend towards more equality, not less – lead inexorably, very simply, to all their policies, across the debt-stricken developed world.

But there are principles on the other side, too; the advantage on the left is a set of beliefs that are actually true, and observable in real life. People do sometimes act in their own self-interest, but mainly on quite trivial matters. Self-interest is, if you like, the fingernail of the body politic; it exists, and life would be inconvenient and even slightly painful without it. The beating heart is something else entirely. Everything important, we do together. Every real effort we make is for one another.

The wellspring of left-wing thought is not hatred of the rich, but the knowledge that the profit motive doesn't come close to what we're really about; a belief that most of us won't be happy prospering if we think it's at the cost of another person's penury ... and that it's a moot point anyway, because in the long or even medium run, most of us won't prosper in the rat-race.

The data proves the power of these arguments like iron filings clustering to a magnet; but we don't make enough of the magnet itself: the magnetism of society, we social creatures working together, beavering away, creating a landscape that we're proud to look at.

We are driven to look after one another not by

legislation, but because that's all we really care about; we are driven to acts of greatness not by competition, but by empathy; we unleash the best of our minds in the service of each other. Markets don't tend towards equality; they tend towards a social injustice that, over time, becomes grotesque. There is nothing inherently incompetent about the state: it is our pooled sovereignty, there to protect us from predators; it is as good or bad as we can be bothered to make it.

Market fundamentalism is stupid: there is nothing wrong with a bit of honest, profit-based competition when you're trying to thrash out who sells the best Martini, but not when you're trying to answer questions that relate to justice, generosity and the future. And those are the questions that matter.

The story of human progress is the story of generosity – we have shared our ideas, and shared our resources to make them happen, and that's how we made discoveries and leapt forward. The idea that we were all hefted to each new level by some plucky industrialist who philanthropically created all the wealth and then allowed it to disperse: that idea is incorrect. It sits at the centre of almost all arguments for inequality, but unfortunately that doesn't make it any more correct.

The story of human prosperity, meanwhile, is the story of justice: the only reason we've ever been able to invest anything, build anything, share our resources for any plan for the future is that we have found ways to make promises and keep them.

None of this alters very much over time. We are as generous and just as we have ever been; we are the same people who created the NHS, who abolished slavery and child labour, who brought in National Insurance, who fought for our civic spaces and our civilised laws. There is nothing modern about dismantling the social safety net, nothing modern at all. People have been fighting for squalor, and for poverty, and for workhouses, pretty much since the moment anybody started fighting against them.

The wealth of a country is in its people – we don't have anything else; we don't have copper mines and, even if we did, heavy industry could not hold a candle to what the citizenry is worth, and can produce, given the chance. The economy is here to serve us, we're not here as meat for the economy. The idea that you might find some political system that created growth, but resulted in a huge amount of hardship, for people who couldn't afford education, who had to be badly paid, who had to live in squalor, and yet that was somehow a good outcome because growth had been achieved: that idea is nuts. Not even the most red-blooded capitalists ever conceived of growth as a good thing for its own sake. The only point of anything – any economic policy, any social endeavour – is to create the conditions in which people can flourish.

Markets are social spaces; they need morals as much as any other space where people meet each other. Often, even quite sober commentators use phrases like 'gangster capitalism' and 'gangster finance', to describe the normal, everyday ways in which banks and corporations screw their customers and screw one another. This cannot become the new normal: we can't just shrug and say, 'That's a global system for you'. A system that isn't founded on honest principles is just a heist.

We have the technology to answer the pressing environmental questions; or, at least, the technology to bridge our needs while we figure out the rest. All we need is for stupid people not to be in charge.

What's stopping you from feeling hopeful? What's suffocating the idea that things could be different? Is it, by any chance, thinking that nothing real can happen outside Westminster and, inside it, nobody wants anything real to happen? Is it thinking that politicians are getting worse: more cynical, less ambitious? Is it worrying that everything outside parliamentary democracy – clicktivism, protests, consumer boycotts, crowd-sourced outrage – is all just a smokescreen, an anaesthetic, a meaningless diversion to counter a sense of generalised impotence?

What movement ever originated in Parliament? What great achievement, what civic moment, ever started as a conversation between one MP and another? Not one, not ever. We do not have to wait until we have permission for change. We do not have to wait for a decree to be handed down from the universe. We do not have to wait for a Private Members' Bill, or a rogue lord to say a halfway-decent thing. We do not have to wait for the mood music to change, for the atmosphere to become more generous. We do not have to wait until economists tell us it's okay to get involved and ask questions about what is being done in the name of the numbers. We do not have to wait until the coast is clear. We do not have to wait to be invited in, like vampires. We do not have to wait until we have framed some demands that are modest enough to be taken seriously.

It's easy to feel powerless, but you don't lack power, and nor do I. Irresistible power is when we all start going in the same direction. What do we want the future to look like?

Does poverty still exist?

I took my kids on a playdate and ended up sitting at a table with a hedge-fund manager, a currency trader, his wife (a woman who works for Deutsche Bank) and another guy in private equity.

I'm not trying to pretend that this company was beyond my wildest dreams and I was pressing my nose against its rarefied glass like an urchin. There's nothing to stop me moving in circles like this, except that I find them boring, and they find me loud and probably boring as well. My kids never clean their plates, so I was looking around the kitchen for somewhere to throw the scraps. We live in the same borough, Lambeth, so even though I was outside my social comfort zone, I knew my way around their local authority recycling protocols.

'Where's your food bin?'

'Food bin . . .' said the hedge-fund manager, the owner of the house. There was a quizzical pause.

'Yes. You know. It's a little bin, and you put food waste in it. Then the council takes it away.'

'And then what happens to it?' said the currency trader. 'Do they give it to the poor?'

I used to tell people that story all the time, for about a week after it happened. And then I stopped, because they all said one of two things. Some said, 'Are you sure he wasn't joking?', as if the possibility of irony might only float into my consciousness a week later, via a third person. (I mean, he wasn't joking. I can tell when people are joking. But even if he was, what kind of joke is that? 'Poor people eat eggshells and chicken bones, given to them by the council.' Indeed, if he had been joking, that might have been worse than the fact that he wasn't.) The others said, 'Why didn't you walk out?' That left me absolutely stumped. If someone makes a sudden remark that jolts the mask, and allows you to see round its edges the extent of their lack of interest in other people's hardship, are you allowed to just stomp off? What would you say? 'You, sir, are not interested in equality!' Seems so rude.

A totalitarian slum

To some people, inequality is not just a fact they're prepared to tolerate; it is an end in itself, a useful spur to progress: as Keith Joseph, advisor to Margaret Thatcher, once wrote, 'Making the rich poorer does not make the poor richer, but it does make the state stronger ... The pursuit of income equality will turn this country into a totalitarian slum.'[1]

Joseph's position is wrong, as we will see shortly; not wrong in my opinion, but factually incorrect. Yet this thinking is tenacious. It stems from the idea that superior people must be allowed to get on with things. They must be enabled to accrue all the wealth they want; otherwise they wouldn't be incentivised to engage their superior brains. It's pretty circular – 'How do I know I'm superior? Well, look at all my wealth. How did I come about my wealth? Well, dur, with my superiority.' And the value system is riven with contradictions. Rich people always claim not to be motivated by money, while at the same time maintaining that, if anything happened to interrupt their cash-flow, their creativity would be snuffed out.

Their double-standards are not our problem; the problem is that this position leads to some pretty extreme views. If wealth is merely the outward symptom of personal excellence, then poverty is a sign that you are rubbish. Since those people only came to be poor by being inferior in the first place, it stands to reason that they would want to eat used teabags. When you believe inequality to be a good thing, you expect poor people to be less intelligent and less industrious than you are; then the fact that you rarely meet them keeps that fantasy aloft.

This is the one part of the picture that makes perfect sense; a small cadre of people at the top doesn't care about poverty. The entire basis for their lives and the way they live them is that some people are simply better than others. They may take a philanthropic interest – they probably don't want to see people starve to death – but as far as they're concerned, there is nothing wrong with a system in which some people are extremely poor. I completely get why they're not interested in having this conversation. The real mystery is: what happened to the rest of us?

Poverty is a thing in this country. The UK is the most financially unequal country in Northern Europe, containing the richest area – inner London – and fully nine of the ten poorest areas (the only one of the bottom ten not in the UK is Hainaut, in Belgium).[2] The poorest 20 per cent in the UK are poorer than any of their equivalents in North-western Europe (closer to the poor of Slovenia and the Czech Republic).[3] Average wages have dropped 4 per cent since 2010,[4] and had been flat since 2003. Since 2008, real median weekly wages – income determined by its purchasing power; that is, a calculation of wages relative to prices – have fallen by 10.2 per cent[5]: only wages in Greece have fallen by more (granted, quite a lot more: 23 per cent). Our train fares are the highest in Europe, we have the second-highest levels of fuel poverty. Don't get me started on housing (see Housing). As of 2014, after housing costs, 14.6 million people were in poverty[6] – this is 23.2 per cent of the population, and 3.5 million of them are children (this is slightly over one in four kids). One in five families cannot afford a trip to their nearest beach.[7] 900,000 people went to the Trussell Trust in 2013 alone for food;[8] and this is not the only food-bank chain in the country.

Poverty in this country has been rising since the 1980s. We've been patching it up with personal debt, which went up three and a half times faster than national income in between 1977 and 2008.[9] But all of us – from the Office for Budget Responsibility, to the Centre for Social Justice (a right-wing think-tank), to the Resolution Foundation (a left-wing think-tank), to the Churches, to the food banks, to the schools, to the activists, to the person standing behind the person at a cashpoint who's freaking out – we all know this problem is there. It is like a suppurating wound; it hurts, and often we can smell it. Yet something stops us from taking off the dressing and having a proper look.

Don't complain until you're dead

Conservatives who like to style themselves 'caring' won't talk about poverty because they don't think it's real. Authentic poverty, to them, is the international measure of living on $1.25 a day; it's the difference between being able to afford clean water and losing your children to cholera. It's the gulf between subsistence and aspiration, the 50 cents between just about holding it together so that you don't starve and getting at least one of your children to a point of literacy. That is true poverty, and anything else going by the name is a masquerade.

Don't complain that you're hungry until you're starving. Don't complain about workplace conditions until you're in Bangladesh and a building has fallen on your head. In other words, don't complain until you're dead. You see a lot of this in feminism as well, incidentally – 'How dare you Western feminists talk about the pay gap when there are women in Sudan being raped on their way to a water-butt?'

Now, it's not entirely on the money because, since the recession, people have starved to death in this country. A woman and her baby boy died of hunger in Westminster, within one mile of Parliament, in 2010. A 44-year-old man named Mark Wood died in Oxfordshire, in 2013, after his benefits were stopped because Atos Healthcare declared him fit for work; he weighed exactly five and a half stone. But in both these cases there were other factors: the mother had a brain infection; Mark Wood had a number of phobias, as well as Asperger's syndrome. It would still, in this era, be quite difficult for a person in perfect health to die from lack of food. This doesn't seem to me like a very grand statement for the twenty-first century, but I don't dispute it. The 'straight-talking' right – embodied for me in the person of Edwina Currie – also loves to ask how it is that people who use food banks can ever be overweight. It's actually really easy to be malnourished and overweight, by a combination of cortisol, stimulated by scarcity, changing your palate (making you overeat when food is there, and also eat the wrong foods), and sugar, having been overeaten, changing your appetite mechanisms. But I am bored of explaining that to the right-wing, because they're so in love with the simplicity of their observation that they will not listen.

Anyway, back to the point: we no longer measure poverty by how many of a person's ribs we can count, or how many of their children they have lost to disease. Instead we say someone is in 'relative' poverty if their income is 60 per cent of the average at any given time; and we say they are in 'absolute' poverty if their income is below 60 per cent of the average as it was measured in a particular year – currently, the median in 2011/12.

So relative poverty goes up and down with the median income; the numbers in relative poverty actually reduce during recessions, because the median income has come down. This is deliberate: relative poverty is a sociological measure, to gauge how many people are being excluded, by their low incomes, from doing the normal things that everyone else does. However, this makes the right dismiss it as a 'political' calculation rather than a factual one.

Absolute poverty, on the other hand, is designed to be a measure of whether or not you can afford basic things: are you skipping meals so that your children can eat? Are you choosing between heating and eating? This really is much closer to the right-wing notion of poverty – can you, or can you not, keep body and soul together? – but here there's a fresh element of scepticism. Most politicians underestimate how much it costs to live. We know that instinctively, which is why we always ask MPs how much milk is, and they can never answer. But it's nothing to do with political myopia – it's just money. The richer people are, the less accurate their estimates of basic expenses. It's not their fault. Budgeting is a use-it-or-lose-it muscle. They don't have to check the cost of what's in their basket; a natural optimism bias makes them think it probably all costs about what it cost last time they checked, in 1997.

This is what led Iain Duncan Smith to say, in April 2013, when asked if he could live on £53 a week, 'I could if I had to' (half a million people then signed an online petition asking him to prove it; he declined). He simply couldn't; but I'm not in any doubt that he genuinely thinks he could.

The week of that IDS story, I lived on £53 a week for an article. It was a cheat – it wasn't even commissioned until Tuesday night, so I only did half a week: seven quid a day *pro rata*. I left the kids out of it, because nothing used to annoy me more in my own childhood than being roped into one of my mother's 'eat for a pound a day to help the children of Africa' wheezes. I was thinking it would be easy. I'd cycle everywhere. I'd eat rice and lentils. I thought the main challenge was going to be writing an honest diary, while trying to reflect sensitively upon the experience of someone without my social capital (my bike, my bills all paid, my phone on a contract, the ability to leave the kids out of it). In fact, it was absolutely impossible. I nearly fainted on the second day because I was trying to cycle on insufficient food. So I blew two quid on a Lucozade, which I had no idea would be two quid, and still felt too light-headed to get on the bike. By that time public transport wouldn't have got me to school on time for pick-up, so I had to get a cab. Excellent reportage; attempting to live on 53 quid a week, I blew £32 in 40 minutes. Oh, and I didn't lose any weight, incidentally; even though I was so hungry that I almost passed out.

And this is the problem the left has, with talking about poverty. Even though I was more sympathetic than IDS, I had a no more realistic impression of poverty than he did. I broadly assume that the experts are right – the Joseph Rowntree Foundation and the Child Poverty Action Group – but I haven't actually had to count the money down the back of the sofa since I had a County Court Judgment against me for unpaid credit-card debt in 1995. There are not enough poor voices in the public domain. You'll get poor families appearing as case studies in a report done by a Not-Poor-Person, but you simply will not get that unmediated, human voice, directed right at you, describing what it's like.

Those of us who are not poor are embarrassed by everything – talking about the poor as a separate species is skin-crawlingly awkward. Yet pretending that some of your best friends are poor is almost as embarrassing and, furthermore, probably a lie. There's some confusion over whether well-meaning people are even allowed to say the word 'poor', whether it's an insult. I've seen graphs of educational attainment in which the 'disadvantaged' are plotted against the 'non-disadvantaged' – not only do we not say 'poor' any more, but we're not even allowed to say that rich people have advantages.

Talking about poverty funnels you down one of two paths – either a piteous one, where you come over as the embodiment of soft-hearted Victoriana, the industrialist's wife in the high-necked blouse, hanging by the factory gates, cooing, 'Look at their dirty children! Look at their tired eyes!' Or a political path, whereupon starts up the chorus of 'If you care so much, why don't you give away all your money?' (I never heard an answer as good as Julie Burchill's: 'In the long term, I'm a communist. But in the meantime, you're not just having mine.')

Who cares about inequality if it makes us all richer?

A key principle has been lost, or forgotten: other people's welfare is my business, and your business. You don't have to be in a situation to talk about that situation. You don't have to be of a class to ask questions about the conditions of that class. It isn't patronising or intrusive or hypocritical to say, 'That person's income is not high enough.' It is okay to talk about poverty even if you've never been poor.

Nevertheless, a lot of people prefer to talk about inequality, and I can see why, since it shifts the focus and makes it less personal, more of a systems

23

error. It doesn't matter how much you earn, if you're talking about inequality; it doesn't matter how much your poor-friend-who-isn't-really-your-friend earns. Inequality is measured by international bodies, recorded in indexes with decimal points; nobody need become emotional – it's just maths.

Here, though, you will get ideological pushback by people who say: who cares about inequality, if it makes everybody richer? 'Inequality of wealth and incomes is the cause of the masses' well-being,' wrote the economist Ludwig von Mises in 1955, 'not the cause of anybody's distress.'[10] I want to be really clear about why this is wrong, otherwise it ends up sounding like an argument about why I'm upset because someone else has a Porsche and I don't think my children will be able to afford one.

Money is never just money

Inequality is not bad because some people end up with too much; if an aristocrat could own a postcode or a dictator could have gold taps without that causing any damage to the society around them, I wouldn't care. Nor do I buy the notion that the world has a finite amount of money, and a rich person snatching too much necessitates a poor person going without. That is not true – money is weird (more in Finance) – and, anyway, it's not the point. The problem with inequality is that it fatally weakens your bargaining power. The poorer you are, the more dependent you are on your job, and the more you have to roll over to the whim of your employer, however outrageous that is.

This has been the story of wage stagnation in the UK, and in the US; and, indeed, of everywhere that wages have failed to reflect growth. First, a right-wing government destroys the power of the unions. Membership goes down. The proportion of British workers in unions has halved in the past three decades.[11]

The weaker your union movement, the greater the share of national prosperity that goes to your top 1 per cent, and the greater the inequality;[12] the reason is really straightforward. Unions bargain, collectively, for pay increases. The output of any enterprise is divided between pay and profit. If no-one fights for pay, then an ever-greater proportion goes to profit, and that's exactly what we've seen. The workforce received between 58 and 64 per cent of output, all the way from the end of the Second World War until the late 1970s. Since then it has declined to its current 51 per cent. But even that doesn't tell the whole story, because it includes in 'pay' the wages of the CEO, which are immense and should, realistically, be classed as profits. You can't seriously think of a £7 million salary as an indication of how hard that CEO worked. There aren't enough hours in the day. The CEO's wage can only really be understood as a cut of the profit, to spur him on to prioritise shareholders over employees.

Over that period we've started to talk about an hourglass jobs market, in which there are jobs at the top, jobs at the bottom, and nothing in the middle. Since 2009 almost all of the new jobs 'created' have been in self-employment (where people are paying themselves atrociously) or in low-productivity sectors. During this government, only one in 40 new jobs has a legit, full-time contract. Of course, some middling jobs are made obsolete by technological advance. But don't accept this too readily: that we just have to get used to a new world in which there is plentiful low-skilled work, which will always be of low value and will be paid a small amount. These aren't laws of the physical universe; these are merely decisions about how money is distributed; decisions that are made increasingly in favour of the shareholder, as the shareholder increases in wealth and power. That's the problem with inequality.

Who are you calling low-skilled?
So, for instance, a corporation might get a contract to run a prison and decide that being a prison officer is low-skilled work. It gets people with few qualifications, and doesn't invest in training. Those POs are then paid low wages, where in the past this was a 30-grand job, with prospects, career development and kudos.

A job that previously would have been 'middle-class' now, in likelihood, requires supplementary benefits from the government in order for that person to pay their rent. It's expensive for the state and it immiserates the employee (not to mention the prisoners), and for what? So that the shareholders can make more money. There is nothing modern or inevitable about this. It's nothing to do with global rebalancing or technology. It's a straight split between labour and profit.

The depleted strength of the unions shows itself in other ways: a lack of dignity in the way employees are treated; a lack of trust in their probity. The first time I noticed anything was in 2005 (though it was old news in supermarkets by then), when the GMB union lodged an objection to the fact that AA call-centre workers were being treated 'like battery hens'. What caught my attention was when the AA announced 'dataveillance', which meant that employees would be tagged, to make sure they had a maximum of 82 minutes away from their computers in a given day. Taking out an hour for lunch and a 15-minute break, this essentially budgeted their loo-breaks to seven minutes. I rang the press office, to see whether the AA made any exemptions – say, if you were allowed to announce, whenever you got in, that you had constipation. The lady was extremely offended, but that's the Victorian worker model in a nutshell: treat everyone like shit, and then expire with horror when they actually say, or even hint at, the word 'shit'.

It all seemed pretty droll at the time – the result of some efficiency brainstorm by a roomful of MBA graduates, never likely to amount to anything, still less to last. But since then things have become really unpleasant. The AA's tagging no longer looks either amusing or notable. There is no way I would get that story into the newspaper now, because this kind of practice is so widespread. As the US journalist Barbara Demick notes, 'Being a low-wage worker means being robbed by the very employer who is monitoring you so insistently for theft.'[13] Amazon tags its employees to make sure they're moving across the warehouse fast enough; it constantly checks and rechecks their bags. Cineworld in Wandsworth makes its staff walk around with clipboards saying 'Here to help', as though they're incapable of conveying this by setting their face into a helpful expression. Pure Healthcare in Bournemouth makes its employees sign a zero-hours contract with an exclusivity clause, for minimum-wage work that includes their accommodation. If they want to leave before six months are up, they have to keep on paying for their room, but are not allowed to live in it. In the Costa Coffee in Channon retail park I saw an advert for a job of no more than 16 hours, for which prospective candidates had to be free from 6 a.m. till 9 p.m., seven days a week. I met a woman in the Newcastle station Starbucks kiosk who'd come into work for a one-hour shift.

I can only say any of this because they are things I've seen with my own eyes, heard with my own ears: there is no transparency from the companies themselves. They have no obligation to tell you anything, and so they don't. Freedom of Information requests don't mean squat to Cineworld. I went back to the AA today to see if it still did dataveillance, or whether – per my expectations – its attempt at control had been thwarted by the undulations of human bowel health. This was the AA's reply: 'I can't give you any figures, but the way we monitor and measure our contact-centre operations is in line with standard industry best practice.'

I don't even know what that means, to be honest. I didn't ask for any figures. I just asked whether or not they still practised 'dataveillance'. Maybe everyone checks their employees' loo breaks. Is that what they call best practice?

The way these jobs are structured now, classic unionisation wouldn't even work. There are 1.4 million zero-hours contracts in the country.[14] This corresponds exactly to the number of people who, in 2013, reported that they would like to work more hours than they were given.[15] Buckingham Palace advertises for zero-hours staff, as does the Palace of Westminster when it places an ad for a Hansard reporter.[16] All these jobs would once have been counted as decent, solid employment – maybe not a dream, but certainly a goal. They are now jobs in which people are kept deliberately insecure in order that they never build up rights or confidence; that they can never plan for how they're going to get to the end of the month. How could a union fight for you, in these conditions? The employer wouldn't even join you on the battlefield; they just wouldn't give you another shift.

So that's the problem with inequality, from a

human point of view. It also carries an untenable economic burden, which is what makes Keith Joseph and von Mises wrong, even by the lights of their own moral stage. When massive corporations pay wages so low that they impoverish their staff, they erode their own customer base. 65 per cent of GDP (gross domestic product) comes from consumer spending. If your consumers can't spend because they're also your employees, this puts a serious dent in your business model.

When a pay rise is not a pay rise

As misguided as alchemists, the Labour government tried to simulate equality by boosting pay packets with in-work tax credits. Ed Balls came into the *Guardian* offices partway through this Coalition term, to give an 'I'm still alive' briefing. He said, with a mischief that I must say I found endearing, 'What we did with Working Families' Tax Credits was the biggest back-door redistribution a government has ever done.'

Er . . . yes and no. New Labour brought people out of poverty with what they called a 'tax credit', but is more properly understood as an in-work benefit, a governmental supplement to an income which they saw was too low. But it wasn't a redistribution, unless you mean redistributing money from middle-weight taxpayers towards the lower-middle and the bottom. What they were effectively doing was subsidising corporate super-profits.

A group of supermarkets, keeping a workforce of nearly one million people on poverty pay, would, in a normal world, soon enough reap the consequences of that in declining sales and, possibly, protests.[17] But if the pay packets are topped up by the state, the sales keep coming in and the protests never happen.

Advisors from the Blair era get furious when you talk about low wages. They say, 'You can't hope to solve the problem of poverty with wages. The world is too complicated now. There is too much else to consider.' 'What else?' you might ask. 'Housing. Family size.' Well, yes, the housing market is messed up, too. But family size? As a reason that a salary can no longer be expected to cover a life? Do they think we're stupid?

Funnily enough, we've tried this before. The Speenhamland system was devised in Berkshire in 1795, by a group of local magistrates worried about workers who, through a combination of low wages and high grain prices, couldn't afford to eat.[18] They really meant well, as is so often the case with magistrates; they came up with the idea that wages would be topped up by the parish, according to the price of bread and the number of children in the family. Substitute 'bread' with 'housing' and you pretty much have New Labour's entire benefit system (except for the fact that the Speenhamland magistrates never did a massive accidental overpayment, then try to get the money back from a load of poor people who'd already spent it).

It took about 30 years at the start of the nineteenth century for people to realise that this was a 'universal system of pauperism', one that enabled – indeed, seemed to be devised for – employers to underpay and food producers to overcharge, without having to suffer the consequences of their community starving or rebelling, or simply not turning up to work. It's coming up for 15 years since the start of the Working Families' Tax Credit. We must be twice as quick on the uptake as the people of the 1800s, surely? We have the Internet.

If governments can mask the effects of poverty pay, so too can debt, but not for ever – and the overhang of debt from the boom years has made poverty at the bottom even more painful than it would normally be. Three and a half million households in the UK are spending more than a quarter of their gross income on debt repayments.[19]

The past three or four years have seen very determined attempts to turn the poor into some kind of circus act of dysfunctionality, their tough lives a consequence of moral degeneration and personal inadequacy that just happened to coincide with a recession. Poverty happens because pay is not high enough. I've seen the numbers. Yet still that presentational bias has got into my system: so that when I think 'underpaid care-worker', my brain helpfully supplies a downtrodden, unambitious person; not thick or lazy, but certainly no good at negotiating for herself.

There are 1.75 million people working in the care industry. It has an annual turnover of £15 billion. 11 per cent is still run by local authorities and there's a small amount of charitable provision, but private companies run the vast majority, and they do so for a profit.

A 12-hour day for 4 hours' pay
The first care-worker I interviewed had to be anonymous. I didn't find her in what you'd call a journalistically clean way: she was the girlfriend of an academic I half-knew, and she herself was doing a PhD. None of that is relevant to the way she was treated: but it's hard to get a sense of the true, grinding oppression in this business when your subject is just doing it as a stopgap.

'You could have a list of clients to go and visit, and the shortest call would be 15 minutes, the longest an hour and a half. When I was there, it was paid per minute, so it was 14 pence per minute. You log in when you get there, you log out when you leave. Travelling between calls, you're not paid anything at all. You're scrimping and saving, you've earned £3.50 here and £4 there, and then 45 minutes of nothing.

'The clients wouldn't be upset with me. It's a difficult position to be in anyway, letting a stranger into your house to bathe you. In a lot of cases, because I was white and English-speaking, a lot of people were really pleased to see me, and they would then slag off the African girls who they normally got. There was a hell of a lot of racism towards the 99 per cent of the other workers.

'An average day that I was doing at the time, I'd start at nine, do 45 minutes with one person, another 45 minutes at ten, a half-hour at twelve, a break, a quarter-hour at four, another 15 minutes at four-thirty, a half-hour at five and another hour from eight till nine. So that's a 12-hour day for four hours' money.

'We were all on zero-hours contracts, so basically they weren't obliged to give us any work. There are hundreds of people out there working like this – I'd meet people all the time, for jobs that required two carers, and I never met anybody who was being paid any differently. I know the hours for tax credits have changed now, but most people were on Housing Benefit.'

She was just passing through. She'd be a doctor soon. Probably not a millionaire; but at least her time wouldn't be measured out in quarter-hours.

Then I met Rochelle Monte. Wry, funny, good-looking, hard-boiled but sweet, she's the kind of person who people gather round in a room.

All the circumstances she describes are the same, except that she's been doing it for her entire career – she's my age and is on the same hourly rate, adjusted for inflation, that she was on at 18. She is based around Newcastle, and public transport doesn't exist that would get her from one appoint-ment to another. She has a car, gets paid 15 pence a mile, so if she puts in £40-worth of petrol, she'll get

£10 back. It's the little things that really ram home what's going on here. How does that meeting go, corporately, where they say, 'These women who are paid the minimum wage by the minute, whom we don't pay travel time even though travelling is half the job, who are using their own cars to do work that we've commissioned – shall we just offer them a quarter of the true cost of their petrol? See if that flies?' She has to pay for her own phone to make her appointments, and she uses it constantly. She is, she said laughingly of her employers, practically paying them.

She also described for me what a 15-minute appointment might look like. 'It might be a medication prompt for an Alzheimer's patient, where I make her breakfast as well. But I'll go in, she's got dementia, there'll be faeces smeared all over her. I sometimes find rubbish in the washing machine. I have to check all this without her noticing, because if she does, she'll get really angry. In 15 minutes!'

That's why she is where she is: not because she would be unable to do anything else, nor because she fails to push her case for a pay rise, but because of a fundamental belief in care and compassion that makes her do this work, regardless of what she's paid for it. Which is to say: the very human traits that make this business possible are used, cynically and relentlessly, to keep those humans' wages down.

It was in describing her that I had an argument with an economist. It doesn't matter who it was

– he's not a leftie, but you wouldn't call him right-wing. He's a serious economist, not some idiot with a PPE degree who can't remember anything, except that he knows it all and nobody else can possibly understand. And we were both drunk and on holiday. That's probably relevant.

I said: this isn't going to work, this situation with the care-workers. The women are being treated – in the words of one Low Pay Commission report – 'instrumentally'. Nobody's thinking about them: what they're worth, their right to fulfilling and dignified employment. They are just instruments of someone else's care package. There will soon be two million of them, and the sector's set to grow by between 24 and 82 per cent over the next 15 years.[20] The care companies get parcelled from one private-equity firm to another, and someone always walks off with millions of quid, while this huge workforce is bled dry.

He said (he was finding me really annoying): 'Why do you think that is, Zoe?' He paused. 'I think it's a rebalancing of the global workforce, but it might not be. It might be the decline of the unions. It might be pay at the top. It might be outsourcing by local authorities. But why do you think they outsourced? University economists don't know the answer to these questions. What makes you so arrogant that you think you do? You don't have the data, you have a series of bottom-up interviews. That's not going to work – it'll take too long. You need to talk to labour-force experts in the UK, in China, in South

America, or you're going to make yourself look stupid.'

My immediate riposte was that I didn't say I had the answers to everything; I was merely naming the problem. I was somewhat piqued by the assumption that I knew absolutely shit-all about anything. But I had just enough foresight to write it down because I knew there was something in what he said.

It's not good enough to say, 'I'm merely naming the problem': nobody would bother doing that if they didn't think there was an answer, and one that they could put their hands on quite readily. And there is a hell of a lot that I don't know. I know, for instance, that 60 per cent of London care-workers and 20 per cent of care-workers nationally are foreign-born.[21] But I don't know if this is 'rebalancing the global economy' – which is to say, whether it will simply continue until the lowest-paid British worker is paid the same as the lowest-paid Bolivian, and that's what globalisation means. I don't know. The people who'd tell you that halting immigration would solve the problem of low wages claim to know, but they don't know, either.

I know that unionisation – or, rather, its decline – has had a deleterious effect on wages. But this doesn't correspond precisely to care-work, which was never part of the unions' proud history of heavy industry anyway. It could be an effect at one remove – other low-paid sectors bringing down expectations of what wages should be. I don't know. I have a hunch that it's partly because care-work is female-dominated. The private sector does not, in the main, take equal pay seriously; besides which, if you're running a workforce that is predominantly female with the long-term intention of paying as little as you possibly can, the Equal Pay Act isn't going to help. It's not as though you're employing a load of men on higher wages, whom the female employees can benchmark themselves against.

I know that the private-equity firm Terra Firma bought the care company Four Seasons in 2012, for £825 million. I know why private-equity firms buy companies that deliver care services: the stock price goes up, in the expectation that the service will be run more cheaply. That is based on the fact that private-equity firms cut costs, either by cranking down pay and conditions or by separating the operating company from the property company (selling the buildings to some other investment company, keeping the profits, then renting those same buildings back to their operating company, which is then left sliding into the red, owing rent on buildings it previously owned: it's called an 'opco-propco' deal). Every care-home scandal you read – from Southern Cross nearing bankruptcy and needing a government bail-out in 2011 to Care UK workers going on strike in 2014 – springs directly from the attempt by incredibly rich people to screw money out of incredibly poor people.

But can I show exactly what happened, when Blackstone walked away from Southern Cross, or after Terra Firma bought Four Seasons? I cannot. There is a huge amount I do not know. Some of it is commercially confidential. Some of it is contested territory and couldn't be 'known' in a classic sense – different people have different opinions. Some of the results aren't in yet, and patterns predicted today won't be demonstrable for another ten or 15 years.

So how dare I comment, on things that even experts don't know? Partly it is because I don't trust that this evidence will ever come in. I don't ever see the messenger boy running over the hill, yelling, 'People! We have properly, definitively proven that treating care-workers like this is bad for the economy in the long-term.' There is a political agenda even to the way questions are framed: the difference between 'How can we afford adult social care?' and 'Can we afford to treat workers like this?' will give you pretty different results.

There is also this tiny flaw in the economic modelling, which is that their answers are often wrong. Gordon Brown predicted in 2006 that, by 2020, we would only have 600,000 low-skilled/low-paid jobs in the entire economy.[22] Labour market analysts put that estimate – the number of low-skilled jobs in the market right now – at between 11 and 13 million people. How many there will be by 2020 depends a lot on the political decisions that we make over the next five years, but I will tell you as a certainty that it won't be 600,000. Gordon Brown, holder of the largest brain anyone had ever come across, was simply wrong. The university economists advising him were wrong.

Let the children go to school

Journalists are notorious for putting the mistake on the front page and the correction on page 37, in teeny-weeny writing. But, with economists, the correction never comes. They never come out and say, 'Oh, it looks like we were wrong about inequality; it doesn't boost GDP after all, it merely stimulates unmanageable public and personal debt and leads to great instability in the global markets' (more in Finance). They never say, 'Oops, sorry, it appears that our modelled scenario was out by about ten million people'. TEN MILLION PEOPLE!

I don't like to shout. But we're supposed to bide our time, button our lips and withhold our judgements on the economy we live in, while we wait for an answer from these guys?

Beneath all of that sits this fundamental difference: the economist argues from the standpoint of economic verities. He looks at what's economically possible – considering global competitiveness, inflationary pay increases, efficiency – and figures out how people can serve that economy. I, conversely, think the economy is there to serve the people. So in the end, while I'm interested in why poverty pay has ended up the way it is, because it informs the route back to prosperity, I actually don't care very much. From the economist's perspective, if the reason for

40

a situation is good enough, they'll accept it as necessary. I will not accept it as necessary.

A parallel: in 1831 the campaign against child labour first gathered speed, and a worker and parent, Samuel Coulson, came to give evidence to the House of Commons about his daughters, who were ten and eight. He was asked about the high season, when the mills were operating 18 hours a day and all the workers, children included, were sleeping three or four hours a night.

'Were the children excessively fatigued by this labour?'

'Many times; we have cried often when we have given them the little victualling we had to give them; we had to shake them, and they have fallen to sleep with the victuals still in their mouths many a time.'

Textile manufacturers put up a fight, a furious, thundering, doom-laden picture of what life would be like if child labour were regulated. Households would be impoverished because they were relying on the income from children. Companies wouldn't be able to fulfil their orders, and they'd all go bust. England would lose its international competitiveness. Everyone would go back to the agrarian age, and these very families bleating about their tired children would all starve to death.

Sod it, said the nation, after a really long time. We can't have children so tired that they fall asleep while they're chewing. We'll take our chances. Let the children go to school, and let this fragile industry do its worst.

It was fine, by the way.

How was slavery abolished? How was child labour abolished? Why aren't we allowed to buy kidneys and babies off each other? Because, when you really drill into it, human dignity comes first.

We are indeed all in this together

> British workers at all three stations in life have less in their pay packets than a decade ago.
>
> Tom Clark and Anthony Heath, *Hard Times*

There is no such thing as a corporate culture that decides only to screw people at the very bottom, while continuing to treat those in the middle decently.

If you think the middle and upper-middle classes are doing okay, you're dreaming. Since the late Nineties wage growth has either been very slow (top 10 per cent), even slower (50th centile[23]) or non-existent (bottom 10 per cent). Since the economic crash, everybody's pay has declined sharply. Zero-hours contracts are an issue for senior health-workers as much as they are for people who work in McDonald's. The only people winning from the labour/profit split that we currently enjoy are the top 1 per cent, whose wealth is increasing so fast as to make their income pretty much irrelevant.[24] Everybody else loses to a different degree, but everybody is losing.

Conditions in middle-ranking jobs are necessarily harder to erode because the people who do them are not considered so interchangeable. The market for middle-class jobs still tends to look a lot kinder; people have security of tenure, proper contracts, pension contributions, paid holidays, sick pay . . . all the things that someone my age would think of as a normal part of being employed.

If you want to get ahead, don't be young

However, this more civilised environment is nothing like certain for those under 30. The inexorable rise of the unpaid internship is often cited as a problem for social mobility: it gives all the opportunities to kids whose parents can support them through it, therefore effectively erasing poor young people, however educated they are, from the careers that everybody wants to do. And that's all true, but human rights are one-size-fits-all. You either believe in a fair day's work for a fair day's pay or you don't. Just because the kids doing the internships are privileged doesn't mean they're not being exploited.

All the expense of training, which when I graduated was considered naturally to fall on the employer, instead falls upon the employee. Oxfam will, on the one hand, produce reports about a 'Perfect Storm' of poverty, while on the other hand classing interns as 'volunteers' so that it can use them for eight months without paying them. MPs will talk about how to get young people 'engaged' with politics, while running their offices on a constantly replenished pool of free researchers (most have stopped using free interns, because of bad publicity: instead they use students as part of their 'professional development', or have researchers paid for by huge companies, as a sort of embedded lobbying[25]). The message here is pretty plain: engagement from all young people would be wonderful, but we only want a certain type of young person in the building. This pattern is repeated across the whole range of competitive careers: the arts, the media, fashion, TV, film, publishing, IT. But instead of saying, 'Look, these unpaid young people have rights as well; they're very highly educated, and they're being skinned alive', we talk about them as though they're part of the problem – if the unpaid intern isn't the midwife of inequality, isn't it a bit suspicious how he's always there at its birth?

David Graeber, the American anthropologist, recently zoned in on this intern issue, and why it contains the particular seeds of social division that it does:

> I tried to grapple with the power of right-wing populism, especially with the way that 'we hate the liberal elite' and 'support the troops' seemed to have a very similar, deep resonance, even to be a way of saying the same thing. What I ended up concluding is that working-class people hate the cultural elite more than they do

the economic elite – and mind you, they don't like the economic elite very much. But they hate the cultural elite because they see them as a group of people who have grabbed all the jobs where one gets paid to do good in the world. If you want a career pursuing any form of value other than monetary value – if you want to work in journalism, and pursue truth, or in the arts, and pursue beauty, or in some charity or international NGO or the UN, and pursue social justice – well, even assuming you can acquire the requisite degrees, for the first few years they won't even pay you. So you're supposed to live in New York or some other expensive city on no money for a few years after graduation. Who else can do that except children of the elite? So if you're a fork-lift operator or even a florist, you know your kid is unlikely to ever become a CEO, but you also know there's no way in a million years they'll ever become drama critic for the *New Yorker* or an international human-rights lawyer. The only way they could get paid a decent salary to do something noble, something that's not just for the money, is to join the army. So saying 'support the troops' is a way of saying 'fuck you' to the cultural elite who think you're a bunch of knuckle-dragging cavemen, but who also make sure your kid would never be able to join their club of rich do-gooders even if he or she was twice as smart as any of them.

What he's describing I would once have called a peculiarly American phenomenon: their armed-forces fetishism, their intern culture – I've seen this on TV all my adult life, and generally thought of it as Americana.

Here in Britain, we have our own kinks – the class system, in which everyone gets to feel their own sort of shame. A middle-class person is ashamed to speak about the conditions of the working class, because to speak of them is to speak for them. An upper-class person can be shamed out of considering anyone outside their own circle, since it's their privilege that suffocates everyone else's potential in the first place. And since a working-class person hardly ever appears in the shared cultural space unless they try to sound middle-class, or they're talking about football, they are shamed into thinking no one wants to hear from them at all. The exception is if you're talking about individualism, consumer-ism, doing what you want and pleasing yourself: then, it doesn't matter how posh or common you are. It's only social solidarity that bears the burden of this quintessentially British embarrassment.

Yet the landscape is the same in both countries: complete silence around conditions of people on poverty pay; exaggerated soldier-worship, in the shape of Help for Heroes or Support Our Troops; myopia on the subject of unpaid internships, because those over-privileged kids are just getting what's coming; and the relentless appropriation of the money by the profit class, instead of by the people doing the actual work. So you have to wonder: is it time we stopped feeling so sheepish about our class privilege, or lack of it, and actually woke up to the fact that we're all getting stiffed by the same mechanism? Do you think that the people doing the work, even if they're incredibly inexperienced and don't know what a fax machine is, are still adding value to that process, which a shareholder is not? Is it plain to you that, when profit comes first, everybody else comes last? Then reject the false divisions between one class and another, the metropolitan elite versus the knuckle-dragging hicks, the strivers versus the skivers. We are all on the same side. The fact that we care about one another is nothing to be ashamed of.

Rhetoric dismissing the unions has been so widely adopted, so often repeated, that it has acquired the reassuring lilt of common sense. Union leaders are just angry warhorses with greasy hair, who hate success and modernity, who just want to make you late for work by calling a Tube strike.

On the contrary: unions are there to fight for your wages; they are there to make sure you get sick pay, that 'flexibility' doesn't leave you scrabbling for ten hours a week, that you get a weekend. They are there to make sure that the industry you're in recognises your contribution to it, recognises the value of your experience or your enthusiasm, doesn't treat you like so much interchangeable meat. They are there to tell your employer that you're a human being. They are there to remind your employer that they're in a relationship with you – one of mutual care and duty – and you're not just a pool of labour that they can dip in and out of. It really doesn't matter what their hair is like.

I said that classic union structures wouldn't work now, because workplace insecurity has made it impossible to be a troublemaker. But we no longer have to be on the same shop floor to talk to each other. We could build an online union that would make collective demands without exposing individual workers whose managers can quietly fire them. University lecturers have already experimented with pop-up unions – temporary, single-issue groups that campaign on specific issues, and that disband when they've won. Unite has set up a community union for the unemployed and low-paid, to campaign against the 'bedroom tax' and benefit sanctions.[26] Look at what 38 Degrees and Change. org can achieve: imagine that transplanted to the world of work. Twenty-first-century unionisation could be as flexible and agile as modern businesses claim to be. Its purpose would be to end poverty pay, and that would reverberate all the way up the pay spine. We don't all have to see our living standards steadily decline for the sake of gargantuan CEO salaries and shareholders.

The thing about politicians is that even the best of them can't fight your battles for you. All they can do is stuff you a metaphorical fiver when they can see you're really struggling; it's like going to see your gran in hospital. It's touching, but it's not going to help. What they can do, and what charities are calling for them to do, is acknowledge the problem. They have the power of data. They need to formally assess the causes of poverty; stop pretending it's because people have too many children, or are inherently lazy, or on the make, or useless; forecast the future of hardship and admit its magnitude. Otherwise, it's up to us.

Hovering over all of this is a cloud of fear; the stock response from businesses is always, 'We cannot afford to pay more. If you keep on insisting, we will go bust.' Pan out, and you can see that this is not true. There is no economic law that says shareholders must take more than half of the nation's output in order to survive. There is no productivity principle whereby CEOs must be paid 300 times what cleaners are paid. They take it because they fight for it. It's time to fight back.

Has the NHS had its day?

We who live in Britain are not proud of the NHS for sentimental reasons. It didn't lodge in our hearts ahead of every other national institution[1] because of nostalgia, or *Carry on Nurse* or *One Born Every Minute*. It is for this simple fact: we took something universal, and damaging, and unjust – illness – and forged from it something unique, and generous, and fair. The NHS, as it was conceived in 1942[2] and built from 1948, became the template for the provision of universal healthcare across the world.

Between the White Paper in 1944,[3] and the goose-pimpling leaflet that read 'Your new national health service begins on the 5th of July. What is it? How do you get it?' in 1948, the fighting was fierce. The arguments from the Conservatives in 1946 were exactly as you'd hear them today: one, we can't afford this magnificent thing; two, greedy people will misuse it.

In the words of Mr Law, MP for Kensington South, '[This would be] a society in which everybody pays to the state what he must, and takes from the state what he can. This is not the kind of society which will be very attractive to the people of this country.'[4]

This is known as the 'freeloader' argument; if we attempt to build things together and share them, some people will grab more than they deserve. In real, observable life it isn't true: most people are generous, not grasping. People might visit the doctor for something that turned out not to be important. I went myself for an itchy ear. But almost nobody visits the doctor in order to extract some kind of personal advantage. It is only in economic modelling that people are persistently arseholes. If all of that sounds familiar to us, it also sounded pretty familiar to the denizens of 1946.

'Let me remind Mr Law,' said the Liberal, Mr Clement Davies, MP for Montgomeryshire, 'that it was his father who opposed the National Insurance Bill of 1911.'

And Mr Law Senior had exactly the same reasons: we can't afford it, and bad people will misuse it.

In short: Conservatives started off hating the NHS. They have never not hated the NHS. Davies noted at the time: 'They could not say yes and they did not dare to say no, so they invented a sort of new, middle Conservative way of trying to get the best of both worlds.' Back then, that middle way meant tabling amendments to derail the bill. Today they create chaos with new legislation, then turn round and say, 'It's impossible to run this organisation. It's in chaos!'

So how did Labour win, back then? First, by being a lot less useless than they are today. And second, against a backdrop of the war, which had brought both scrutiny and moral urgency to public health. The Peckham Health Experiment found that only one in ten people – in that deprived area – was in good health; 60 per cent had a disorder they were unaware of; three in ten were actively sick. From this and other cohort studies, the estimate was made that in 1936 recognised disease cost the nation £300 million in lost productivity. Since funding for a National Health Service was budgeted at only a bit more than half that (£152 million), the pragmatic case was easily made: we can afford it, because without it we're spending more. Just because you don't have proper healthcare for everybody doesn't mean that you don't spend money on it.

And perhaps the freeloader argument was trumped by the war; people who would die for their country were plainly not in it for whatever they could get.

Instantly, everyone loved the NHS. No politician in my lifetime has fought an election with the promise to reduce funding for the Health Service. Even Margaret Thatcher, surfing the tide of anti-state feeling, peddling the 'vigorous values' (energy, adventurousness, independence) over the 'softer virtues' (humility, gentleness, sympathy) never suggested that ill people could use a little more vigour. Thatcher fought the 1979 campaign saying, 'It is not our intention to reduce spending on the

Health Service. Indeed, we intend to make better use of what resources are available. So we will simplify and decentralise the service and cut back bureaucracy.' That. Old. Chestnut. She fought in 1983 with the line: 'Let me make one thing absolutely clear. The National Health Service is safe with us.'[5] I was ten at the time, living in a hard-left cell (my mother was a member of Battersea Labour Party and sometimes had her friends round). The NHS, they said, was not safe with the Conservatives, who were circling it like vultures, waiting to privatise. I thought they were mad, but with the benefit of hindsight and the National Archive, it appears that they were right.[6] The Cabinet had a meeting in 1982 at which they established that privatising the NHS was a really sound economical idea.

The NHS: safe in whose hands?

I only return to this ancient history because one idea that depresses the hell out of me is that modern politics is uniquely bad, and modern politicians are uniquely mendacious. It isn't, and they are not; politicians have been claiming that the NHS was safe, while privately planning to privatise it, for as long as I've been alive.

In 1997 the political offer was a little bit more lavish than 'We can see you like this thing, we promise not to break it': Tony Blair promised to cut waiting lists and treat 100,000 extra patients, which would be paid for by cutting the £100 million wasted in red tape. That target was met by 2000 but, like all targets instituted everywhere, was observed to be perverting the outcome, as everybody concentrated on the target rather than the treatment. So they made it a better target – waiting times, rather than waiting lists – and this changed the results again, but again was found to be interfering with the business of healthcare, by overriding the judgement of the professionals and forcing them to prioritise a measure that politicians would be able to count. The approach was characterised at the time as 'targets and terror'. Health policy analysts often write about the 'targets and terror' approach, attempting to measure its efficacy, but I've never seen any sustained enquiry into what it does to the morale of those who are being terrorised by these targets. Doctors have pretty muscular unions, so are widely believed to be able to look after themselves. Yet this still leaves a gigantic 'why' over the territory – why train these people, and employ them, and trust them, just to undermine them with terror and distract them with targets? I think we could come up with a better way to get the best out of each other.

The winning promise, since the late Seventies, has always been that the service would be maintained or improved, while the same money would be spent (just differently). For about five seconds in 2000, Labour rejected those terms. Per capita spending would be increased to bring it into line with the EU average;[7] it sounded a lot as if spending would be increased for its own sake, simply because we were a civilised nation, and why shouldn't we spend the same as other civilised nations spent?

This was a break in the clouds that had been greyscaling the terrain for years: the basic assumption that, given the choice, we would always prefer to spend less rather than more. Unfortunately that moment came accompanied by some catastrophic private-finance deals (more on those in Privatisation). It's like trying to discuss the *Titanic*, starting with, 'But apart from the iceberg, a lot of the safety features were actually pretty modern.' And yet linger, to consider how easy it is to break this spell; all it takes is for one person to say, 'No, I don't want everything to be as cheap as possible. In fact, I think we should spend more.' And everyone goes, 'Sure. So do I.'

This is the point at which, if you're in a pub, or on the Internet, or some place where people are rude, someone will say: 'There is no money left. End of.' Then sit back, delighted with the brevity and inarguability of their point. Paradoxically, the alternative they suggest – a constantly economising NHS, always looking to contract out its services to a lower bidder – is much more expensive. The lowest bidder tends to be the largest entity, cross-subsidising their bid with other contracts, probably also given to them by the government. Then, when the contract is won, the costs start to go up, whereupon the government is in a very weak position to negotiate, since all the smaller bidders who could have done the work have gone out of business.

The Conservative promise in 2010, I may not need to remind you, was: 'The NHS: Safe in Our Hands'. In other words, it was almost identical to Thatcher's, and was, like Thatcher's, a lie, to mask the intention of dismantling it. We probably should have seen the Health and Social Care Act coming. I feel a little sheepish about what a shock the threat to the NHS, posed by the Coalition, has been. There was one other big clue of the Conservatives' plans, from five years before, when Andrew Lansley, then Shadow Health Minister, announced his blueprint for the future of healthcare, 'drawing on lessons from utility privatisation'. Any normal person would look at utility privatisation – incredibly expensive energy, thanks to the predatory privatised encrgy market (see Privatisation) – and think the first and only lesson to draw was 'Don't privatise your utilities'. But what normal person was listening to Andrew Lansley in 2005?

So, what has happened to the NHS, supposedly 'so safe'? The Health and Social Care Act was passed on 27th March 2012. It relieved the Health Secretary of his responsibility for all of our health; the post has carried that duty since the NHS was founded. This makes it possible, for the first time, for people to slip through the gaps of universal provision, without that being the Health Secretary's problem. However, on its own, that would be merely symbolic. To do harm, it needs this other change: instead of care provision organised by geographical area, in which those areas were contiguous, it is now divided by Clinical Commissioning Groups. It's a layer of management that's supposed to be GP-led, in which you're eligible for care via your GP, and technically ineligible if you don't have a GP. Surgeries are already starting to de-register patients in their thousands: 1,500 in one go from a single surgery in Norfolk; an entire nursing home in Edgbaston. The Royal College of GPs estimated that more than 50 million people would be unable to get an appointment in 2014, which is one in nine.[8] It's not the surgery's fault that they are underfunded, and it's not the population's fault for living too long. Some plucky media outlets are looking to blame migrants, but the population didn't suddenly become too big for its healthcare. This is a funding issue and, knocking on from that, a staffing problem. The greater peril is that, in the new structure, when you don't have a GP, you have no automatic access to the NHS at all. These CCGs were supposed to be run by GPs, but more than one-third have already lost the GP on their board. Without a medic, these boards just become another tier of management.

And one more thing – the private sector. £13 billion worth of contracts have already been put up for tender;[9] £2.6 billion worth have already been delivered to profit-driven companies, including Virgin Care, BUPA and Care UK.[10] £1.5 billion has already gone to companies with links to 24 Tory MPs and lords.[11] One-third of NHS walk-in centres have been closed, and half of all ambulance stations are earmarked for closure. The reorganisation has already cost £3 billion. Waiting lists are at a six-year high, Conservative ministers are privately already blithely admitting that there's not much the government can do to control the health system – which is true, once you've contracted out all its services – and the whole thing smells of corruption. 144 lords (equally split between the parties) and 81 MPs (mostly tories) hold shares in the same companies that are bidding for the contracts.[12] In 2012 the head of the NHS's Cooperation and Competition Panel (CCP), Lord Carter of Coles, was simultaneously employed, for £800,000 a year, by McKesson, an American health company. It caused a brief stink which he weathered, quietly quitting when the CCP was merged with Monitor the following year; only to turn up again, as NHS chair of Procurement and Efficiency – which is to say, the person overseeing which company gets which contract – two years later.

The NHS is one of the greatest humanitarian projects ever undertaken in peacetime, anywhere in the world. But that very fact weighs against it; in the current climate, all conversations start with the baseline assumption that only self-interest can drive efficiency. So we accept with the NHS that, since it was the moral, collective thing to do, it must therefore, in its everyday running, be crap.

In fact, we are the best at nearly everything?
In life-expectancy terms, at 81.1, we rank jointly

with Luxembourg, Austria, Canada and South Korea. It's not the highest life expectancy in the world, but well up there with affluent, advanced nations.

But life expectancy is a blunt measure and you get some perverse results. You could get a country whose healthcare was mediocre but whose people only ate fish, and they'd do pretty well.

What you really want is an international comparator study conducted by an apolitical body, measuring a large number of different outcomes, reaching some reliable conclusion; which, by extraordinary good fortune, we have. Called the Mirror, Mirror study,[13] this compares Britain to ten other developed nations – Australia, Canada, France, Germany, the Netherlands, New Zealand, Norway, Sweden, Switzerland and the US, and puts us at the top, for almost everything. NHS stalwarts love it, but they had no hand in its creation: it's compiled by the Commonwealth Fund, borrowing some data from the World Health Organisation and the Organisation for Economic Co-operation and Development (OECD). Quality of care, access, efficiency, equity: we top the charts, falling down slightly in timeliness of care. It's no big deal, as we're still third: but the fact is, with centrally planned healthcare provision, you either provide too much and are called inefficient, or people sometimes have to wait for stuff. We built a system that is the best and the cheapest in the world; why change it so that it follows the principles of the worst and the most expensive?

We fall down a lot on healthy lives, coming tenth. The Institute for Health Metrics and Evaluation bluntly puts this down to dietary risk.[14] Obesity (along with its public-health twin, type-two diabetes) is a perennial theme in the argument for paring down or privatising the Health Service: it's always either obesity, diabetes or an ageing population, and the conclusion is always the same. 'Unaffordable,' they intone, all mournful and premonitory. 'You refuse to look after yourselves, which makes you prohibitively expensive to treat, which means we can no longer afford this public health system. And, let's be honest, you don't really deserve it.'

Now, nobody can deny that we have an obesity problem, but the last way to solve it would be to undermine the principles of a public health system. When people talk about obesity, as a reason to give up on the NHS, they're basically using a variation on the freeloader argument: grasping people are taking the piss, and that's why we can't pool our resources to buy things together.

If you called obesity 'metabolic syndrome' (which is what costs the money), people would start looking round for a medical cause. Call it a weight problem, and greed is instantly the underpinning behaviour. So, the argument runs, those people who misuse the NHS are greedy; they're taking more than their fair share. What makes you think they're greedy? Well, look at how fat they are. The malady itself is proof of their natures, which then manifest in their wanting the most of everything: of NHS resources, of space on buses, of chips – of everything.

The 'ageing population' motif creates a different mood: obviously nobody would accuse old people of staying alive on purpose. Rather, this introduces the dual themes of resignation and decline: they can't help getting old; we can't get out of looking after them; we just have to get used to the fact that things we used to be able to afford we no longer can.

It's a swizz; affordability isn't a constant measure, it's about what you raise and how you allocate it. Besides which, it is factually wrong to say 'unaffordable' in relation to healthcare; when people are ill, they still have to be treated. You can flip the whole thing into private hands, rely on charity for the people who can't afford it, carve up health-spending any which way, but the money is still spent. The correct phrase is, therefore, 'If we allow X to continue, we'll still afford it because it'll have to be afforded; it's just going to become really, really expensive.' The restructuring of the NHS, I cast-iron guarantee you, will not save the public purse any money; castigating fat people will not save any money; bemoaning old age will not save any money. While medical care is still free at the point of use, the money will still be spent; the greater the role of the private sector, the more of it will be lost to profit.

But let's imagine – using obesity or ageing as your fig leaf – you abandon your commitment to free healthcare for all; now the cost will be much greater, to much less effect, at the additional cost of huge amounts of misery. We will see why in a second. But just quickly, first ... It would be really easy to tackle obesity; that lies with the food industry. The connection between a global pandemic of weight gain and multinational corporations adding sugar to processed food is as easily observable and widely acknowledged as Newton's laws. If they were spiking our food with arsenic to make it last longer, we would regulate, and we *can* regulate this. It's really no big deal.

If anybody marshals obesity as an argument for greater privatisation, or less universal provision, in the Health Service, they're being disingenuous: privatisation won't make anything cheaper, and it won't change anybody's behaviour. It is exactly the debate they had in 1946, modernised with a fat suit.

In 2012, just after the Health and Social Care act had been passed, I interviewed Stuart Hall (the intellectual; not the disgraced sex-offender DJ). He was dying then, but quite languidly and with a wry approach. He had end-term renal failure, and had undergone dialysis for seven years. 'Five years is the best; after that, it's killing you and keeping you alive at the same time. Have you any idea how much dialysis costs per session? Do I believe in a public health system? I sure do. With bells on.' It is incredibly bloody weird talking the politics of public health with someone who is dying in front of you. Hall said that the left had failed. 'The principle that someone shouldn't profit from someone else's ill health has been lost. That's what matters about the failure of the analyses of the left – they don't articulate where we are. If someone says an American health company will run the NHS efficiently, they can't think of the principle to refute that.' We were in his kitchen, and the way the light was streaming in made it hard for us to see each other through the weak English sunshine, and I remember being a bit grateful for that, since I felt a part of the politico-cultural collapse that he described. I hate using moral arguments; one person's moral truth is another person's unrealistic liberal bleating. What I like best is the argument of the Mirror, Mirror study: let's do it our way because it's the best way.

There's a further data set, covering a bit less ground: what kind of life expectancy do you get for each dollar spent? Some of the numbers are pretty obvious: Indonesia spends very little money, and has very low life expectancy. We spend a bit less money than Denmark, but have higher life expectancy, in what may be the only recorded instance of us doing something better than Denmark. By this measure alone, we're not the best in the world. Yet the difference between us and the very best – Japan – is not vast.

It's all quite curious: if our bureaucracy is so incredibly bloated, and the public sector is so terrible at running things, how on earth are we managing to make up the numbers? How do we make up for all those pitiable, state-sponsored inefficiencies that creep into the system?

I am sorry to say it, but this is only half a story about how brilliant the state is. The other half is about how ineffably hopeless, rapacious, grasping and savage the private sector is. That bit is a really ugly story about profit.

A spurt of American sadism

America has a bullish exterior, and the rhetoric that comes out of it can give you the impression that they know what they're doing, as they do with motorways, and air-conditioning. But underneath it is a shambles. Their costs are alarmingly high, per capita, and their life expectancy is, believe it or not, worse than it was in the 1970s.[15]

Broadly speaking, the inefficiencies of US healthcare are due to the fact that a profit-based system overtreats the rich and undertreats the poor. The rich will have the smallest thing investigated and spend a lot of money establishing that it's definitely piles and not bowel cancer. The poor will present much later, by which time even if some humanitarian programme is in place to treat them, their disease is worse and more expensive to treat. You often see this described in places like *Forbes* magazine[16] as a cultural idiosyncrasy – Americans prefer to see specialists, and their use of primary-care doctors (GPs) is low, so of course the costs are higher. But really this is about money and about waste: you don't need to see a dermatologist when you have a bit of eczema, or an otolaryngologist if you have an ear infection. Most illnesses are well within the grasp of most GPs. But if you're working on the principle that you get what you pay for, obviously the drive is towards specialisation for the rich, and makeshift temporary clinics in gymnasia for the poor.

Anyway, nobody disagrees with this: when you assess the whole system, you find that one unit of good health costs an unnecessarily large amount of dollars. When you put that to economists, though (especially American ones), they always say something along the lines of: 'Ah, but you're including uninsured people in the data.' Their point is that you can't evaluate a system by including in it the health of the people who aren't covered by it. So if your healthcare is insurance-based, the 15 per cent of people who can't afford insurance don't tell you much about the system itself. Annoyingly, for the economist's view, international data comparisons still insist on evaluating each country on the basis that all of its citizens' lives are of equal worth.

But even when you park that broad and obvious built-in inefficiency, there is the architecture of profit, the managerial money it costs to make sure the right people get paid for the right thing. People who truly trust market forces are incredibly pernickety about public-sector waste, and yet enjoy an almost infinite tolerance for the money it costs to keep the market functioning properly as a market. In the US they typically spend 36 per cent of their healthcare budgets on management.[17]

This isn't fraud or mismanagement or error; it's just what it costs.

And then there's fraud

False billing, over-billing, strike forces, takedowns ... doctors charging for imaginary wheelchairs ... pharmacies, physicians and patients forming little crime leagues. The annual health spend in America is $2.7 trillion, or 17 per cent of GDP. No one even knows how much of that is embezzled, but in 2012 Donald Berwick, a former head of the Centers for Medicare and Medicaid Services (CMS), and Andrew Hackbarth of the RAND Corporation, estimated that fraud (plus the fighting of fraud) could add as much as $272 billion across the entire health system. I know, I know, what does 'as much as' mean? It could be less. It could be $200 billion.[18] So I guess it's starting to make sense why it's so inefficient. But there is also, distinct from fraud, the small matter of almost everybody, almost everywhere, being flayed alive.

On the 2nd April 2013 – at 6.15 p.m., he tells us helpfully – the Serbian-American poet Charles Simic wrote this painful paragraph:

> This is the new face of American sadism: the unconcealed burst of joy at the thought that pain is going to be inflicted on someone weak and helpless. Its viciousness, I believe, is symptomatic of the way our society is changing. Everything from the healthcare industry, payday loans, and

for-profit prisons to the trading in so-called derivatives, privatization of public education, outsourcing of jobs, war profiteering, and hundreds of other ongoing rackets all have that same predatory quality. It's as if this were not their own country, but some place they've invaded in order to loot its wealth and fleece its population without caring what happens to that population tomorrow.[19]

He was talking not broadly about the mean old world, with the generalised message that life, everywhere, by some incomprehensible mechanism, has become irreversibly worse. He was referring to a report about costs in US healthcare,[20] in which the journalist Steven Brill discovered that hospitals – even non-profit ones – charge whatever they like. An aspirin might cost you 100 times more than it would in Walmart; a chest X-ray ten times more than Medicaid would pay. Basically, hospitals use their patients to cross-subsidise one another. A gold-plated insurance company, with really expensive policies, will negotiate the hospital down to $3,000 for a dose of the cancer drug Rituxan, say. Maybe the hospital only just breaks even on that – for the drug itself, plus the staff to prescribe and administer it. It doesn't matter, because they can make the money back by charging an uninsured person, or a person with lesser insurance, $13,702 for exactly the same thing. I know, we're a long way from home here – but it's vital for us to see this, because this is the precise opposite of the NHS: a system in which the weaker you are, the more you have to pay. It is, as Brill put it, 'the ultimate seller's market'.

Costs no longer bear any relation to what people can afford. In 2000 'nearly half'[21] of American bankruptcies were due to medical bills. By 2007 it was 62 per cent,[22] of which – this is the chilling bit – 78 per cent were insured. Most medical debtors, the authors noted, were well educated, owned homes and had middle-class jobs. So the US made this huge advance in getting insurance for the uninsured, in ObamaCare, but meanwhile the ecology of the system had morphed and grown a new tumour; the power balance between the medics and the ill had become so skewed over time that even the middle classes were now one chronic illness away from going bust.

There's something about the weakness of the flesh that has its own particular humiliation: being the schmuck with cancer who can't afford to have cancer; wanting to live so much, and simply not having the wherewithal. We did something amazing when we created the NHS; we took the price tag off a priceless thing and showed each other how much we understood.

Whenever you look too closely at America, someone will point out that the US and the UK have two completely different systems, that to compare them is meaningless and that the NHS will always be free at the point of need. We'll never have to pay for it, so it can never bankrupt or divide us.

Never write off how big a deal this is: whatever private-sector deals are struck, it is highly improbable, it seems to me, that we'll ever have to find £30,000 because we're diagnosed with MS. The American way isn't the stone-cold ghost of our Christmas future; rather, it is an illustration of what a profit motive actually does in healthcare – it swarms the arena with people who are not interested in promoting health. I have lived for so long in a political discourse where every sentence that starts with 'private sector' ends with 'efficiency' that I had forgotten how frequently those two things worked against one another.

I don't blame politicians for all this. There are Conservatives, as well as Liberal Democrats, who – I believe – would rather die than fleece their own constituents for the sake of their share portfolio. But the fact that so many of them don't feel like that is, I think, a signal of political despair. They're not protecting their honour, because they don't think they have anything to protect; we already hold them in such low esteem.

Arguably, politics has so far sustained more damage than the Health Service has; it has become really difficult to distinguish between political conviction and self-interest. The Conservatives have broken the whole system open to the private sector, when they expressly swore that they wouldn't change anything, but PFI (private finance initiative) was rolled out by New Labour. What they have done to health, more than in any other single area, has destroyed our ability both to trust political parties and to differentiate between them.

Is competition good for you?
New Labour, characteristically, tried to find somewhere halfway between public ownership and a thrusting, competitive market. Enter: non-price-based competition.

Such an ugly phrase can only have been dreamt up in recent history, and it describes a very Nineties/ Noughties idea: if, for some reason, you cannot compete on price, institute a sort-of market system based on some other thing. So the Department of Health set the prices, and hospitals competed for patients. A number of studies evaluated it, notably a long-term look by the King's Fund[23] and a paper by a group from the London School of Economics.[24]

These studies are wild. They are name-checked constantly – by David Cameron, Jeremy Hunt and, previously, Andrew Lansley – as proof that competition benefits the NHS; this is not what they show. What they actually show is the way your mind works when competitive systems are all you understand.

So, for instance, the King's Fund evaluated what people thought about choice in 2002, when waiting times were more than six months in many cases. Well, people loved it, because it meant they didn't have to wait. But what they really approved of was 'not waiting'. Researchers asked people what informed their choices, when they chose. Most people said, 'What my doctor recommended', which is the same as saying, 'I didn't choose.' The largest other factor was 'Where the hospital is in relation to my house'. 'Never mind!' concluded the study. People may not like choosing, but they like not waiting; and since choice was introduced partly in order to cut waiting times, this means people like choice. See what I mean? Wild.

The number of people who ever used the NHS 'Good Choices' website (now 'NHS Choices') was 4 per cent. This is the bit where researchers in think-tanks roll their eyes about how bovine we all are – that we won't even take a consumer choice that's handed to us free, on a plate. They don't understand exactly what it is that we're saying: 'I'm not a consumer. I'm a person. I just want you to look after me.'

I was given a choice of hospital when I had my first child, which by coincidence was due the same month as my sister's second. I didn't want to go to Chelsea and Westminster because a friend said they were all incredibly mean and, if you asked them to pass you a glass of water, said, 'It's not a hotel, you know', even if you had 17 fresh stitches across your abdomen and a baby. I didn't want to go to St George's because I spent three months there when I was a kid. I didn't want to go to King's because that's where my sister would be. So I went to St Thomas's, which is where the GP told me to go in the first place. What I really didn't want to do was give birth at all, which I think is a pretty common state of mind when choosing a hospital: really not wanting to go to any of them. You do not look at metrics, you ask people you know; no amount of transparency will tell you whether or not the midwives are mean, and no amount of hospital excellence will undo a bad experience from 29 years before. Moreover, the entire idea of choice is that, once you've chosen, you don't care what the alternatives are like: indeed, you hope that they're woeful, to make your choice even more intelligent. That's not at all what I want from a hospital. I don't want a round-the-clock midwife to myself in St Tommy's while women in King's are sharing one between five, even if my sister does not happen to be there. I don't want Chelsea and Westminster to have really low mortality rates while St George's has high ones. I don't need a specialist to do a routine birth. A fine job is as good as the best job. I don't want to choose between excellent and unsatisfactory. I want it all to be fine, for everybody.

In medical circles, they have a codeword for healthcare policy written by fit, young men: they call it 'bollocks'. If you must allow a fit young man to write a policy, they entreat, at least make it a doctor, who has met some ill people. No dice, medics. Unfortunately, fit young men in think-tanks are all they've got.

In 'Does Hospital Competition Save Lives?', researchers took hospitals in which there was a choice for one procedure – hip replacements – and measured the results for a different event: heart attacks. The finding was that, in hospitals where there was a nearby competitor for the hip operation, institutional standards were driven up so much that survival rates improved for the major event. Okay, that sounds like it makes sense; management cultures are everything in large organisations. A better culture is better for everybody.

But it's contested: other health researchers say that hospitals with nearby competitors are the ones that are situated in large urban areas. They get good results because that's where the specialists are. The specialists are there because that's where the population has the highest density. Who would put a specialist heart unit in Beamish when everybody lives in Newcastle? 'Aha, but we have controlled for that,' say the first lot. 'It is impossible to control for that,' say the second (I'm paraphrasing to make this argument go faster[25]). Survival rates for heart attacks have been driven up by the steady accumulation of knowledge. We learn, and then we share our learning, and then we refine our practice, and then we share our practice, and then we learn some more, and we end up better at it. That's why large hospitals get better results than small ones. Not because they're trying to do better than the guy down the road they always lose to at squash, but because it's where the people work who know the most.

Clearly, I am not an expert in hip replacements, percutaneous coronary interventions or epidemiology, but I know this: you cannot distinguish the effects of competition from the effects of sharing knowledge and pursuing clinical excellence. Politicians can bring in any targets they choose, and they can simulate any market conditions they last learnt about on their MBAs, but they cannot stop well-educated, passionate professionals pooling their ideas in an ambitious way to save lives. Cooperation does the work, and competition gets the credit. The Devil, as ever, has the best PR.

In fairness, I understand the way the story is told: competition is fun to watch, whereas cooperation is not. But it is just a narrative device; it's not a law of the physical universe. I've read so many times that 'competition drives innovation', and it's just unfathomable to me why we accept it; innovation is driven by the human urge to share ideas.

Competition is great for proving what you already know; if you want to get somewhere new, you have to share your homework. And every one of us understands this; everyone except a small number of economists, to whom we have lately decided to defer on almost everything.

I interviewed Zack Cooper (one of the authors of 'Does Hospital Competition Save Lives?'), and he said this interesting thing:

> I think one of the reasons our work was so controversial in England is that doctors are viewed as almost omnipotent. If there's a problem, it's the fault of the patient or the government. Doctors are simply there to do God's work.

If you just look at the annual fights over doctors' pay, that should be enough to say that doctors aren't motivated exclusively by the desire to do good. And if they're not exclusively motivated by altruism, and you force them to compete, that's going to make a difference.

He's right about one thing: the weird relationship we have with our medical profession, in which we do (let's be honest) think they're Gods. It is not a function of our craven British desire to obey; or, if it is, only because that went into the DNA of the Health Service. It's the principle on which the NHS was built: treatment on the basis of need. But who determines need? We can't evaluate our own needs relative to one another's; we need medical experts. But Cooper is wrong about another thing: his binary understanding of altruism, whereby any person not entirely selfless must instead be understood as entirely selfish, and join the fray.

I think some paternalism is warranted; the reason health isn't suited to the free market is that there's an asymmetry of knowledge, so you've got to expect that any system we arrive at instead is going to have quite a lot of respect in it. But, sure, doctors aren't purely selfless, nor are they omniscient; if you worship them as such, you're going to end up a little bit disappointed. Their human qualities – of intelligence, empathy, insight, wisdom – will vary from one to another, as is the case in any profession. Since our respect for doctors grew out of love for the system, rather than some innate, standardised wondrousness of the doctors themselves, other countries are bound to look at us and think we're a little bit nuts.

It is, furthermore, true that doctors are not shy about making demands for money. In 1945 Aneurin Bevan, the Minister for Health, designing the NHS from scratch, did a crafty thing: he based his salary offer for GPs on the tax returns they were handing in. They knew this was going to end up with less income than they were on, but couldn't say so without admitting past tax avoidance; instead they complained in a circumspect way, and he offered them a little bit more, and that was basically the settlement they were stuck with. No politician has ever thought of anything so wily since and, as a result, Whitehall always comes out of pay negotiations feeling as though it's been stiffed. But I don't have a problem with medics being well paid; they work hard and they bring huge social value.

What's more, I totally reject the analysis that to prove your authentic 'goodness', you must eschew all self-interest. It is right for doctors to want their training and expertise recognised in their pay; it is right for midwives to strike when their pay, in real terms, goes down yet again. A sophisticated society manages to pick a course between screwing out the highest salary you possibly can and 'If you care so much, why aren't you doing it for free?'

This is a perversion of our age: the more you assert your job as having some value besides making money, the less you're supposed to want to be paid for it. It's the logical extension of the bullshit adage: 'If you're so smart, why aren't you rich?' If you're so good, why aren't you poor?

Why should firemen get the pensions they were promised when they joined? Why should legal-aid barristers carry on getting paid right to the end of the case? Why should the head of that environmental charity be on £100,000 – why doesn't she give it to the dolphins, if she loves them so much? Anybody who actively asserts that their job is bigger or better than buyer and seller should be able to demonstrate that, by accepting the minimum wage to do it. It's the petulance of the market fundamentalists: if you won't accept our rules, then you can't play with our ball. Unfortunately they think the whole of money is their ball.

Doctors are motivated by human kindness and the quest for excellence and they argue collectively for the wages that befit their knowledge and experience. There is nothing contradictory about this.

How do we protect the NHS?
What would be helpful – to debate, to policy and to the frontline – is if we moved the conversation along from 'keep it public' versus 'privatise'. Just forget the private sector. Start by saying that the NHS got to be the best in the world by being a public service; we all built it, we all use it, we all pay for it. That means repealing the Health and Social Care Act.

Almost as important is this: just because you would (almost) die to preserve the principle of the NHS doesn't mean you have to think the institution is perfect. Many of the attacks on the institution, and the professions within it, are so unjust that it's hard to think straight. As I write, the Health Secretary Jeremy Hunt has come up with a cracking wheeze to name-and-shame GPs who fail to send people with cancer for a 'life-saving' scan fast enough. The idea leaks poison like a chancre: nobody misses cancer on purpose. All this does is diminish the general standing of GPs and flood hospitals with healthy patients. As a policy, it fails on every level; yet, as propaganda, there is something about it that works – some tension that it leverages between the patient and the doctor.

Feeling ourselves to be under siege, we assume that defending the NHS means brooking no criticism at all: there is nothing wrong with it; there has never been an overweening surgeon cocking up heart operations; there has never been a useless management culture, blind to failure, punishing the whistle-blowers instead of listening to them. All of which has led to the frankly bizarre position in public discourse where, on one side, any bad event at all that occurs in any hospital is used as evidence of the unfeasibility of the entire institution, while the other side refuses to accept that anything bad has ever happened. A baby dies from a contaminated drip;[26] a psychopathic celebrity rapes and sexually assaults scores of patients, many of them children,

some of them deceased; these become 'serious questions that the NHS must ask itself'. It's preposterous
– the contamination occurred in the private sector;
and the celebrity was depraved, a moral gargoyle, a
man whom, if you met him in fiction, you simply
wouldn't believe. The thing for the NHS to learn
would be: 'abide by the procedures you no doubt
already have in place'.

There are plenty of health problems that the NHS
cannot answer; there's a famous study of life
expectancy in London – they call it the Jubilee Line
of Health Inequality – which shows that, for every
stop you travel east from Westminster,[27] you lose a
year of life expectancy. In 2006 life expectancy
between the best-off and worst-off areas of the UK
tipped over a decade, for the first time since reliable
measurement began. There's a study of infant
mortality that shows a large discrepancy in sheer
survival chances between middle- and working-
class babies.[28] It has become fashionable, even
normal, to point to these divergent outcomes as
though they were a signal that the collective purpose
of the Health Service had failed.

This is just facile; inequalities aren't great and at
times they're woeful, but the Health Service exists
in a generalised atmosphere of social conditions,
and not under a bell jar where everyone breathes
the same clean air of its egalitarian purpose.

However, to refuse all criticism is to reject the
need for change, and this makes you sound stuck,
old-fashioned, an enemy of progress. Tactically,

defensiveness is a mistake. But it's a mistake anyway, because it's based on a needless fear: that if you tug on the thread of any individual failing, the whole thing will unravel. It will not. The Health Service is not some unviable pipe dream, a sweet thing we managed in yesteryear. It is better than it has ever been. It is more viable than ever; the alternatives are so laughably poor. If it has financial problems, that is because it's been either under-funded or skinned alive by the private sector, or both. We don't have to accept a steady deterioration as the price we pay for being modern.

Some things are no-one's fault

There is something monumentally immature about applying the principles of name and shame, targets and terror, or patient choice to a world whose fundamental business is allaying mortality.

My father was diagnosed with secondary liver cancer in October 2004. There was no problem with catching it, since his GP could see it through his actual skin (a 'mass', she called it tactfully, as in, 'I'm a bit worried about this mass', clearly thinking, 'I can see that bloody tumour through two layers of clothing'). By that time it was too late to do anything.

Bonfire Night the year – nearly a full year – before, he had been talking about maybe getting a dog, and said he wanted a small one that would walk at the same pace as he did. I said, 'You'd better make it a three-legged dog, because you're walking incredibly

80

slowly.' If I had interrogated for a second why he was walking at the speed of a three-legged dog (he was only 63 then), he might have been diagnosed sooner. My sister wishes that she had mentioned his voice, which she noticed went squeaky about six months before he was diagnosed. I didn't think a squeaky voice was related to the primary, which was probably in his bowel, and she said, 'Thanks – it's lucky you're an oncologist.' While he was dying, he himself remembered going on a walk that seemed unfathomably long, thinking in retrospect that this was probably the beginning of it. It's such a keen, torturing regret, the too-late diagnosis; it's so painful to blame yourself. I would recommend, if there's even a chink of plausibility to it, blaming the doctor instead.

My father was referred and diagnosed very quickly, and they said from the start that it was terminal, but he might be able to have chemotherapy to survive five months instead of two. This bit was mortifying: each appointment would be a week on from the last; we would often be told some explicit thing, like 'You've got to be strong enough for the chemo; you won't be able to take it if you're already bed-bound.' Then by the next appointment, of course, he would be bed-bound, but he'd be trying to pretend he wasn't. Twice we heaved him up to the door of the unit in a wheelchair, then I ran off to hide the wheelchair while my stepmother sauntered in with him as though he'd walked unaided all the way from the car park, probably whistling.

The oncologist always knew, by looking at him, how ill he already was and had to ignore this awful, vaudeville *Carry On Dying Person* routine. Options were quietly removed from the table. Nothing was ever said; we would just find ourselves back in the car, aware that the momentum had changed and things were no longer such a rush. I usually didn't realise until hours later what had happened – what new reality we'd all just adjusted to.

There's a lot about authority and openness going on in this situation that isn't health-related; my father saw his whole life as a battle of wits between him and whoever had been coarse enough to ask him a straight question. If you asked him the time, he would dick around with his tie, while he figured out if there was an advantage to be had from your thinking it was an hour later than it was.

So he would never have said to any doctor, 'Are you dragging your feet because you think it's a waste of money to give me three extra months of life? Or do you genuinely think it's not medically possible?' Whatever the answer was, he wouldn't have believed it, and he would have seen it as a weakness in himself to ask a question that accurately reflected what he was thinking.

Yet the experts were erecting their own barriers; they never gave us any information that we didn't explicitly ask for, even while they must have been able to guess that, half an hour after leaving their office, we'd realise what questions we should have asked. They were never straight with us. They must have seen that question in his eyes, 'Am I already too ill? Or is there more you could do? Do I just have to ask in the right way?' They must have seen that anguish – of needing an answer, but not trusting the only person who could give it to you. I think they could have been more human; could have said, 'Look, I know what you're thinking. But you are dying, and a billion pounds couldn't buy an extra quality-of-life month for you.' He died on 27th November, not quite six weeks after he had been diagnosed.

This is where the fabled doctorly paternalism doesn't work. It does up to a point. But as soon as there's any sense that doctors know something, but aren't saying it, it undermines the trust we hold them in. Then, to avoid the embarrassment of not being trusted, they disappear behind an authoritarian aspect. Mutual suspicion is a self-tightening coil.

Having said that, they could have been more open and he still would have died; and I would probably now be complaining about the undertaker, who had to turn him on his head because the staircase was too narrow.

We always have this exaggerated respect for specialists, especially surgeons, but they often do the same operation, seven times a day, for their entire career. It's not even as complicated as mending a boiler. And they are quite well protected – not just by our respect, but also by the fact that there's a lot less guesswork by the time you reach the specialist.

GPs, on the other hand, know and recognise pretty well every condition, and torture themselves if they can't. That's how they become so expert, with the tenacity, the stoicism, the verve; they are like Staffordshire bull terriers. Generally speaking, they know enough to judge when they are really at fault, and when people just need to blame them because the alternative is to blame themselves. They need that confidence to stay sane, and we need them to have it, otherwise we'd have to take responsibility for our own, totally specious apportioning of blame. But that doesn't mean they always have to be right, or that we have to treat them as though they are.

Paternalism to partnership

There is a growing trend in general practice: ask the patient what they think is wrong. Half the hypochondriacs can be reassured right off the bat. ('Cancer of the shoulder, I think Doc,' they say. 'Impossible,' he snaps. But for that reassurance, you have to be straight about what you think you've got.) Sometimes the patient's own superstition carries the seed of their real ailment. Once in a while the patient will be right. Health-policy people talk about 'co-production'; how do you give people a sense of power in their own treatment, a sense that they and the medic are engaged together in the search for the same result? By making the relationship as collaborative and human as it can possibly be. Not by naming and shaming anybody, or by endlessly choosing new GPs, or by setting stupid targets. Only politicians would come up with an adversarial system, because adversity is all they understand. If you want your GP appointment to sound like PMQs, put Jeremy Hunt in charge of it.

Market strategies – whether they're ersatz ones like non-price-based competition, or semi-private ones like PFI, or full-on corporate outsourcing – are mainly good at delivering public funds into private hands. They cost the NHS a lot of money; the benefits, so desperately sought by the people who believe they must be there, are pretty contested and vanishing small, when set against the disadvantages.

You don't have to be a consumer in order to participate. 'Choice' is a stupid, callow concept when it comes to health, but that doesn't mean that nobody wants a voice. We can build a different relationship; one in which to be a patient doesn't mean to be passive, and to be a doctor doesn't mean autocratic infallibility.

How do you create a 'participatory' NHS? Lose that word, for a start. It recalls the forced, desperately unwilling jollity of audience participation. Reject ideas that involve voting for committees. They're never popular (they tried them in New Zealand and the turnout was absurd, sometimes in single digits); and the few people who tend to get involved are those who already have free time and civic muscle – traits that mean they are probably democratically over-represented already.

There's no reason why we shouldn't look at health

the same way we look at primary schools. What if there were the equivalent of governorships, roles with meaning, for people who cared? What if the intensity of civic partnership that people feel, when they're engaged with the NHS for real reasons, had somewhere further it could go, beyond 'heal me'? I've seen campaigns for hospitals threatened with closure run by parents whose kids have had 17 operations, and they still find time to bring a judicial review and have a bake-sale. What would happen if we thought creatively about what we needed from each other? If we didn't try to systematise it, or make a duty of it – just accepted that some people could do more than others, that relationships are fluid. If we started with a fundamental assumption of goodwill, where would that lead?

Knowing our NHS to be the best doesn't mean preserving it in aspic. If we trust one another to protect its foundations, we can build something grander still. Can we still afford it? It's the best money we've ever spent, and will remain so.

Have you ever wondered why you can't afford a house?

> Our homes are the slots we fit into in space. Our families are the slots we fit into in time. Making housing harder to come by makes being part of society, even being part of a family, all the harder to achieve.
>
> Danny Dorling, *All that is Solid*

A room at the top(ish)

I bought my first flat in Camberwell, in South-east London, in 2000, when I was 27. The estate agent was a wiry man, nearing retirement; he was one of those booze-hounds who cultivates a pompous, easily offended manner, as if to offset the message of his face ('I'm probably pissed. Try me!'). It was the first time a man had given me a lift in his car as a potential client. It was absolutely brilliant. I used to stick my head out of the window like a dog.

I was already outside the scope of the 'average young professional' – I had been left £27,000 by a relative. I was earning £40,000, which is a lot more than a journalist of my standing (low) and output (lower still) would earn today (I don't want to rub young people's noses in it, but for a while there, as the last century ended, some of us were really overpaid).

Still, there we were, driving round Camberwell, looking for a flat for £150,000; he would point to beautiful, cavernous penthouses, converted from Victorian banks, and say, 'I sold that for £80k, just five years ago!' I would feel anxious, sour and inadequate. 'It always feels like that,' he said once, in a rare flash of empathy. 'You always feel like you missed the boat. If you didn't, you'd be in a depressed market, and you'd be worrying whether anything was worth anything.'

Anyway I bought a flat in Dagmar Road, which has converted Victorian houses down one side, lower-rise, yellow-brick council stock down the other. At the end where it joined the main road, a barrier had been erected. Traffic could only join the road in the middle, and the dead-end became an impromptu second-hand car dealership. The surveyor's report said the proximity to social housing could decrease the flat's value, and I thought it strange how openly snobbish a surveyor was allowed to be: to say that even living within 20 yards of a poor person might impact upon your investment.

I sold it in 2007 for £300,000. In my imagination, I had massively increased its value by getting my sister to paint a feature wall in the living room; in reality, this was roughly in line with all London house-price increases between 2000 and 2007, whose average went up from £180,000 to nearly £300,000.[1] The buyer, by coincidence, was a woman I was at university with, who worked for Control Risks, the security analysts. Which is to say that, after seven years had passed, the flat had changed in a more significant respect than its feature wall: it was no longer affordable by a 27-year-old feature writer; it was now only within the reach of a 34-year-old analyst. I haven't checked what the pay grades are at Control Risks, but I know broadly that jobs with the word 'analyst' in the title are better paid than jobs with the word 'feature'.

Last year I went to see the same flat – middle- and top-floor maisonette – in a house a few doors down. The area hasn't changed at all (though Peckham, half a mile away, has, beyond all recognition). The houses opposite are still social housing. The shop round the corner has gone from a Spar to a Nisa, but the people who run it are the same. It all smells the same, the kerbside feel is the same, the heroin addict in the park – against the odds – is still alive. I did what I always do when nostalgia taunts me like that, and the past is so close that the impossibility of ever going back hits me like sudden news: I bought some cigarettes. I could tell they were symbolic because I didn't buy matches. There was a kid in front of me who couldn't afford both his bananas and his sweets, so I gave him 20p. Which always happened.

This other flat – with no feature wall and, by some architectural quirk I couldn't figure out, a much smaller kitchen – is now on the market for £650,000. If you'd saved 10 per cent for a deposit, so you needed to borrow £585,000, you would still have to be earning nearly £200,000 a year. Clearly there's some latitude here: you could take on a very long-term mortgage, and someone might lend you that on a slightly smaller income, but not much smaller. You could commit to spending a large amount of your pre-tax income on the mortgage and you might be able to raise that amount on £150,000. Nevertheless, this is no longer a flat for an under-30; it might do for a professional couple in their mid-thirties, but they would have to be pretty professional: GPs, heads of department in secondary schools, barristers and, more to the point, travelling in twos. What single person earns £200,000? A banker. We currently have a housing situation in which unremarkable flats in areas nowhere near a Tube cost so much that only a small tier of people working in financial services can afford them. In 2014 the average Southwark property 'earnt' more in a year than the average solicitor: £89,708. The data analyst who did that work, Tristan Carlyon at the National Housing Federation, said: 'If you want a pay rise, the way forward is clear: be a house.'

If this flat continues to double in value every seven years, by 2028 (this is when my kids will be

27-ish), it will be £2.6 million. Is there anybody, seriously, anywhere who thinks wages are going to keep pace with that? Will there even be enough bankers to buy properties at that price? If this sounds far-fetched, there's an asset-management company, London Central Portfolio, which predicted in 2014 that, by 2050, a one-bedder in Mayfair would cost £36 million. They retracted this some months later. Yet nobody is predicting that the market deflates to the point that an ordinary earner could buy an ordinary house. That idea, now, would be completely extraordinary.

Across the UK house prices rose only sixfold between 1983 and 2007.[2] I say 'only'; of course, wages have not risen sixfold. The OECD found in 2013 that UK house prices, on average, were over-valued by 31 per cent in comparison with rents, and by 21 per cent in comparison with incomes.[3] Even that doesn't give a true picture, though, since it takes a national average of prices, against a national average of wages, and doesn't mention that you could never live in that average; the cheap housing that brings down the average is in the North, while the better wages that bring up the average are in London and the South-east.

The inequalities in house prices are fascinating, and newspapers like the *Daily Telegraph* (chief recorder of the national housing obsession) love to produce maps[4] to show how many square feet in a cheap place you could buy for one square foot in London. For 231 square feet in the capital (this is a

91

tiny studio flat), you could buy 4,031 square feet in parts of Wales (this is majestic-scale splendour of five bedrooms, plus garage bays, whatever they are). That kind of bizarro, Alice-in-Wonderland difference in scale – the idea that you could pay the same price for such different things – is meant to create the illusion of choice. Instead of looking at the box studio for which you pay way more than you can afford and thinking, 'This is nuts. Why can't I afford something normal?', you're supposed to think, 'It is my choice to live in a box. If I minded that much, I could choose to relocate to a mansion.'

But choice is nowhere, when it comes to housing. You cannot move to Wales if your salary springs in the South. All that matters is how much your costs are, relative to your earnings in that area. This ratio throws up some data showing that, even while London is far and away the most expensive, housing relative to income is steeper in rural areas, mainly pretty ones – Cornwall, the Cotswolds – places where people have second homes. In South Buckinghamshire the price of an average house has gone above 20 times the average wage.[5] Not even Northern Rock in the good old days would give you that kind of mortgage.

I mention this only because there is a growing tendency to write off unaffordability as a London problem – like rudeness – that Londoners just inexplicably have. On the contrary, anywhere people want to buy houses, prices outstrip wages. In the event that, one day, London becomes full and everybody moves to Bristol, the same thing will happen there.

We'll deal in a second with what this does to people at or near the bottom – what it does to rents and Housing Benefit bills; what it does to people who are cast out of prosperous areas by scrambling local authorities; what it does to disposable income; how long it would take for a couple on the average wage to save a deposit (actually, that's quite easy – 31 years[6]); how this changes the amount of money people have to spend and the way people have to live.

Right now, I'm fascinated by the situation with the top 10 per cent of earners, not because I think we're more important, but because I am amazed that there isn't more pushback.

Nobody can seriously believe that this is a good system: one in which people under 40 have to either inherit or work in financial services to buy a place they can live in. Adam Smith himself, grandfather of neoclassical economics (which is what our hyper-rational underpinnings are supposed to be all about), would turn in his grave to see this. An economy based on rents? Markets work when the buyer and seller can come to a mutually advantageous arrangement; they don't work when almost everybody is working to service the debts they owe to a very small number at the top.

Even if you are in your forties, and you did manage to grab onto the ropes of this hot-air balloon – let's say you bought a flat-to-let while the going was good – you'll still have children, probably. Or if you don't, you'll know people who do. Or if you don't, you might not want to live in a city where only the offspring of the rich can live.

And, of course, if you are under 40, you are living this experiment: wondering how it is that you're in a job so respectable that you're allowed to witness other people's passport applications, and yet your salary wouldn't buy you anywhere closer than 300 miles to your office.

This should be the easiest place in the world to find agreement. But try flying this kite. Try saying: this can't continue. I've heard the most ridiculous rationalisations – that the problem is actually with old-age care, because the money we should be inheriting from our parents instead goes on their care-home. I got into a Twitter row with a young guy on *The Economist* magazine. It doesn't matter what he's called; there are tons of them, mainly on *The Economist* and the *Financial Times*. Their line is that there's no problem with young people being unable to buy, because all the cool people rent anyway. Europeans rent. Renting is more flexible; it lends itself better to the international job offers that will inevitably cluster around the cool, flexible person. 'But, but . . . you're not renting out of choice. You're renting because you can't afford to buy; since you can't amass the money you need to buy, you're building up someone else's fortune.' Actually, came the urbane reply, the additional expense of being responsible for things like boilers makes buying (contrary to my old-timer's folly) much more expensive and much more hassle.

Now, never mind that renting is not a European paradise, because we in Britain don't have any of the regulations that Europeans have; never mind that landlords become ever more rapacious and unreasonable, as their power grows (though, in the end, we're going to have to talk about this) . . . The crucial point here is this: these young men are economically literate, more than literate. They must know that the changes to housing costs over the past three or four decades will ultimately make their lives worse. If and when they do buy a house, it will be smaller and farther out than it would have been; they will spend more of their time commuting, a greater proportion of their wages paying for it, and they will take longer to pay it back. If, on the other hand, they stay in their rental accommodation for the whole of their lives, then they will never build up the wealth that their predecessors did; this will change their old age, and change the prospects of their children and grandchildren. They know all this! If they were really the perfectly rational, perfectly self-interested individuals that their worldview insists upon, they would see that this situation is untenable.

The debate is permeated by the desperate preservation of the status quo. The government's answer is the 'Help to Buy' scheme: it underwrites first-time buyers' debts so that they can get mortgages. It is the ultimate sticking-plaster policy: they justify it on the grounds that, unless borrowers go bankrupt, the government won't have to spend anything. But the reason first-timers couldn't get mortgages in the first place was that their earnings were out of kilter with the debt they wanted to incur. So the government is basically fixing it for them to take on a debt they can't afford, which will alter their lives; and fixing it for the mortgage companies not to have to take a risk, when the entire justification for the profit they make is that they took a risk to make it. To put that even more bluntly, the government here takes the core principles of productive capitalism – investment, lending, risk – and neuters them. To what purpose? To make sure an unaffordable market is briefly affordable for some people. Senior analysts called this 'moronic', on-the-record.[7] Even the Bank of England, well-known lair of rebels, said this was a bad idea, because it would only make house prices go up, and they were already too high. The International Monetary Fund gave the same warning: 'the result would ultimately be mostly house price increases that would work against the aim of boosting access to housing'.

I do not say this for partisan reasons; Labour messed up housing, too, and it was Margaret Thatcher who lit this dancing bonfire. No, I say this because it forces the question: why, when it clearly does nothing to solve the real problem, and when even your own team say it's a bad idea, would you execute such a stupid policy? For the same reason that building societies have started to call first-time buyers 'young' at 42, because they would rather contort the language than admit that this market is no longer open to the young (42! Not even the beauty market would try to get away with that). And for the same reason that people keep arguing with me.

Fundamentally, everyone believes that the market is bound to crash. Four months before my trip down memory cul-de-sac, the market for dwellings in Camberwell was even hotter. A garage at the end of Dagmar Road sold for £550,000 in April 2014, despite the fact that it didn't have planning permission. It was the most expensive garage ever sold in Britain, and prompted a lot of frustration among economists and geographers: can't you people see this is a bubble? Don't you know anything? At around the same time there was a spate of stories about people not even bothering to tidy up when they were selling, flats going on the market heaped with junk, fresh animal faeces on the floor. The obvious point was that the market was so strong that sellers no longer had to pull their thumb out of their arse: buyers would buy anything.

The deeper second point is that the value of the house no longer bears any relation to what the house is used for. You're selling a flat for half a million pounds to a person who earns £50,000. How can that person's shelter cost them everything they earn – all their waking hours – for a decade? It makes no economic sense; it makes no human sense. So you can see, in the mess and squalor, an irresistible truth: what's the point of cleaning up, of making it look like a home? This isn't a home, this is a commodity. The fact that some poor schmuck also has to live in it is their lookout.

A crash will happen, because no market expands for ever. It may take 15 years, because so much of the bubble is fuelled by foreign investment, or it might happen this year. By the time you read this, it may have already happened – in August 2014 Rightmove recorded the biggest-ever summer fall in house prices, of 2.9 per cent on the preceding month. A natural summer contraction or the beginning of something? I don't know and, more to the point, it doesn't matter: a slow deflation will not bring houses back into the reach of average wages for decades. And a fast deflation is called a crash. These are not benign, market-regulating things. There have been four crashes in this country since the 1970s; they have done nothing to normalise the housing market. They hit the country unequally. They infect markets larger than their own (the entire global financial crash, bear in mind, started with the 2007 crash in American house prices). Some places recover, and other places take scores of months to find their true bottom, by which time the whole area is depressed. Inequalities – between places and people – deepen. And the most buoyant places (the ones, if you like, that are most to blame) are the fastest to recover. Looking at a problem like our housing market and thinking it'll be okay because of the inevitable crash is like looking at climate change and thinking, 'Not to worry; we'll probably have a gigantic war, in which so many people are killed that we hit our emissions targets effortlessly.' All of that may be true, but there are better ways to solve problems than just waiting for them to be eclipsed by other, larger problems.

And this brings us to the small matter of Armageddon. If half of our resistance to change is the complacency that things will change with or without us, the other half is genuine and understandable fear. If the housing market is inflated, let it remain so; because what exactly happens in a crash? All those things I just said, and more: housing represents 58.1 per cent of the total net worth of this country, which is £4.3 trillion.[8] 76 per cent of all bank loans in Britain go to property, 64 per cent of that to residential mortgages.[9] What happens to our net worth if that market crashes? What happens to our bond market, our international standing? Are those banks overexposed enough to crumple and, if so, do we bail them out? Are we looking at a market that is too big to fail? From this perspective, you would do anything to avert a crash; but what is really unforgivable about politics is the shameless time-span they put on their thinking. They don't want to avoid a crash for ever; they just want to avoid a crash on their watch. Help to Buy is plainly designed to keep the show on the road until the next election. New Labour's final term was loaded with initiatives to lend money to people who couldn't afford a deposit.[10] They should have been asking what had gone wrong with wages and prices, that people couldn't save their own money. Instead we got Open Market HomeBuy, MyChoice HomeBuy, Ownhome and HomeBuy Direct: they could all have been grouped under the umbrella Votebuy Direct, and probably, in some corner of Whitehall, they were.

Thatcher's Right to Buy may have been a massive popularity purchase, but at least it wasn't cynical: she believed it was the right thing to do. More recent governments have been doing whatever will cost the least and hold things together the longest, to the advantage of their own party. This stinks. I think it distresses me more than individual acts of corruption; at least delinquency is rebellious. Bland, institutional self-interest, suffocating the future, is not fun from any angle.

But, in the meantime, while we wait for either a political saviour or a massive crash, or more likely the second and then the first, how is the market staying afloat?

It's partly kept up by elite extremes: there is, for instance, a discernible skew in central London properties towards the foreign super-rich. 75 per cent of houses newly released in this premium bracket – houses with Central London postcodes – are sold at overseas events.[11] Developers think the UK rich aren't going to be rich enough, and I'm sure they're right. This contributes to the emptiness of residential Central London (they're buying for a currency haven or a pied-à-terre, not to turn rental income). The high-end bedrooms of W1 are empty;

there is no 'space' left in the other London postcodes for people doing normal jobs. These two facts are not unrelated, but their relationship takes quite a complicated path.

One final thing: it isn't quite fair to say that we have no UK families rich enough to buy UK property. Once the richest (now the second-richest) UK landowner is the Duke of Westminster. This fact seems to me to belong to a different era. If it were Libya circa 2004 and Colonel Gaddafi's son owned half of Tripoli, it would make perfect sense. I struggle to reconcile it with my image of a modern democracy, that in the most expensive city in the world (apart from Monaco), an aristocrat owns everything. But to people ten years younger than me it probably fits the image of modernity pretty well.

Things have changed quite a lot. The problem with the status quo is that it's not static.

A room in the middle

> As always, the worst is never certain to arrive. It is much too soon to warn readers that by 2050 they may be paying rent to the emir of Qatar.
>
> Thomas Piketty, *Capital in the Twenty-First Century*

Relax, everyone; you may be getting poorer, fast, while a small number of people get hugely richer, but it's way too soon to say that everything will belong to one man by the middle of the century. Way too soon.

8.5 million people now rent from a private landlord. The number of people in Britain who are landlords, Shelter puts at around 2 per cent. Tenants are typically spending 40 per cent of their net income on rent;[12] housing is considered unaffordable if it takes up more than 35 per cent of your net income. These figures and estimates are from government sources, they're not from the *Socialist Worker*. Put simply, this means that everybody in the middle is screwed, nearly screwed or totally screwed.

In 1997, shortly before Labour came to power, the Conservatives made the assured shorthold tenancy[13] the default contract between private landlords and their tenants. This had important knock-on effects for the power relationship between landlord and tenant, because from here on in, tenants could basically be evicted for anything; not just rent arrears, asking for repairs (the homelessness charity Shelter calls these 'revenge evictions') or asking in a high-pitched voice. The year before, the buy-to-let mortgage had been invented. It didn't – and couldn't – really take off until tenants had had their rights curtailed; while they were well protected, the investment was too risky and the mortgages not frequently approved. Under the last government, the Rugg Review proposed more regulations for landlords and letting agents. In 2010 the Coalition scrapped those ideas, which only reinforced landlords' untouchability.[14]

Since that time, 18 years ago, buy-to-let returns have outstripped those of every other major asset class. A financial services PR person noted, in congratulatory spirit, 'Every £1,000 invested in an average buy-to-let property purchased with a 75% loan-to-value (LTV) mortgage in the final quarter of 1996 would have been worth £13,048 by the final quarter of 2013, a compound annual return of 16.3%.'[15]

For no reason that I can make out, their mortgage payments are tax-free. Buy-to-let landlords are effectively paid by the Treasury to buy the properties that their tenants would have bought themselves, had the prices not been forced up by the BTL mortgage. So even though you read a lot about buy-to-let mortgages being a two-sided game, and how it's a risk, and a nuisance, the truth is it's a game in which one side has won before it's even begun.

The more people have had to rent instead of buying, the higher rents have become. They're a captive market. In 2013 rents increased by twice as much as wages,[16] but in London this hit the laughable multiplier of eight. Look, we can't blame the housing market entirely; it doesn't help that wages are stagnant. We can't say this is entirely due to landlords' gleeful exploitation, because of course houses are over-valued, so they have to charge more to get the same returns (you could ask, of course, why they needed to get the same returns and couldn't just suck up 10 per cent in profit for a while; just while the other 'team' got back on its feet; just so as not to impoverish their fellow humans. But I don't want to get schmaltzy).

There is a brilliant campaign group called Generation Rent who put a lot of the blame on baby-boomers, which is to say, their own parents. But I think it's reasonable to conclude that we're looking at a constellation of factors, a platoon of enemies: systemic wage decline, individual rapaciousness, governmental failure and corporate greed (both in banking and construction, of which more in a second).

One observable change, besides cost, is that rental properties are becoming steadily more crap. One-third of homes in the private rental sector are officially classified as 'non-decent'.[17] Even besides the revenge evictions, there is something unpleasantly overweening in the way landlords, via letting agents, deal with tenants. I've been guarantor for a couple of friends of mine, and the demands are absurd – I had to swear that I was good for three years' worth of rent, should anything go wrong, in one case (the landlord could evict the tenant after six months). The last guarantor form I signed asked for two next-of-kins, who had to be blood-related to me and yet not reside at the same address. It's audacious: my blood relatives aren't liable for a guarantee that I undertake. How on earth is it anybody's business where they live? Yet of course I couldn't say that, in case the tenant lost the flat, and he was already panicking.

The less secure employment becomes, and the

less likely people are to have three years' worth of solid bank statements all saying the same thing, the more extravagant the landlords' demands become, to a point way past 'unreasonable', and closer to 'cruel'. And perhaps landlords would respond that now tenants aren't typically in long-term, steady employment, they need more security. But this is against the spirit of anything like decent capitalism, which is that profit comes with risk attached. Instead, the more profit landlords generate, the less risk they are prepared to stomach, and the more humiliating hoops they make their tenants jump through, to prove this unprovable thing: 'whatever your next outrageous demand, I'm good for it.'

In the event, my guarantee failed. The letting agent turned me down because I lived in London and Darren Brook lived in the East Riding of Yorkshire. 'If we have to take you to court, we have to attend your local court, which would work out very expensive for us. You have to look at the bigger picture.' It was moonshine and they knew it. Court proceedings for costs are done online anyway. It was obvious to me that they didn't want him because he was disabled. In 2013 the BBC did an undercover investigation that showed London letting agents weren't showing black people round their properties.

I take the view that they don't actively hate the disabled, or races not their own, these agents; they're just trying to protect their client from poverty, and their prejudice tells them where poverty, disability and race coincide. But when you're at the wrong end of the decision, it feels as it must have felt in the Sixties, when boarding rooms carried signs saying 'No Blacks, No Irish, No Dogs'. 'I bet if I was still able to work, they would have taken our money gladly,' Brook said. 'We've been made to feel like some kind of vermin.'

A room at the bottom

> The party in power, whose late twentieth-century figurehead, Margaret Thatcher, did so much to create the problem, is responding by separating off the economically least powerful and squeezing them into the smallest, meanest, most insecure possible living space.
>
> James Meek, *Private Island*

Just before the most expensive garage in the UK was sold in Camberwell, a local Labour politician called Tony Belton was trying to get me to go round a little flat that had come up in South-west London. It was ex-council and was on the market for £1.2 million.

I grew up in Wandsworth and have known him since I was 14, when he was the Labour leader of the council. Then, he was considered quite centrist by his more radical leafleteers. Now, even his Labour colleagues consider him the last barnacle of the hard-left. The nastiness of this now-Conservative council is gobsmacking. The ideas they've run up the flagpole include: charging parents to use playgrounds; selling Wandsworth town hall for flats, and getting the council workers to work from home; evicting the entire families of people who participated in the London riots. Vindictive, impractical, often illegal, very naïve, their vision is like a cocktail made by children: all shampoo, bath salts and orange juice. You'd never swallow it; all you can do is look at it and think how disgusting it is.

Today's Labour members on the council are plucky, but pretty busy. They certainly do not have time to linger on the mistakes of the 1980s, and how a little ex-council flat on what used to be an estate full of drug dealers came to be worth 48 times the inflation-adjusted salary of the average-income earner for whom it was originally built. So it was just left to this guy, like a dogged Hercule Poirot, trying to solve a whodunnit in which – while the victims are alive and kicking – all the suspects are dead. I didn't go with him, in the end. I knew what the flat would probably look like.

But just out of interest, where does that person, who would once have lived in that modest but not poky flat in South-west London, live now?

In 1979, the year before Right to Buy, the number of households in social housing – that is, stock owned by either the council or a housing association – hit a peak of 5.5 million.[18] In the 35 years since then, a lot have been flogged off, almost none built; there are now 1.7 million homes owned by councils, 2.4 million owned by housing associations, 4.1 million households in total living in social housing. The term 'affordable' is rarely meant literally and housing associations are often no protection against impossible rents. It is incredibly hard to qualify for social housing and, even if you do, the waiting lists are huge. Those two concepts have come to run into each other, two sides of the same coin of 'scarcity'; but actually, they're quite distinct problems. You may qualify for social housing with bells on, but if your local authority doesn't have any, your qualification means nothing. It's like knowing how to do dressage in a town with no horses.

Councils sometimes try to take the heat off themselves with a promise to do things differently. So, for instance, in March 2013 the cabinet minister for housing at Hammersmith & Fulham Council told LBC Radio that there was a change in store for people who wanted to go on the housing waiting list. You could hear the waves of approval from presenter Nick Ferrari to Andrew Johnson, the housing officer. Addressing himself particularly to Bulgarians, Johnson said: 'For those people who want to come here and work and make a contribution, fantastic. For those who don't, I'm afraid there won't be a council house for them.'

This is such utter bullshit that, even listening to it now, I break into an incredulous smile. (I kept it as a podcast. I had a feeling I would need it.) They don't have any housing. They have 13,000 homes (all full), and at the time they made that announcement their waiting list had more than 8,000 people on it, some of whom had been waiting for years. The idea that a lazy Bulgarian might – previous to Mr Johnson's intervention – have been able to arrive in the UK and saunter into a council flat is fantasy.

His promise didn't do anything to boost supply or change demand; all it did was slash the council's waiting list, from 8,171 in 2012 to 768 in April 2013. Those people were never going to be socially housed anyway. The council simply decreed them no longer a problem.

So that's one downside of social housing: that, when you need it, bureaucracies have no problem just magicking you away; you'll get Housing Benefit – or Local Housing Allowance (LHA), as it's called for private-sector rent – and sink or swim in the private sector with the rest.

When you're dependent on social housing, you are very vulnerable to policy change. It's often made by people who don't understand the system they're messing with, or who don't care to understand it, because making a mess is part of the point.

The 'bedroom tax' is a good example: by this new law, introduced in April 2013, if you're under-occupying, you lose Housing Benefit: 14 per cent of it for one spare room, 25 per cent of it for two or more spare rooms. So you either have to move or make up the difference from your other income. Except that if you had other income to spare, you wouldn't be eligible for social housing in the first place. And if there were a smaller place for you to move to, you probably wouldn't be under-occupying.[19]

There's a chance that the reason you have a spare room is some recent event – perhaps your child has died. Until recently you were allowed a year's grace period for the death of a family member, which has now been reduced to three months.[20] So now you either have to spend your non-existent spare income or move to a non-existent smaller property, on the back of a life-destroying loss. It's not very pretty, this policy. It is also inept, incredibly expensive to administer, creates costs in other areas (food banks, debt services, evictions) and, even leaving those aside, is likely to save much less than projected. Iain Duncan Smith spoke of probable savings of £415–500 million a year.[21] A York University study disputed this, putting the likely figure at 60 per cent of that.[22]

To put that money into perspective, the free-school-meals policy that Nick Clegg made up on the hoof, to allay his fears of being egged at his own party conference, is going to cost £1.15 billion. This is why it's no joke being a social tenant; at the stroke of someone else's pen you might find that your life is impossible, to save money that in another governmental context would be pissed up a wall on a PR exercise.

That's actually slightly too kind to policymakers: people on Housing Benefit are deliberately scapegoated, as a cover for the shambolic situation. The benefit cap (part of the new Universal Credit system) is always justified with this line, which they clearly have on a giant Post-it in Tory HQ. 'How can it be right that a family on benefits is bringing in more money than a family in which both parents work?' Well, good question: how can it be right? It doesn't make any sense.

It's right because rents are increasing faster than wages. So if you want people not to be homeless, you have to give them more money than an employer would pay them. But this is a pretty stark truth, lifting the lid on a snakepit of system failure. Blame the benefit claimants instead, and you create a more manageable picture of a system that would work fine, if it weren't for those brazen slugs at the bottom.

What can people do otherwise? There is a huge constituency – one-quarter of adults under 35 – still living in their childhood bedroom.[23] It is droll that Margaret Thatcher, the person who (allegedly) said a 26-year-old still using a bus could consider himself a failure, is directly responsible for a generation of 26-year-olds who are still using their Snoopy duvet cover. This has spurred lots of lifestyle articles about what it's like to discover that your mum now takes 15 minutes to get out of a chair and your dad has hair growing out of everything, but the real kicker about living with your parents into adulthood is that you can't get laid.

So either we change our attitudes and become more like Italy, or the eighteenth century, where there is – or was – nothing unusual about living in your childhood bedroom (but also, now that I think about it, it is – or was – difficult to get laid) or we accept that this market makes people's lives less fulfilling, less independent, less free. If you described this as a communist system ('In Soviet Russia circa 1989, a quarter of adults had to live with their parents' or 'In Singapore, due to government land controls, under-35s can't own property') people would say, 'What a horrible system, imagine living in a country that didn't care about personal freedom.' Because our system results from a free market, it is taken to mean freedom for all. The opposite is true. It brings varying degrees of financial benefit, to 2 per cent of people, and it means one-quarter of under-35s cannot get laid. (No, to be a bit more rigorous about the data, the ones who already had a boyfriend or girlfriend when their living arrangements were different are probably doing okay.)

If you can't, or won't, or aren't allowed to move back in with your parents, but you are in the very significant group whose wages do not cover rent, there is Housing Benefit. This started in its current form in 1982, just after the Right to Buy. This was the plan: sell off council houses to the responsible, hard-working people who live in them; they will all now be housed – job done. But in the unlikely event that a few cranks or misfits don't take up our generous offer, we will tide them over until the market has coped with the shock and private provision has caught up with demand. That's what it was supposed to be, an obscure benefit for weirdos, like Widowed Parent's Allowance. Its administration was passed over to local authorities from central government, on the basis that local authorities were the ones who knew best what their local market conditions were like.

Even by 1989 it cost £5 billion. All the proceeds of the housing-stock sell-off went to central government; and local government was suddenly responsible for the people who couldn't afford to house themselves. And that situation still abides today. Imagine if any Thatcher-era politician had spelt this out, 'This benefit will balloon until it is the single largest element of social security, one-third of the entire welfare bill, and over five million people are on it, many of them working full-time; most of the flats will end up in the hands of buy-to-let landlords. Local authorities, with very little stock of their own, will no longer be investing in their own properties for their own citizens, but rather jetting out money, like a carotid artery, to the private sector' . . . There might have been a few more reservations expressed about the Right to Buy policy.

In the spending period from 2011 to 2014 the amount allocated to Housing Benefit – £94 billion – was nearly 20 times that allocated to new housing: £5 billion.[24] Things were no different under Labour, though the sheer number of people claiming has gone up since 2009, when it was 4.2 million, to 2014, when it was 5 million. This is the inevitable consequence of declining living standards and the erosion of workplace rights (more in Poverty).

Housing Benefit is now paid to 21 per cent of residents;[25] it's the highest number who can't afford their rent in the OECD, and the plainest possible signal that the market is broken. The extra claims over the past five years are almost all from people with jobs. In 2009 there were 450,000 employed HB claimants; in 2014 there were 1.1 million.[26] This is not a story about scroungers or the idle, or about a creaking benefit system. This is a story about wages not being high enough, and rents being too high. I find there's something really cheering about it: 1.1 million people doing a job that doesn't even cover their rent, for the sake of their sense of self. Look at that work ethic; in some classes, we're almost German. Contrast that with (is this a low blow?) the average MP, who sees no dignity in work for its own sake; indeed seems actively dismayed by the kind of people who travel anywhere and don't keep the receipt.

There's one more group: the housing 'pinched', the proper definition of which[27] is households that spend half their income on housing. These, by the way, are mainly not people on Housing Benefit, because that's taken as a direct subsidy. They tend to be those with just too much to qualify for support; nearly a million working households, containing 2.2 million people. Almost all of them are in the bottom 20 per cent of income; 830,000 households have £60 a week to live on, after they've paid their rent. These are the people you see being interviewed at a food bank, whose situation doesn't make sense: they're employed, they're not on any benefits, they don't have a heap of children, they're not disabled, they're not full-time carers. They are just one bad event – a broken boiler, a parking ticket – away from not having any food. And there they are, in the queue, in a tidy size-ten trouser suit, picking up chickpeas, unable to believe this is happening.

How will it end? Nobody knows for certain. It is much too soon to start warning people that they'll end up in cardboard boxes. In the short term, interest rates are bound to go up at some point, and that will make life a lot harder for home owners with mortgages, who are currently under-represented in the 'pinched' group. That will have a knock-on effect on rents, too, making the pinch even harder.

One study[28] adumbrates the picture for the young. By 2020 a large debt hangover from university, coupled with house prices being so much higher than salaries, will reduce home ownership among 18–35-year-olds from nearly 35 per cent in 1997 to around 12 per cent. All those people who would have owned, by the same projections, will go into the private rental sector. If that process continues, uninterrupted by regulation in lettings or policy levers of any sort, they are going to get fleeced. The National Housing Federation found in 2012 that the cost of privately renting a home had risen 37 per cent since 2007, and would rise another 35 per cent by 2018. The people just below these renting professionals will be knock-on fleeced, and the people below that. The prediction was 400,000 under-35s unable to buy or rent. With changes that significant, it's hard to say what will kick in, between parental bail-outs and 'chaotic pathways' (that's what you're on, if you spend a portion of a given year homeless, or sleeping on a sofa).

This cannot stand. Society has a pretty solid track record of ignoring things that only happen to poor people, but we cannot sell out an entire generation. They won't have it.

Here it becomes necessary to linger briefly on whose fault it was. Not for pleasure, just for answers. The lesson of Right to Buy is that, if the state is going to take responsibility for housing people, then it needs to own housing stock. If it owns nothing, it is reliant on the social and the private sector. Housing associations do some valiant work, but many behave like businesses navigating pesky regulations, rather than pro-social enterprises. The private sector absolutely rinses the public sector; they know people must be housed, and they own the housing. How did it come to pass that, in every postcode, in every county, the smallest, crummiest flat is available to rent at exactly the cost of the maximum LHA for a flat that size? Because they're gaming the system, and I don't blame them; the system deserves it – it's rubbish.

Part of the money spent on Housing Benefit should be used to build new homes. The guaranteed income of that rent, which the government is going to be paying anyway, needs to be used creatively, in the sense of: let's create some places for people to live. There is an environmental angle to this, which is that the housing we need for the future – food-neutral, energy-neutral, run on edible walls and its own solar-powered windows – will not be undertaken by the private sector, which isn't far-sighted. It can only be built by the state and, when it is, it will be awe-inspiring. The notion of council housing as a ghetto for the underclass will evaporate (more in Environment).

There's some debate about who should own this social housing, once it's been built. The spectrum runs from 'sell it on the open market and build more' to 'keep it in state hands for ever'. Between those two positions, there are original ideas. People could buy them, but they would do so for security and a sense of belonging, not for speculation and investment. The council would set the price at which they would buy back. The market would be a lot more boring, but affordability very often does sound boring on paper, yet there is much more delight in living it. It could be crowd-funded, a classic nineteenth-century building-society model, turbo-powered by the Internet. The state provides the land, one million small investors provide the money, it works as an investment vehicle with meaning, one that is accessible and creates winners, not losers.

Building new homes would only be good enough

if the high prices were down to a shortage of supply. In fact, the high prices are down to more than a shortage of supply, and the shortage of supply is down to more than the fact that we're a teeny-weeny island that mostly comes under the protection of EU wildflower-meadow regulation.

Second point first: if it were just about shortage, then the empty homes there are would be filled, the land that has planning permission would be developed, the flats that need renovating would be renovated, and it would be in everybody's interests to cooperate to fill the space. In fact there is a huge amount of land – enough for 400,000 homes – that already has planning permission and yet remains undeveloped. There are 80,000 empty homes in London alone. There's a small amount of wilful under-occupation by rich people living in Russia or Switzerland. But the hoarding is principally done by the developers themselves. Land prices go up much faster than housing prices.[29] When you build a house on land, you realise its value in the price of the house: you're already dropping some of its price as a speculative asset, just by turning it into a place that people can live in. If you absolutely have to build, all the incentives are for you to make as cheap a house as possible, to mitigate the money you're already chucking away. It's custom-built, this system, to create poor-quality housing, incredibly slowly.

There's an old-fashioned tax solution to that, which is to tax land. This isn't necessarily a redistributive tax, although naturally the money raised would go into the public purse. But it would exist to discourage the hoarding of a thing we all need. We don't need to make housing unprofitable, to make this work. We merely have to make it unprofitable to keep it deliberately empty.

While we're there, we have to change the council-tax bands. It would be redistributive, because at the moment people whose house's real value is £2 million are paying the same as people with a house worth one-quarter of that. But the main reason is that it makes us look ridiculous, to have a tax based on property values that we last checked 22 years ago.

When everyone's losing, who wins?

> The housing market is not really a market for houses. The housing market is driven principally by the availability of finance, mainly mortgage debt, but sometimes bonuses, inheritances, or hot money from abroad.
>
> Faisal Islam, *The Default Line*

Corporate perversion of this market doesn't end with the construction industry. Indeed, from some angles, the builders wouldn't even get a footnote. Banks – partly with the bonuses to their own employees, mainly with the liberalisation of the mortgage market – made this mess.

119

Credit, purchasing power, money itself – these things are not created by government, but by banks. Some money is 'created' for human capital (student loans), some for commercial real estate, a small amount for productive investment – the vast majority, 85 per cent, is for residential mortgages. Banks create the money that lets us buy the homes that are then too expensive because the money was created imprudently, with insufficient heed to our salaries. Being flooded with credit does more than accelerate debt: it pushes up prices, so that you have to get into that debt to buy the thing that, previously, cost less. You could call it a free market, in so far as banks are free to create as much money as they like. But you, with your million pound mortgage, or your £300,000 studio flat – how free are you?

The scandal in the early Noughties was the self-certified mortgage: you didn't have to prove anything, you just had to certify your made-up salary yourself. The length of the repayment term was increased at around the same time, so that it became normal for it to be longer than 25 years. Then there was a short, insane period when the loan-to-value (LTV) could be anything up to 125 per cent. 'Cashback' or 'underwater' mortgages, they called them, after the cute American term for negative equity. Northern Rock called its 125 per cent LTV the 'Together' mortgage. 'Together, we can go bankrupt faster . . . it'll take you too long if you try it on your own.' Interest-only mortgages – you only pay the interest, and after 25 years still owe the original sum – were merely the contractual incarnation of the banks' underlying attitude: 'We don't care how you plan to pay this back, or where you'll live at the end. Who do you think we are – your dad?'

The banks soaked the market in credit. There are two interpretations of this. The centrist, acceptable reading is that the housing market became something else, a market for buying and selling debt. The Marxist reading is that 'use' value came unstuck from 'exchange' value: the commodification of the Thing – that is, the money to be made from exchanging it – set the value. This left the people who actually wanted to use the Thing unable to afford it. These are the same arguments, really. It's just that people are still scared to reference Marx, even – especially – when he's right, and this leads to a ridiculous reinvention of principles that were established and understood 150 years ago.

Just after the financial crash I interviewed Andy Haldane, the chief economist at the Bank of England. It was weird, like meeting the man behind the curtain. He spent an hour with me, and then said at the end that it was off-the-record. Obviously my time is not money, but surely his time is money? I reckon I casually relieved him of a thousand pounds.

Anyway he said this one, puzzled thing, and I recall it here impressionistically. The lending markets had to open up a bit, he said, because in the Seventies you couldn't borrow anything, you had to be personally known to your bank manager, and he would decide what you were capable of, based on what he knew of your father, even your grandfather. But when the markets have opened up so much that people are taking on debts they could never hope to justify on their salaries, this will have a number of consequences.

In the worst-case scenario, the debts turn bad, and there will be a massive global financial crash, which of course is what had just happened, starting in Florida. But even in the best-case scenario, this lending will force up prices, which will price people out, which in turn will encourage more lending. We are still in the habit of calling that 'risky', even though it is clear, now, that the banks took no risks. They were bailed out. In a paradox that I would call 'delicious' if I lived in the future, the risk is borne by everybody except the people who claim to be taking a risk: the borrower and, via the Treasury, the taxpayer.

Sorry, that last bit was me, not Haldane: he ended on 'force up prices'. Exuberant lending, such as the high-street banks did in the years up to the financial crash, forced up prices. Let's not dwell on why they did it, whether simply for profit or because they genuinely don't like to say 'no'. We can't leave something so serious to people who do not take it seriously.

You're always fighting yesterday's war with a bank: I could say that we need regulation to stop deals that are underwater before they even begin;

but the next debacle won't come from an underwater mortgage. The next thing will be a scam they're inventing right now. I could say that building societies need to go back to being not-for-profit, but I'm not even sure that would help.

Banks need two things: they need to be able to go bust; and they need morals. They won't remember their morals until we let them go bust. Lending someone five times their salary is a social act, between human beings, with huge human implications. If you don't care what happens to them at the end of it, it doesn't work.

The last, and perhaps obvious, thing is the rental market: it's unlikely that any of these measures will cause an instant and radical upswing in home ownership, so the rental market needs to be civilised. It works in Europe because tenants can get a bit of security – five years instead of six months. Everything in the UK market plays to the landlord. The standards are poor, the energy-efficiency is woeful. Most landlords understand property only as an investment and have no expertise in actually providing housing. It's just absurd: the whole country subsidising one investor bracket, at the expense of . . . the whole country.

Doing housing differently is a pain. It's complicated and fraught, rife with pitfalls, crackling with conflict. A lot of the answers aren't obvious. But imagine what it would be like, facing this system, if you were the only one. In fact, you're one of millions. You're one of almost everybody, except the affluent over-40s, and even we hate it. The hard bit of any process is building support. That's not going to be the hard bit here.

Are taxes for the little people?

> The reality is that the history of social justice is to be found written in the tax laws of most countries.
>
> Richard Murphy,
> *Towards a New Tax Consensus*

If tax is going to work, you have to love it. You can't just see it as some almighty ball-ache that happens to raise lots of useful money. You've got to love the principle itself: love the act of putting in your share, love the scope of the ambition it embodies, and then love the grandeur of the plans it makes possible. You've got to love it like you've just met it; love it like a community of medievals drinking filthy puddle-water who have just figured out how they could afford plumbing. You've got to feel your chest puff out with civic and human pride at the thought of what you did.

This sounds improbable, this state of mind, but

actually it isn't. What's really difficult is drumming up a sense of pride in things you've done on your own. Think of any magazine interview, with anybody, where the question is 'What are you proudest of?' They always say, 'My children.' 'When were you happiest?' 'When my son was born . . .' [a pause, probably, that the interviewer is too polite to record, while they remember they have two children] . . . 'Sons! When my sons were born.'

Now the birth of children (followed by their continuing existence) is a precious and wonderful thing, but nobody really believes they're an achievement: they are their own achievement; they do all that hard work to make themselves what they are.

It is hard to take pride in individual achievements because you sound like a wanker. Material goods are supposed to give you some frisson of enjoyment, but try naming them out loud. You sound appalling; you sound like a cartoon villain, the dreck of every sitcom.

This isn't because of some social mistake, a cultural hangover from a Judaeo-Christian fear of the sin of pridefulness. It's because amassing things, then boasting about them, is petty. The smallness of the endeavour shames everybody involved.

Immaterial achievements are different, but they fail in different ways. Educational success I always thought of as a fluke. Good work was always a collaboration. I'm not saying this to be modest; I'm saying it because it's true. Maybe if I did triathlons I'd feel differently.

A surprised sort of pride

Ask me, on the other hand, what I'm proud of as a British national (besides the obvious NHS). I'm proud of the BBC (even though it also drives me mad with its saggy, authoritarian news agenda and proliferation of father-figures), for the astonishing chin-out tenacity, the tear-jerkingly ridiculous way it holds onto the idea of itself as a global public service. I was amazed to find myself proud of the Olympics, the volunteers, the wildflowers, Greenwich Park, Bradley Wiggins. I'm proud of the universities – a surprised sort of pride at their international status, like when you have a half-sister who last time you checked was 14, and then she turns out to be an astrophysicist (this really happened). I'm proud of steel, railways, Viagra, IVF. Look, we can argue about Bradley Wiggins some other time – everything else, we built together. Everything else, we built with tax.

Obviously there's the huge matter of size and significance – you have universal healthcare on the one hand, and you have an item with a touchscreen and a steadily deteriorating battery life on the other. There is just no comparison. Of course collective achievements are more fulfilling. They're bigger.

But there's something else, some deeper psychic point about what it means when we buy things: 'consumerist' used to be a dirty word in the Nineties; before then, lefties used to talk about greed and waste. I think this is wrong – wanting stuff is basically social. It's just a way of sending signals to one another, the same urge to communicate that gets 175,000 people into a field in Glastonbury, or makes people all want to live in the same town. It is an unfortunate perversion that when the consumer identity is amplified, we can't think of another way to express togetherness than by all buying the same thing. But this act of consumption is never a collective act. We're chasing the crowd through the act of ownership; so when it comes to flaunting the thing, we realise we can't. There's a hierarchical tang – I can afford this thing, therefore I'm the best – which is aggressive and poisons the universalism that was the only thing driving the desire in the first place. It was meant to bond us – the iPhone, or the bag, or whatever it was – but all it does is isolate us.

This is why the satisfaction is so fleeting, the desire replaced almost immediately by the desire for something else. The minute you own it, you've failed at the thing that made you want to own it.

Building infrastructure, creating the conditions necessary for discovery, constructing tangible things that make life better for everyone – it's all a bit more coherent. Again, the urge is social, but here the outcome is also social. Anybody can be proud of the NHS, and anybody can use the NHS. You can say you're proud without preening, because your part in it was both vast and minuscule. Nothing could be more material than a school or a hospital, and yet look at what they give us – beyond education and health, the knowledge that we're capable of anything, so long as we do it together.

This, incidentally, is why philanthropy is no substitute for tax. If we turned up some really sound philanthropists, who were prepared to take a broad spectrum of advice about society and what it needed (which, by the way, is extremely unlikely), we might end up with the same facilities. But what we wouldn't have is the unbounded horizon, the exhilarating vastness of what we might do next.

That is why tax is beautiful – not for all the beautiful things it can buy, not even for the fact that it 'buys' us a society, but for the sense it bestows of our own power. It turns us all into adventurers. It is beautiful in itself.

The low-tax consensus

So when I hear an apparently educated person launching an argument whose foundation is that, in normal life, normal people want to pay as little tax as they possibly can, I am suspicious. I think that person has never really given much thought to what money does, what it can buy, what it can't; how much we can do alone, and how much we can do together. I suspect that person is just parroting the consensus that self-interest should be what guides us; that, if we're all left alone to look after ourselves, society will work better than if we try to cooperate. The problem with the me-and-mine philosophy is that even people who believe passionately in it can never get very passionate about it; it's so narrow and uninspiring, so small-time and shamefaced. It's like reading a Lakeland catalogue instead of a book.[1]

Let's not forget what we have done, as a nation: besides steel and the railways, we invented the pub and the round. We invented saying sorry when it was the other person's fault. We invented the old ladies who will fight to the death to pay for one another's hot drinks (though I met a Tunisian once who said they invented that). We transposed the word 'Blitz' from 'large-scale bombing event that destroyed all our property' into a byword for 'helping one another even when we had nothing'. Rabid possessive individualism is not our style.

I met a guy at a conference whose dad had just died; I didn't find out much about him, and I definitely didn't accurately transcribe what he said, but he embodied the tax dilemma so well that I'm going to paraphrase him anyway. Coming up for 50, with a decent but not enormous income, a house in London because he was born at the right time, two children nearing university; characterwise, he was a pro-social person who would never quibble with the purpose of tax. His father left, say, £100,000, and some accountant gave him advice on how to pay as little tax as possible. He was not in favour of tax avoidance. He was especially not in favour of avoiding tax on unearnt income. And yet, when it came to it – that difference between what he should pay and what he could get away with paying, that sum plagued him. He felt like he was throwing that money into a black hole.

There are two things going on here: the first is that you always trust yourself to do something more sensible with your own money than the government will. Your saving it, or investing it, will do something better for your family than your paying it into central government. This is still good for society, because you're making your own unit self-sufficient.

But the truth is that unless you have a serious amount of money, your future security is pretty tenuous. You might save enough to pay your kids' university fees, but you'll never be able to save enough to assure their standard of living if, say, they're not that smart, or they'd prefer to do a job that society doesn't reward very well, or they're not healthy, or they're quite wild. You might be able to save enough for one narrow path; you can never save enough for a spread bet. You would be much better off sinking that money into society, on the basis that higher education will be free, and the living wage will be enough to live on, and health services will be good, and the safety net will let kids be wild and bounce them back up again when they're finished. But – and this is a huge but – you have to trust that that's what the government is going to do. So when you see successive governments chipping away at higher education as a public good, allowing (and indeed encouraging) wages to stagnate, selling off the Health Service and constantly questioning the 'viability' of the welfare state, it is reasonable for you to hunker down and start thinking of ways to protect yourself.

Or, rather, it's reasonable in the short term, but irrational in the long term – just because you don't trust the politicians you can see with the money that they want is not a good reason to give up on the social project. The more we distrust MPs, the more sheepish and reluctant they become about raising taxes, as though they could make us love them again by asking for less. This seals as a truism the line that nobody really wants to pay tax. Whereas, in fact, just because you don't want to pay tax to this government doesn't mean you don't love tax. If you felt that you were building something beautiful – a bridge, a housing project, a future – you wouldn't think twice.

The second thing that's going on with Inheritance Man is that, once you have money in your fist, it's yours. It's a primal thing. I had a VAT 'situation' at the beginning of 2014, which is to say, I'd been underpaying my VAT for a decade. I was paying it on net amounts, not gross amounts. It was an accident, okay?[2] The net result was that I owed them £18,000, and when I discovered that, the shock was visceral. I felt sick, the bottom fell out of my stomach, my palms started sweating. It was a bit like being held up at gunpoint, except that it was over the phone, by a Welsh person. And I'm in favour of tax; imagine how I'd have felt if I hated it.

I would have felt exactly the same. Money is weird. We do more with it than spend it. We form our identities with it, express ourselves with it, make it the conduit of our dreams and our futures, use it as a proxy for status and value. So when a faceless bureaucracy takes a load off you, for a moment you are rocked to your foundations. Her Majesty's Revenue & Customs stimulates nothing for you, emotionally; and the money stimulates everything. It just seems so wrong. But money is not all those things; it's not love, or happiness, or worth, it's only a proxy. So I got over it pretty fast. This is the genius of deduction at source: that it doesn't put your social instincts into competition with your less rational, finders-keepers, 'I want it because it's mine' instincts.

True love died (between us and tax . . .)

I can remember where I was when I heard the news (on my sofa; it's a numbers game, more than a memory; I was always on my sofa in the Noughties). A YouGov poll had asked students what their biggest fear was, for the future. It was the year 2001. What were they scared of? Hilariously, almost nothing that was really going to happen – nobody talked about a financial crash. I didn't write my first piece about the credit-crunch until 2007, and even then I mainly focused on what characteristics it shared with the stomach-crunch (it might be a little bit painful, but it won't kill you, was my considered opinion; this turned out not to be 100 per cent accurate).

Nevertheless, there were some pretty solid threats on the horizon by then; climate change was A Thing;

globalisation as a driver of inequality was A Thing, although at that point the conversation was mainly about wages in the developing world, and nobody talked about wages in the UK;[3] housing was not A Thing; terrorism was A Huge Thing. And yet what really terrified them, these students, these young, skint thinkers with their future ahead of them? High tax. 75 per cent of them said that their major fear for the future was high tax.

I was gobsmacked, pacing about, talking to myself. Don't they understand? Has somebody tampered with their WKD? Why can't they see that high tax will benefit them? Don't they know that there was a time when students were allowed to claim Unemployment Benefit during the holidays, and had their accommodation paid for – and all those things were thanks to tax? I remember feeling quite defeated and depressed, and I can't remember what happened next, but it probably ended with me writing a column about it: how Thatcher's children had been fatally affected by her mindset, and their beliefs had been replaced by a kind of listless, impotent paranoia.

In fact, they had realised something that I – a decade older and fogged by old-fashioned assumptions – hadn't. Rich people had already stopped paying tax. Nobody sends you a memo when that happens. Nobody makes an announcement that, from now on, corporation tax will be a little more negotiable, and top-rate income tax a little more avoidable. It just slowly becomes normal. When rich people stop paying tax, the middle and bottom are dead right to be worried, because they're going to end up paying it all.[4]

How did the rich manage that? Partly, there was a shift in the way taxes were levied. Income tax and corporation tax were slowly whittled down. Indirect taxes like VAT were increased. The impact of this is that the poorest now pay a higher proportion of their income than anybody but the top decile.[5]

Nobody – literally nobody – would ever argue that it is a good system to have the bottom ten per cent paying the joint-largest proportion of their earnings in tax. It doesn't make sense on the level of justice, it doesn't do anything to help the economy, it doesn't raise revenues, it goes against the very principles of taxation and democracy. At a pinch, you could say this was a return to the fifteenth-century model, where peasants paid a load of tax to keep Henry VIII in velvet knickerbockers and rare meats. But even he had a preference for raising money from institutions, rather than the very poorest people in the kingdom.

Before we get on to how that happened, why do we have variable tax rates in the first place? Why doesn't everyone just pay the same percentage? This is Nigel Farage's big idea, on the basis that it ends tax avoidance, evasion, errors and everything, in one go; this is not only incorrect, it is the exact opposite of the truth.[6] And yet plenty of sensible people say this, too: periodically one of those nice younger guys who writes for *The Times* will say, 'What was wrong with a flat rate of tax, anyway?'

Here's what's wrong with it. First, if tax is about investing in the future and helping others, it's unrealistic to expect people to do that when they're struggling to survive. You need to cover your basics – food, shelter, warmth and enough stuff so that you don't feel terminally inferior – before you can contribute to society. The 'shelter' part is already unaffordable for many people (as we've seen in Housing); and the warmth part, in cold winters, is out, too (as we saw in Poverty). People who can't cover the basics shouldn't be expected to pay tax at all. But if they were taken out of the tax equation, then by necessity everyone else would have to pay more.

Second, there is a difference between proportional and absolute effects: what it means to take 10 per cent off someone on £20,000 is not the same, by any reasonable measure, as what it means to take 10 per cent off someone with £2 million. Third, a pound does a different thing, depending on who has it. Rich people,[7] left to their own devices, take their money out of the active economy, salting it away in schemes to preserve it. It's not because they're inherently bad people; it's a burden, having money. The more you feel like it validates you, the more desperate you are not to lose it, because you secretly know, if you have any sense at all, that it's not validation; it was mainly luck.

Anyway, when they're mediumly rich, they buy property as an investment, which drives up rents; and when they're hopelessly rich, they spend money on things, from assets to luxuries, that tend not to plough money into the society around them. This will eventually become a rentier economy, with one entire class making its income from the rents paid by another class. It adds up to something quite crude. Modern societies thrive, partly, because even the poorest are active within them; the more money there is in the poorest pocket, the more liveliness there will be in the market; poor people spend what they've got.

Fourth, rich people – again, I say this without chagrin, they don't do it on purpose – get most benefit from the life that tax buys. They have the most property and wealth to protect, so they get most from the maintenance of law and order. As employers, they reap the rewards of an educated and healthy workforce, who arrive at work via transport infrastructure. If they're not employers, they probably inherited their wealth, in which case they have tax to thank for all the blessings of stability, the steady accretion of civilisation, that has brought them to this merry state, where they can remain rich without anybody trying to overthrow them. There's another category of people, who are neither major employers nor inheritors, who had a stunning idea or talent and turned it into something that everybody wanted to buy. It's not very large, this group, comprising mainly pop stars, entrepreneurs, some footballers and Richard Branson. If you really want to push it, let's imagine him as the libertarian's hero; never ill for a day in his life; either educated privately or educated shittily, so with nothing to thank the state for in that regard; has a helicopter, so doesn't need roads. We're now down to Richard Branson and Wayne Rooney, but stay with it. Even the ones who take nothing from the state, who pride themselves on taking nothing, even these people still need a living, breathing, prosperous society, otherwise there's nobody to buy their stuff. Entrepreneurs do not thrive in chaotic places. You don't get many supergroups out of South Sudan. We're nothing without one another; we can't even get rich without one another. And once we have got rich, we have more of a stake in the rest of society than ever.

Anyway. This all starts with the Rolling Stones
In 1971 tax rates at the top were really high by today's standards, but had actually just been cut, from 90 per cent to 75 per cent (this was on incomes above £20,000; adjusted for inflation, £176,000). They were raised again in 1974 to 83 per cent, but there was also a charge on unearnt income of 15 per cent, which meant that money from investments could, theoretically, be charged at 98 per cent. When the Beatles sang, 'There's one for you / nineteen for me / 'Cause I'm the taxman', they were, astonishingly, being fiscally accurate – Harold Wilson had a 95 per cent supertax in place for a short time.

The Stones, under the instruction of their accountant, Prince Rupert Loewenstein, moved to France for the avoidance of tax: to the sumptuous

Villa Nellcôte on the Côte d'Azure. Photos of this time, shot mainly by Dominique Tarlé, have them all looking painfully beautiful and languid, in stately belle époque ballrooms. It is impossible to take your eyes off them; you could imagine that you were looking at genius, frozen in time. However, this is like looking at Robert Capa's photos and concluding that the Second World War must have been really fun and quite sexy.

Exile on Main St was the result. Loewenstein used to say proudly that it was the only album he could think of that referenced its tax planning in the title. 'Planning'. Ha! The other noticeable thing about it is that it's rubbish. As *Rolling Stone* magazine wrote upon its release, 'With Keith, however, except for a couple of spectacular chording exhibitions and some lethal openings, his instrumental wizardry is practically nowhere to be seen ... It hurts the album, as the bone earring has often provided the marker on which the Stones rise or fall.'

Keith Richards famously hated the Nellcôte basement studio, which was too humid and warped his guitar strings; they couldn't even get to the end of a song without having to retune. It's interesting to consider those 'lethal openings' in the light of that – perhaps, if they could have played the whole bloody thing without stopping, they might have arrived at a song that was lethal all the way through.

The main reason for Richards's ghostlike presence on that album, though, was his heroin habit; he took up the drug in earnest, having scraped his back in a go-karting accident. Naturally, this wasn't the first time he'd done drugs – he'd been found guilty in the Sixties of allowing cannabis to be smoked on his property. However, I bet you it was the first time he'd been go-karting. Who, living a full life in the society of their own choosing, acts like they're on a stag weekend organised through Groupon? It is pretty well established that Richards arrived in France clean and spent the next decade on smack. He often maintains that drugs were the engine of his brilliant songs, which would be something to consider if you thought his songs were brilliant. What basically happened is that he unplugged himself from the place that built his psyche, abandoned his national grid and tried to get his energy from drugs instead. The wreckage of this tax avoidance is so laughably expensive.

These are all counterfactuals, which are impossible to prove – any of that could have happened in Abbey Road (apart from the humidity; and, I'm afraid I insist, the go-karting).

Nevertheless, there is a kernel of behaviour here, which is common to many tax avoiders: one way or another, it costs them at least as much to avoid tax as it would to pay it. Sometimes it's a purely financial swap, spending hundreds of thousands on tax advice, to avoid an amount that might not be much higher. More often the loss is something other than money – you might be a hedge-fund manager who moves to Guernsey and can't visit his wife and children for months;[8] or you might be party to some aggressive tax-avoidance scheme that, once it is widely known, casts you in a different light for ever. If someone were to come up to you and say, 'I offer you £10 million, to live away from your family', you'd refuse it. Likewise, if someone offered you £500,000 for your reputation, you wouldn't countenance it. These things aren't for sale. But tax avoidance isn't really about money.

People who cannot stomach paying tax at the top feel like they're being mugged. They feel that, for reasons they often call 'political', they're on the receiving end of some blatant injustice, some massive government levy whose purpose they know not. From where they're standing, the state takes their money to placate the resentful mob. Here, it becomes a game of cat-and-mouse, or man-against-mountain; they're the plucky individual, in a radically uneven battle against the omnipotent government, whose might they can only defeat with pure cunning. It's the classic stuff of fairytales: one bold hero who finally stands up to the unreasonable dragon; from this angle, it is totally obvious how much identity they have tied up in their non-compliance. Corporate tax avoidance is different, much more strategic and not really emotional at all – individual tax avoidance is, when you see what people sacrifice for it, possibly the most emotional financial moment they have. Until they get divorced.

No top rate of tax would be low enough to ensure that nobody tried to avoid it. Governments have been trying that for years – it's gone from 90 per cent at the top, to 45 per cent now, and tax avoidance, combined with evasion (they call it the 'tax gap') has never been higher.[9] The highest estimate of all the missing money combined (from VAT fraud, like mine wasn't, to the tax affairs of Google or Vodafone) is £120 billion. The deficit, on which basis we're eroding our social safety net now, so that there are kids in Stoke going through wheelie bins for food,[10] is £105 billion. All of that could be cleared, not even by putting up taxes, but simply by collecting what we're owed.

These are, necessarily, just estimates – it could be half that. Let's say HMRC is right, and it's only a quarter of that. £35 billion is still enough to plug the £20 billion NHS hole, or to pay for HS2, or to double the investment in energy infrastructure. But with that money, however low or high it turned out to be, we could finally escape this political swamp, where the terms of engagement are 'there's no money left'. We could build something better.

Anyway. Let's not dwell.

Solid government at low, low prices
The drive to get taxes down, while it's always billed as great for everybody – great for your pocket, ding-ding!, and a great way to tackle avoidance – is actually just following through on the Nineties political consensus: what voters want is 'value', solid government at low, low prices.

In the Seventies, Labour's tough talk about

squeezing the rich till the pips squeak unearthed a political paradox – people didn't like it. Whether because they aspired to be rich, or thought the rich were the engines of the whole nation's prosperity, or merely thought the rich hadn't done anything to deserve this cruelty to their pips: for one reason or another, they failed to respond to Denis Healey's call. What he was actually talking about was property speculation – taxing landlords till their pips squeaked. All he was saying was that if property owners gain too much power over people who rent, those renters will never be able to buy houses, and the inequality will be fixed like . . . well, a little bit like some kind of nineteenth-century class system. He was just saying it 40 years before it was as plainly visible as the nose on your face. So you can forgive people for thinking it was a bit much.

The left didn't drop their high-tax rhetoric until Neil Kinnock's 1992 defeat, which was put down to his announcement of a 'tax-and-spend' budget too close to the election. And that was the end of that; no Labour politician has ever, to my knowledge, made a public case for high taxes at the top ever since. The closest they've ever come is the promise of a mansion tax on homes worth more than £2 million – it's not insignificant; it'll raise some money, and it at least broaches the fact that London's status as a good, stable place for an oligarch to squirrel money away is making the capital rather expensive, and also a bit strange and quiet and obsessed with mediocre, overpriced fusion food.

But it misses the point: those high, 75 per cent-plus tax rates existed to discourage vast salaries. It doesn't matter hugely what a Rolling Stone or a member of Take That gets paid; they're not at the head of a pay spine, their high wages don't have a knock-on effect of lower wages across the company, and they aren't reliant on shareholders for bonuses, so they don't have poor incentives to maximise profits at the expense of long-term business goals . . . You can, in society, pay a pop star whatever you like. I know that inequality is bad in itself; that when we reach a point where one person's worth is 20,000 times that of another person we have lost sight of the fundamental truths of human existence: that we are born equal and we want the same things. But while they can mess with humanity's equilibrium-setting, pop stars cannot, whatever they're paid, mess with the day-to-day running of society in the way that an overpaid CEO can. This is probably why Gary Barlow struggles to understand why he has to pay higher-rate tax, especially after all that incredibly hard work he did, standing next to a yellow bear, asking people who were already on the breadline themselves to dig a little deeper for the children in the wheelchairs.

Critics of high tax rates claim they reduce productivity; and that people, realising they won't keep much of the money they earn above a certain threshold, stop trying. This would hold more water if productivity and high pay were related, but they aren't.

In 2012 the average FTSE 100 executive was paid £4.3 million, which figure had doubled in ten years; that same decade, of course, saw the financial crash. Not even the most stalwart defender of Big Business would say that productivity had doubled over that period. This £4-ish million is 160 times the salary of the average worker. It is not humanly possible for one person to be 160 times more able, skilled, industrious, educated, talented or visionary than another person. Wage rises no longer reflect productivity at the top, and at the bottom wages haven't been rising at all since 2003 and don't reflect the fact that everybody in a company – however badly you treat them – adds to the value of that company. These facts are all connected; not because you could take that £4 million, divide it by 50,000 and everybody on the pay spine could have a bit more – it would give all the other employees 80 quid more a year. That wouldn't help.

No, the problem is that CEOs gear all their decisions towards shareholder profit, because that's how they get their pay and bonus agreed. The shareholders have almost no interest in the company, beyond the immediate profit from their investment,[11] and the CEO has no interest beyond what makes the shareholders happy (which state of affairs has a name: 'shareholder value maximisation'). This has had a massive effect on the way companies are run: the more they prioritise shareholder profit, the less they invest in research and development. This is no small thing. You can't run an industrial base where everybody is trying to cash out and nobody's inventing anything. Well, clearly you can, because we do, but you can't forever.

The other major neglected investment category is people. If you're a boss who is connected to the company, connected to its future, connected to the idea that it's producing something worthwhile, you would accept without question that training, career progression, wages and job security were the pillars of whatever deal you'd struck with your workforce. You'd probably still, if you were a red-blooded capitalist, have battles over how much profit was distributed to you and how much to them. But that's fine – that's what unions are for.

What we have instead, as a consequence of outlandish executive pay, is a professional managerial class (very small, incredibly powerful) with only very short-term commitments to each company, and shareholders whose roots are even shallower. They don't really see themselves as being in a relationship with the people who work for them. Not only has pay flattened out, but job security is shot (see Poverty).

This is why tax needs to be so high, above a certain point, that there's not even much point fighting for more money. If CEOs had to prove themselves to one another, to the world, in some way other than with this salary arms race, they might take more pride in the business they were in, take a broader view on it, perhaps include in that view the contributions of other people besides themselves.

Or they might not; they might just have to start a CEOs' tug-of-war. But the destabilising, impoverishing effects of limitless top-end pay, businesses changing shape to service the mad, unspendable demands of their executives – this is no good.

I know what you're thinking, because I'm thinking it: there's something sad about this solution. Capping income feels like capping ambition. It feels Soviet (but also a bit Welsh) and small-town, where limitless wealth is glitzy and American. It feels like the big earners will go off to frolic in the *Great Gatsby* while we're left in some rain-drenched parlour full of lonely people in a novel by Turgenev.

But money and ambition are not the same. Glitz is a thin, predictable attraction and you don't need to be in the 1 per cent to drink Martini. Almost everybody on these gargantuan salaries, when asked what motivates them, will say anything – everything – but money. They're not even lying; they don't want money, they want to be openly, publicly valued above all other people similar to them, and money is just the easiest, most demonstrable way to measure value. They might be narcissists, but they're not greedy. To most of them, it won't make any difference at all to the work they do if their salary tops out at £1 million, or a bit less. A few people will, inevitably, walk away in disgust. But to be honest, those people probably already live in Guernsey.

How high would that top bracket be? And what would tax-take be above it? There is no evidence of high tax affecting productivity below 80 per cent.[12] François Hollande, Europe's biggest pinko, brought in a 75 per cent rate on salaries of more than one million euros in 2012, which was his biggest, most memorable election promise. Who left? Gerard Depardieu moved to Russia, to pay 6 per cent tax on his massive fortune. He didn't have to worry about seeing his family, because his daughter hates him and his son is now dead, but, before that, hated him. Otherwise, it's hard to assess so far. The most trenchant opponents of high tax at the top seem to be financial commentators, who line up to talk about 'economic suicide' and the inevitable exodus of all the talent. The number of French people in the UK is trotted out constantly as proof that high taxes don't work (London is known wryly as their sixth-largest city). But that 75 per cent tax rate has yet to be enforced, and the French diaspora has been huge for a decade. The real message for those worried about a brain-drain is that French rich people leave anyway, whoever's in charge and whatever their tax rate is.

The very fact that François Hollande has tried it makes a high-tax solution look even more impossible to British politicians: not just political suicide, but also lunatic Frenchness. But this alternative: governmental thundering about tax avoidance while senior members of that government are using exactly the avoidance loopholes they're complaining about;[13] simultaneously cutting top-rate tax and encouraging high pay at the top, while mandating poor conditions at the bottom – all of this ultimately undermines both justice and long-term profitability. This alternative absolutely sucks. It suits hardly any of us.

Corporate tax avoidance always used to be seen as something that only happened to poor countries. That was incorrect: tax avoidance has always, since its incipience, harmed trade, productivity and transparency globally. But it's true that large companies never used to be quite so brazenly fuck-you in developed countries as they were in developing ones.

The instruments used to avoid tax at this level are pretty well innumerable, though the act of trying to count them would be an interesting, though sullying insight into just how petty, craven, dishonest and tight-fisted they are.[14] However, the central manoeuvre is very simple: you move your taxable income from a country with high corporation tax to a country with lower tax. In its most benign incarnation, you move your whole business from the US, say, to Ireland, which had a famously low tax rate in the years running up to its going bust. The argument is that you, the company, create jobs in that country, so the tax the government forsook to get you there was worth it. It's a moot point whether or not it *is* worth it: a foreign employer bringing low-skilled jobs for purely tax-avoidance reasons isn't going to do much for your knowledge base (which is what really drives prosperity) and is going to disappear at the inducement of some other tax regime that's even lower.[15] It will always be right at the worst possible moment, as your currency is collapsing. But at least it's on the level: Dell moved to Ireland and made it their manufacturing base and, while it lasted, it provided manufacturing jobs.

Much more common avoidance involves large corporations simply basing their HQ in a low tax dominion: companies from the quintessentially British (Boots) to the new transnationalist (Amazon) all behave in the same way. They set up in Luxembourg, where corporation tax is negotiable and often opaque to outside regulators. That's not where they do most of their business – it is merely where they declare its spoils.

Businesses so booming that they have a shop every twenty yards (Starbucks) will then turn round and say it's a profitless operation in the UK. Amusingly, when pushed on the matter in a public setting, they will say, aghast: 'But we do pay tax, we pay National Insurance, and we pay VAT',[16] and then rattle out some large numbers of how much their VAT comes to. This is intended to quieten critics, as we imagine all that lovely money raining into the Treasury; perhaps picture ourselves taking a bath in it, like burlesque dancers. In fact, all it rams home is how much tax they should be paying, but aren't; if they are generating that much in sales, and employing that many people, it is simply implausible that they're not profiting from it.

Recently, I have noticed a change in tack, among the defenders of large corporate tax avoiders: that it's good for them to avoid tax, because it brings down the prices on our coffee or our sinus spray. If we were to tax them more rigorously, they would simply pass on the costs to the consumer.

The first problem with this is that it's a redistribution of benefit, towards people who can afford frappuccinos, away from people who can't. When you allow tax instruments – or, for that matter, regulations around the treatment of employees – to be sidestepped on the basis that the leaner, meaner business will be better for the end-user, you order everybody into a consumer hierarchy, where those who buy the most gain the most. It's often not clear that this is where the argument's headed, since its proponents usually present it in terms of the people at the bottom, who can only just afford that cappuccino, and if it were twenty pence more expensive as a result of tax, they'd have had their choice to drink coffee removed by an overweening state. But obviously the true beneficiaries of a consumer hierarchy are the already-wealthy. It's an upwards redistribution, which defies the point of tax. It also traduces the essence of tax, which is to build things of beauty, value and purpose together that none of us singly could afford. Not a coffee, in other words. The opposite of a coffee.

But there's an interesting assumption underneath that already totally facile argument, and when I say 'interesting', of course I mean 'wrong': viz., that all the savings corporations make from not paying tax are passed on to us, the consumers. I'm perfectly happy to put this to the test: tax them properly, like normal businesses throughout history. If they are already operating at such slim margins that they have to pass the cost straight onto us, nobody will be able to undercut them. If, on the other hand, they try to pass the costs onto us and some other coffee shop manages to sell coffee that is just as good and cheaper, it will be plain why (and in whose benefit) the coffee and its tax affairs had to be arranged the way they were. This would be called competition, which is the only thing the free market is any good for. Markets aren't just good – they are brilliant at solving small problems, ironing out kinks; brilliant at making sure the bar on your road is the best it could possibly be for the people it serves; brilliant at nailing the person who's pretending to sell half a pound of chestnuts when in fact it is 220 grams.

We don't need to accept huge profits, vast CEO salaries and tax avoidance as the price of a coffee industry. We have managed to sell each other hot drinks perfectly well since the dawn of time.

The managing director of John Lewis, Andy Street, once complained that tax avoidance didn't just dent the Treasury; it made it quite difficult for businesses that did pay their tax to compete. This stood out, a respectable, apolitical, middle-of-the-road voice, saying 'This isn't going to work'. Margaret Hodge is taxation's Joan of Arc; she calls in the head of Google to the Public Accounts Committee and calls him evil. 100 of her could remake the whole global system; ten of her could do it, with us on her side. Richard Murphy is an accountant who loves fair taxation, which I think – to the profession's modern incarnation – is like being a doctor who loves germ warfare. Yet the reason these people are rare gems, and you couldn't name many more of them, is that people who openly extol taxation in public life put themselves outside the range of what's considered 'respectable'. In a respectable world, to be in favour of high tax is ideological, while to be in favour of low tax is practical. As a reading of reality, this has its arse on backwards. 'Ideological' means clinging to an idea in defiance of all the evidence – and nothing could be more ideological than the low-tax lobby. They may refer to the Laffer curve, which postulates that, above a certain rate, the Treasury's real income from taxation will be zero, because people will simply stop producing. Or they may cite the trickle-down effect, a mechanism by which they claim the rich will fund the rest, so long as they're allowed to become rich enough. None of this is observable in real life. Very few economists believe in the Laffer curve.[17] It is a political construct dressed up as a demonstrable fact.

But let's go back to the calm of John Lewis. The respectable middle ground is not served by tax avoidance. If you were to imagine John Lewis as a person, he would almost certainly be on PAYE, which is to say, his tax would be deducted at source. The respectable middle – your solid, Civil Service, unexcitable, Cheddar-eating middle – could not avoid tax even if it wanted to. Respectability has allowed its accepted wisdoms to be hijacked by people with whom it has very little in common. You don't have to be left-wing to love tax. I don't know if it even helps.

The question then urgently becomes: what do we do about it? What do you actually do about tax avoidance, when the people who're meant to legislate against it also engage in it? How do you change a 'public attitude' to high taxes, when it feels as though it's been in place for as long as you've been alive? What can individual governments do anyway, when their measures are always countered by the mantra: 'Rich people will just move. Companies will just move. You'll be left with your pro-social tax rates, in a country completely empty of everyone except the unemployed'? The bald fact is that there's nothing you can do as a pressure group without the active intervention of your government. It takes more than a Public Accounts Committee making salty interventions; it takes more than an online petition. It takes laws, and enforcement. It takes active investment in HMRC, which is currently going in the opposite direction and losing staff. It takes the utmost commitment of the people running the show. And even that probably won't be enough – with corporation tax especially, but also with tax rates for the highest earners, countries need to coordinate their efforts, and most probably make some agreement not to undercut one another.

Innocents abroad

Yet none of that will be possible until the atmosphere

changes; and we make the atmosphere. Politicians will only do what they think is 'realistic', and their idea of realism is to reflect what they think we think. If we think tax works, we have to say we think it.

A quirk of the austerity era is the semi-frequent witch-hunt, where a Freedom of Information request or a leak delivers a fresh haul of tax avoiders, and then we all have a fight about how bad or not-so-bad we think their behaviour is. I used to think this was great, if only because it stimulated an open conversation about what tax is for – when Bob Geldof's tax affairs were made public, it was momentarily possible to say out loud that, if people like him didn't avoid their tax so strenuously, we might not need his philanthropic energy. If Gary Barlow and people like him paid tax, we might be able to afford dignity and opportunities for disabled and deprived children from the public purse, without having to beg. This, I thought, was what the conversation needed: real people, with faces, histories, profiles, upon whom we could vent our disapproval. I set about building what I hoped would be a pin-accurate chronology of the great tax haters of our times, from Mick Jagger to Adele. Jo Brand had a great story about going on one of those variety shows at the end of the Nineties, and the producer saying they had to finish by nine because one of the Spice Girls had to be on a plane by midnight, having slept as many nights in England as she was allowed, before having to pay tax as a UK citizen. The timing was so evocative – that tipping point when the reflexive, anti-authoritarian leftiness of Eighties and Nineties comedy ceded to the me-first culture-of-the-self that the coming century would bring. But Brand sounded dispirited by the whole thing.

'They were innocents abroad, they were just being advised by people all the time. Presumably, tax-wise, if someone said, "We can save you 400 grand a year", most people are going to say "yes", aren't they? I don't suppose it even occurs to most people what that's about.

'I've always thought it's very interesting that certain financial institutions advise the government on tax law, and then they advise celebrities and rich people on their taxes. That seems weird to me. Because you need to have an independent body advising on tax, which has nothing to do with the people who are then going to be liable for large tax bills.'

It's always the celebrities that stick out. It's never the families who've made tax avoidance into a tournament sport, going back seven generations. It's never the hedge-fund managers who won't have their photographs printed. It's never the people you see arriving at the Conservative party summer ball, to bid £45,000 on a game of tennis with Boris Johnson. It's never the people who make the policy. The establishment survives by its facelessness, while the famous people with their giant faces take these occasional ejaculations of hate and disapproval as the penalty they pay for acting like money when they're not from money. Maybe they don't care, and

I hope they don't. It's obnoxious; you unleash this spurt of vitriol at Cheryl Cole, and it never amounts to anything. You can't run an engine on bile; it's corrosive.

If we don't trust central government with our taxes, there are better ways to raise them. Tax-raising powers should be devolved to people with whom we could have a real democratic relationship. If we don't think the burden is falling fairly – and it isn't – we could raise tax more on wealth and less on income. Simultaneously, we must look outwards: corporate tax evasion can only be tackled internationally, but that shouldn't put us off. Often, international agreement is easier to reach – having a global summit is like going to Relate, for governments. They put on their best face, and often some good comes of it.

'We would all like a nice playing field in our village, just as we would all like a good rail service to the nearest town . . . a conveniently-sited post office and so forth. But the only way we can be made to pay for such things is by general taxation. No one has come up with a better way of aggregating individual desires to collective advantage.' This was written by the late Tony Judt, in *Ill Fares The Land: A Treatise On Our Present Discontents*, Penguin 2011, a book which you now don't have to read because there it is: we could do great things, which we all want. We can only do them together, and why not?

Was your education bog-standard?

I went to Godolphin & Latymer School for Girls, a fee-paying school in West London, from 1984 until 1991. I didn't have much choice – didn't conceive it as a choice – when I was 11, but I could have left in the sixth form. I didn't really object to private schools at that point. If I'm honest, I was so morose that I didn't think of it as a privilege. The more expensive your education is, the more it encourages you to think of yourself as one of the chosen few. That is the value proposition: your parents drop a load of money, and you emerge with a sense of entitlement. But it never made me feel remotely lucky. It was intensely hierarchical, and yet all the organising principles of the hierarchy were tawdry. Who was your dad? Where did you live? How thin were your thighs? How rich were you? It was like the moral universe of Paris Hilton crossed with that of Katie Hopkins. These are anachronistic examples: then, it was like Madonna crossed with Michael Portillo.

So, yes, I went to a private school, and for some people that discredits everything I could possibly think about education, or any other matter of public policy. The face-value assumption is that everybody born into privilege must thereafter be on the side of privilege. It would be really convenient for the forces of conservatism to have that well-oiled merry-go-round where you'd go from private school, to Russell Group university, to position of prominence, whence you'd argue that private schools were a perfectly fair place to draw all your colleagues from, because those were the schools full of the best people. Plenty would say that's how it works already.

But politics aren't innate, they're chosen. If you wouldn't try an 11-year-old soldier for a war crime, then you can't demand that a privately educated 11-year-old believe in and defend that system for their whole adult life. Not only is it reasonable to be against private schools, having been to one, but for at least some people I think it's inevitable. Private education is weird; in tacit ways, with unspoken assumptions and outspoken snobberies, with stupid hats and elaborate histories, there's a constant insistence that you're all superior, accompanied by the contradictory message that you are inadequate. Exam results are private schools' core business, so everybody's a billboard. There's no sense that you hold any innate interest for them, beyond what you project about their academic credentials. But if you project a good thing about them academically, yet aren't posh enough, that's no good, either. Seven years, it takes, to turn reasonable-ish 11-year-olds into these brittle egos who know they're born to rule, but worry (often rightly) that they were chosen by accident and they're not up to it. Politics is full of them. I can smell their insecurity through the telly. I don't blame the teachers, by the way. I blame the institutional philosophy. And, sure, this is a personal view, and rather a dated one. Eton (motto: Let Eton Flourish) might be completely different.

So there was this great thing, this marvellous, bountiful education, which I reaped the full benefit of, and now I'm trying to stop other people getting it. This is the bedrock of almost every argument against cooperating to improve anything. You want to bring down global emissions? You live in the West, you've already had your emissions and now you want to stifle growth in the developing world. You think growth for its own sake is pointless? You've already had your boom years, and now you want to stop everyone else having them.

Conservatism is founded on self-interest; conservatives think that our natural instincts are to look after number one, and those instincts are the source of progress. Self-interest isn't 'selfish' – far from it, it spurs us on to innovate and produce and be self-reliant. If everyone had the smarts to work hard and save up and send their children to private school, all children would be better educated, and taxes would be lower. Real selfishness is wanting the state to pay for things: what could be more selfish than relying on other people to look after you?

Like One Direction, it makes sense while you're listening to it, but it's complete pap: self-interest is shallow and uninspiring. We might do a minor thing for our own sake, but we'll only do a huge thing for someone else. In education, this means that together we can build something better than any of us could afford alone; but more to the point, let a thousand flowers bloom. Whatever you do, never restrict your hopes and ambitions to the people who have money.

Plainly, these are two opposing worldviews, and that's nothing to be afraid of. That might be the summary point of this entire book: let's just stop trying to accommodate the disciples of self-interest. Stop trying to find the middle ground, for it doesn't exist.

A person who believes in self-interest as the governing human motivation must, therefore, find a self-interested motivation for me, otherwise my very existence calls into question their founding principle. Hence: I'm arguing against private schools because I want to shore up the advantage I had, by making sure nobody else gets it. Or: I'm arguing from a position of envy, because I can't afford a private school for my own children, so I want to make sure nobody else's go to one. I know what my principles are. I don't conceive it as a battle between my own children and everybody else's. I want an equitable education system because I want to see everybody get the chance to flourish. But this is why the private-school debate gets so heated, even amongst people who couldn't remotely afford to privately educate their kids, even amongst those who don't have children: because it's not really anything to do with education. It is pure politics; two intractable views, refracted through children for extra emotion.

While there's nothing hypocritical about having been to a private school, it would be hypocritical to send your kids to one. When politicians do, they take a mind-your-own-business line on it: 'I don't play politics with my children's education' (George Osborne); 'I'm a mother first and a politician second' (Diane Abbott). I prefer that to the people who go on about how great the playing fields are, and who won't let up until you give way and say that: yes, their children probably will end up with a better sporting ethic than yours. But it's disingenuous. Politicians know perfectly well why this is our business: you can't believe in social justice for other people's children. So you can pay for your children's education, by all means, but you cannot thereafter pretend equality is a principle that is particularly dear to you (which, in fairness, I don't think George Osborne does). Many politicians do bow to the obvious necessity that if you want to run state education, you have to use it; but the anguish of their public pronouncements – can Michael Gove possibly take the risk of sending his children to these Westminster state schools, commonly agreed to be the best in the country? – only reinforces the message that state education is harmful and dangerous.

12 per cent of their waking hours

Educationally, it doesn't make that much difference. No reputable study has ever found that more than 20 per cent of results variation can be put down to the influence of the school[1] – the rest is all home environment, influences, pressures, hurdles, expectations. As poverty increases, so the environmental determinants get even stronger, and the educational ones get weaker, for the obvious reasons that it's really hard to learn if you're constantly having to move house and school, if your parents work very long hours, if you're hungry, if you're homeless. Schools cannot take responsibility for solving problems that are social and economic, not least because kids only spend 12 per cent of their waking hours in them anyway. One startling study found not a single school that could replicate the value it had added, consistently, over five years, and concluded that value-added scores were meaningless.[2] A research paper from the US found that, once you controlled for the fact that their pupils were richer, 'the private school advantage disappeared and even reversed in most cases'.[3] A study of the voucher programme in Chile – poorer pupils were given vouchers so that they could go to private schools – found no evidence of improved outcomes across any of the 150 municipalities.[4] An OECD study found that, adjusting for background, state-educated kids did just as well on Pisa scores as privately educated ones.[5] I just put those in as curiosities: obviously British public schools may be very different to private education in America or Chile. Regardless, a child who would thrive at Westminster will, all the research tell us, thrive at Lambeth Academy.

But socially? Socially is a whole other story. The real purpose of private education is, like the date-stamp on an egg, to brand your child with a respectable provenance, so that institutions will welcome him or her. If that's what you're worried about, rather than actual GCSEs, then you are dead right to be worried. And who isn't, really? I don't want my children to grow up thinking they can't be high-court judges or that they won't get into Russell Group universities; I don't want to see them elbowed out of the way by people with more expensive accents. But since the problem is with the exclusive institution, not with the wrong accent, to take refuge in private education seems, apart from everything else, backward looking and a little weak.

While the conversation about private education changes very little over time, the context has changed massively: like the final-salary pension and the manageable mortgage, public schools have slipped out of the grasp of the middle classes. Average day-school fees are £13,000 a year.[6] Assuming two children, you would need £26,000 of disposable, after-tax income: even at the 95 per-centile, average earnings are not quite £70,000. So even if we picture a household in which there are two parents, both in the top 5 per cent income bracket (this, incidentally, would put them in the top 1 per cent for household income), they would still need to spend almost one-third of their net income on a private education. 'Middle-class' was probably a bit of a stretch in the Eighties, but it is now a wildly inaccurate way to describe the group for whom this would be manageable. Amusingly, there are many ways to reduce school fees by paying them out of untaxed income, all of which rely on having a massive capital sum to begin with.

Choosing your bog-standard education

This doesn't mean we can't discuss private education, but if we actually want to talk about education – rather than class and privilege – only comprehensive schools are relevant. The Thatcher era wanted, in the long term, to introduce a quasi-market system, where parents were given vouchers that they could then spend on their school of choice, or could top up in the private sector. This was recognised at the time for the incredibly stupid idea that it was, but it morphed into 'parent choice'. If we couldn't choose to send our children to private schools, politicians concluded, then we would be happiest if we could do pretend-choosing, with no price tag, between a number of excellent state-provided options. For that to mean anything, schools had to be easily comparable against a series of measurable outcomes, and so Ofsted was born, in the Education (Schools) Act of 1992.

Parents don't want choice, any more than hospital patients do: we just want our nearest school to be good, and to have space for our kid. The majority of parents oppose free schools,[7] which were designed as the great drivers of market-like choice conditions. Free schools had some uptake amongst those who were either neurotic about state education because it had been so relentlessly talked-down, or wanted to hive off a school just for middle-class kids, thereby simulating the conditions of a private education; that's why 70 per cent of them opened in areas with low deprivation, and why free schools in the early wave were always sited in the wrong place. Even if we did want choice, that parent sitting between three excellent schools, um-ing and ah-ing about whether to choose the one with the wonderful music or the one that's great for maths – that parent does not exist.

When my kids were five, I wanted them, above all, to go to a school where it was challenging but not pressurised, they got to go on good trips and there was a playground. I wanted them to be seen as individuals, to emerge with the confidence, resilience and impetus to do justice to their potential, which, considering that I also think they're magic (this parental fallacy is universal), is infinite. I wanted them to be people who'd concentrate because they were immersed, and not because they'd been schooled to understand that life for people who don't concentrate is grim. I didn't ever want to have a conversation in which I had to explain why they had to go to school, even though it was boring. I've now had that conversation a couple of times, and it did not please me. It's not under-stimulation that bores them, but the constant testing, and learning how to be tested, and sitting still to be retested. After a while they get used to it and stop complaining; that's sad, too. I don't think any of what I want is unreasonable; it's impossible, if we want every child in the room to advance at a standardised pace across a narrow suite of topics, set indeterminately by a person who has never met them. But it's not asking a lot of education that it should be interesting: a group of 30 children will have a range of interests – legitimate, fascinating, profound lines of enquiry – that is unimaginably vast.

As it turns out, I think my kids' school is great. I think we all have the same values – we could file them broadly under 'education: it's not filling a bucket, it's lighting a fire' – and they do everything they can, while simultaneously meeting a bunch of facile targets. But I could not have discovered any of that from reading their Ofsted report.

Instead I'd have found out what grades they get, relative to intake (the 'value added') and how many kids there are with poor attendance. The last, especially, could not be less relevant. Your kid doesn't care whether or not someone's gone to Sweden in the middle of term for a fake wedding. It only matters because it brings down grades, and grades only matter because they're the target. It is a perfect example of the McNamara fallacy: you start off measuring what is valuable, and you end up valuing only what is measurable.

I never gave much thought to Ofsted. I just assumed that if you're going to have a huge system paid for by tax, you need to monitor it, otherwise it will end up full of people who don't work hard and have egg on their clothes. I interviewed one edu-geek, Warwick Mansell, who made the case against grade targets of any sort. The minute you have a target, all attention is focused on the kids who are borderline, and those who are solidly within their band get less teaching. It's not very equitable. I couldn't argue with that, but nor did I really digest it, since I saw the system itself as above challenge. Who would want to be educated in a system without oversight? Isn't it a bit of a coincidence that the only people who moan about inspections are the ones whom it inspects? In the end, aren't inspectors just public servants like any others, working hard to do a good job?

Yes. On that final point, absolutely: after two decades of hostility between teachers and Ofsted inspectors, you'll often hear a snide remark about how they're all either failed or retired teachers, and either never knew or can't remember how it's done. I'm in favour of taking as a broad premise that people are honest and doing their best, until you have concrete evidence of the opposite (see Finance, Privatisation).

Everything else, however, is founded on mis-apprehension. Constant testing doesn't necessarily amount to meaningful oversight. Often it produces an effect that utterly outweighs any of the antici-pated benefits. Ofsted creates competition of the worst sort: one school gets an Outstanding or a Good, and all the most determined parents try to get into it, so they will move heaven and earth (or, in practical terms, house). They appeal, they move partway through the year; it always takes a lot of energy, and it often takes money. The nearest school that isn't Outstanding ends up with the intake with the less energetic and less wealthy parents – which, considering that's going to account for 80 per cent of pupil attainment, will drive down their results. A virtuous circle for one school will be a death-spiral for its neighbour. It's weird how an organisation so obsessed with collecting data has never even wondered aloud whether or not the competition process improves or screws the loser. Because, to everybody using the schools, it is patently plain.

In business, the theory is that the loser improves or goes bust; in public services, people still need to use that loser, so everyone loses. Though it's called 'choice', it isn't one. Parents are allowed to express a preference, but there's nothing they can do if that preference is not heeded. They have no agency at all. All they know is that there's this one incredibly popular school, which they won't get into, and some mediocre schools around it. The anxiety is paralysing. There's no longer any broad sense that all the schools are pretty good and, if you ended up with one that was less good, you might be able to help. In its place, a pressing fear that to send your children to anything less than an Outstanding school is really your failure as a parent, and if you were pushier (aka richer) you would have averted it.

What else has the target culture done? Apart from treating pupils like units of learning, and characterising teachers as lesson-deliverers, it has steadily eroded the natural assumption that nobody cares more about child literacy and attainment and fulfilment than teachers do. That's been replaced by the premise that you have to constantly watch teachers and grade them, because all they really want to do is scrimshank and eat fig rolls. Politicians try to micro-manage the raw business of teaching with time-consuming and impractical ideas. There is no road map, except 'away from trust'. Whatever the policy would be if we relied, respectfully, on professional judgement – do the opposite. That has been the government line for years. Michael Gove, when Education Secretary, used to call the whole teaching body 'the blob'. It's quite amusing, but in a headline-writing knob-end kind of a way. It doesn't sound at all like a serious-minded person, pro-foundly occupied with the education of every British child. Not at all like that.

We could do this a lot better: have an Ofsted that monitored leadership, then trusted the leaders. Or get rid of it altogether and rely on democratic accountability, exerted through a receptive and transparent local authority and through active involvement with the school itself. All these ideas are founded on trust – trusting heads, the officials of local government, teachers themselves, and Ofsted officials, for that matter. If you wanted any radical overhaul of Ofsted beyond 'test more, fight with unions more, introduce more targets', then you'd have to take as your starting point that everyone involved wanted to do their best by the kids they were educating and would pursue that collaboratively with an open mind. This is a pretty big leap, I grant: that human nature is fundamentally good; but look at the system without trust. It's piled with targets, which teachers then kill themselves to meet, but their very efforts are interpreted as 'gaming the system', which idea is then used to erode trust in them even further. Teacher morale is as low as it has ever been, through a combination of ridiculous workload and political bad-mouthing.

Ranking systems are meaningless: every teacher is an Outstanding some days, and an Unsatisfactory on other days; a lot depends not just on their mood, but on 30 other moods of the classroom (it has been estimated that, to get a statistically reliable view on someone's teaching, you would have to monitor each one for 60 hours a year). A gang of inspectors, with the best will in the world, cannot deem a teacher good or bad – to claim that they can is a crime against statistics. Instead, all they can do is introduce a bunch of things that teachers have to demonstrate, in order to be considered good or bad. One author and ex-teacher, David Didau, observed: 'In one teacher's class, I estimated that she spent about 70 per cent of her day on activities designed to prove to senior leaders that she was doing her job.'

I would take all of that – the targets and the endless counting – if there were proof that it did some good. Probably not as a teacher, and maybe not even as a parent, but as a person in the world who believed in opportunity, I would accept a system based on distrust if there were any proof that it worked, that the highly ranked schools were doing better by their students. But the results don't tell you that: results mainly tell you about what the intake is. The only reasonable demonstration of effectiveness would be if Outstanding schools typically reduced the difference in outcomes between rich kids and poor kids. That is exactly what the numbers cannot show. The difference in results between kids on free school meals and the rest is stolidly, remarkably static, across all bands of school from Outstanding to Failing.[8] It's only remarkable, of course, if you have ignored all the evidence about the factors that determine academic achievement. It's the economy, stupid!

Free Schools for get-up-and-go parents

The academies programme was started by the Labour government, though arguably it began with

Margaret Thatcher (again) and her technical colleges.[9] It has been radically extended by the Coalition: as I write today, 1,338 secondaries are converter academies, 469 are sponsored academies and 1,461 are still run by the local authority. Of the primaries, 1,465 are converters, 689 are sponsored academies and 14,664 are still run by the local authority.

The principle of Academisation now is that anyone can open a school, except the local authority. Decades of expertise is wasted. Even if we assume that it wasn't expertise (it was just accumulated leftie tripe), councils remain the only bodies with any accurate sense of where places are needed, and how many.

Sure enough, in no time, there were wild distortions, especially with free schools – three secondaries were established in Suffolk in 2012 in areas that already had surplus places; there are now nearly 11,000 more places than they need, in contrast to the national picture, a shortage of 240,000 primary places. That shortage will turn into a gap in secondaries over the next few years, as children inconveniently grow. A proper central-education policy would be planning for that; instead, it's trundling out the rhetoric of 'free schools for really zingy, get-up-and-go parents', which in practice means 'extra places in areas that don't need them, for parents who for some reason have taken against their existing local school'. Precisely because of all this ridiculous waste, the Department for Education says the criteria for opening a free school have become stricter, which I don't doubt; it's probably quite a good way to bury the policy without ever having to admit its failure.

Academisation carries on, and the picture is pretty mixed. In 2012 I made a documentary about a chain of academies run by the charity Ark (Absolute Return for Kids). I thought the whole organisation stank: it was set up by a bunch of fund managers trying to 'give something back', originally in the developing world and then in the UK, by taking over schools in very deprived areas. It's just so insulting: fund managers, if they want to give something back, should think harder about what their core business is doing to the global economy; indeed, the mechanisms by which their business creates poverty in the first place. Annoyingly for me, it turned out that their schools were really good. The support for head teachers was really good. The heads themselves were really good. Effectively I spent six months making an advert for Ark, which then aired on Radio 4. Vexing.

The problem with academies is that the picture is very mixed. Some are really good, some are really bad, and there is a fair smattering in between. Whatever you hear from an increasingly desperate Education Department, there is no serious person researching this who would go any further than to say: they cover the same broad range from good to bad as local-authority schools do. That's speaking from an educational perspective. The interesting thing about bad policy is that it cannot help but scoop up some good people; some will succeed. However, things do go wrong with this system that do not happen in schools with local-authority oversight.

First, they open where they're not needed. So a secondary free school in Brixton opened with only 17 pupils, having cost the DfE £18 million, and we only know that because a reporter sat outside the gate and counted them in.[10] Which brings us to the second and (many would say) larger problem, that of transparency and accountability: democratic accountability is shot. The person in charge of your local academy was originally the Secretary of State. This didn't work: there is only one of him (or her). So the DfE introduced Regional Commissioners, but there was nothing transparent about the process – how were they appointed? Why were only one-quarter of them women, when nearly 80 per cent of the educational workforce is female? Why, if the entire problem with education was local bureaucrats, would everything be solved by the creation of a new local bureaucracy?

Related and possibly more important is the dizzying waste of money. Every now and then I'll get whistle-blowers reporting stories of what looks like corruption: a head paid £170,000; £40,000 spent on furniture; IT contracts given to family members. But, when I look into it, I find that the Education Funding Agency has already investigated and cleared it.[11] Apparently that's a fine amount for the head of two schools to earn, and it's okay to have a nice desk. So, for a reputable newspaper, it's not really a story (then the *Daily Mail* runs it instead[12]). I put this, in a public meeting, to the national Schools Commissioner, Frank Green. He said, 'Well, when I was a head, I can tell you, I didn't earn anything like that!' It's difficult to know how to respond to such a completely irrelevant remark; plus I'd already given the microphone back, so I just blinked at him. A councillor from Bradford, Ralph Berry, chipped in, 'I'm living with the consequences in Bradford of this sort of thing. King's Science Academy was run as a family corner shop. Recruiting without proper process, contracting without proper procurement.' Gary Phillips, head of the Lilian Baylis Technology School, said, 'I don't think the present government quite understands the storm that's about to approach them with head-teacher pay.' The National Audit Office found that 43 per cent of Academy Trusts' financial statements showed 'related party transactions', which is NAO-speak for 'giving contracts to someone you know' – worth a total of £71 million.[13] It found that the DfE had no way of tracking the cost-effectiveness of its policies. £5 billion has been spent on new school places: as someone who supports public spending for the good of citizens, I should be pleased, I guess. But not if it's going on furniture, or contracts to people's friends. Frank Green approached me afterwards and told me there were more than 100 investigations pending into local-authority schools; but that doesn't actually tell me very much, because there was no indication of how serious the charges were or, indeed, whether they were true. When the local authority is in charge, it appoints the auditors. This doesn't mean corruption could never happen. But it does mean that, unless the whole council is bent, it would be very difficult for a school to spend money illegitimately.[14]

Where next, then? A few academy chains will continue to be brilliant, some will continue to be bad, and it is an open question, for those bad ones, who they will be handed to when it is finally established how bad they are. Other chains may not want to take them on; it would plainly be humiliating to have to hand them back to local authorities, having based your entire educational plan on the hypothesis that local authorities were useless; that bit will depend on who is in government when the incompetent ones start to unravel. It doesn't seem very likely that a government can continue to treat teachers like this – the workload, the constant slating – without creating shortages. The one thing I can predict with certainty is what will *not* happen: the academy process will not simply continue apace, producing steady improvements in real education (as opposed to meaningless targets), to deliver the results the government claims to want from it, to 'break down the barriers to social mobility at all stages of a person's life'.[15] That's not the way this is going. Good systems aren't built on constant surveillance and monitoring.

Whether or not any school system in the world can break down barriers to social mobility is an open question – it's also a pointless question. Even if you could create a school so dynamic, disciplined and inspiring that it could teach children who were hungry, I'm afraid there would still be pinkos asking why children have to be hungry. We're not going to go away just because three of them get into Oxbridge.

I want something different from education itself – something you wouldn't need a fleet of inspectors to count, and something teachers wouldn't have to spend their evenings trying to prove: schools in which teachers, students, parents, governors, community organisations and local politicians are all responsible for building a democratic, civic institution, rather than a results factory. This is already going on, all over the country[16] – there are hundreds of schools run as co-ops. There's a handful run explicitly as Citizen Schools. Pupils aren't just drilled for GCSEs; they're taught their own power, and how to organise around it. It is actually pretty childish to think you can plonk your kids in an institution and let one super-head sort them all out. If you want things to be better, and to have a say in what 'better' would look like, you have to participate, and know that you are allowed to participate. Everyone has to feel they're part of something larger than just a quest for their own grades.

Your gardener must be able to read
What is education for? What kind of adults do we want to produce? Where will they slot into the jobs of the future? What kind of lives will they be able to build with the things they have learnt? Mass public education, as it was originally conceived, had this idea: you take all kids and you train them in deductive reasoning, and the ones who are really good at it become scientists (or engineers), and the ones who are a bit more poetic become philosophers (or poets), and the ones who are less good somehow manage to shuffle themselves into jobs that don't require deductive reasoning in such large quantities (almost all jobs). It was never designed to educate everybody to the same degree: rather, it started off on the assumption that some humans were inherently superior to others and would always have more sophisticated minds, worthy of more refinement; so you sent those to the Russell Group universities, and you made sure everybody else could read – and we would all arrive well prepared for the role in life that had been determined by our birth. Some Conservatives still basically think like this. I interviewed Michael Heseltine once, and we were talking about equality of opportunity; or at least that's what I thought we were talking about. His answer was: 'Your gardener must be able to read. Otherwise how can he be expected to determine the word "poison"?' Apparently the question he thought I'd put was: 'What's the point of literacy in the lower orders?'

A cloistered elite

In the normal world this view of a society ranked by birth, where poor people learnt to read in order to serve rich ones better, steadily gave way to the idea that opportunity should be open to all, and anyone who tried really hard and was naturally very able ought to be able to get to the top. Naturally, along with this, universities moved from belonging to a cloistered elite to, ideally, being able to accommodate everybody, or at least, 50 per cent of everybody.[17] This took roughly 100 years, from the establishment of the redbrick universities, at the end of the nineteenth century, to the conversion of polytechnics and the mass democratisation of higher education at the end of the twentieth. Prior to the end of the 1800s universities weren't economically purposed, they were just places to send your children while they waited for you to die. That doesn't mean they didn't learn useful things.

Blair made the 50 per cent target partly because he loved targets; partly because the meritocratic Britain that he openly yearned for needed greater access to tertiary education; partly because the obsession with Sino-Japanese educational superiority had already taken hold (in the Dearing Report, begun in 1996, the abiding anxiety was: if the Japanese had higher rates of university participation than us, what would that mean for their global competitiveness?); and partly because it was already understood, by 1997, that students would start paying tuition fees. Dearing accepted that student numbers must go up and, if they did, the state must stop paying, since the whole business had been 'designed in the 1950s for an elite system'. At that time total government spending – on tuition, maintenance, capital investment, the whole lot – was under £10 billion, or about 1.2 per cent of GDP, much lower than the OECD average. What's so depressing, reading that report now, is that it never even questioned the idea that only the elite were worth educating at the state's expense and, once the masses came rushing in, the taxpayer would no longer want to fund it. The person who objected, when the Labour government lifted the fee cap to £3,000 in 2003, was Iain Duncan Smith, who called it 'a tax on learning'.

The recent hike to £9,000-a-year fees was justified using the argument: 'Why should the taxpayer put his hand in his pocket for people who are already part of the elite?' They're not part of the elite; they're the same people of whom 20 years ago the question was: 'Why would a taxpayer stump up for members of society who are not elite, who might just be average?' The argument for fees is full of idle self-satisfied inconsistency, which it can afford because it is so confident of the central premise: that the taxpayer resents every penny spent on learning that isn't his own, and there is nothing in tertiary education that brings any great benefit to anyone except the person who receives it.

The elite, being the only ones who can pay for their children's tuition fees up front, are the only ones for whom this change will not echo into the future. It is impossible to tell what life will look like, for an ordinary kid with a decent 2:1, coming out of a decent university, in 2016. Even if we imagine that the scandal of unpaid internship has been fixed by then, even if secure working conditions are back on the rise, even if wage stagnation has eased off a bit, she or he will still have an average £50,000 debt-overhang, which she or he will have to clear before commencing to save for a mortgage. How rich will you have to be just to live a normal life, in the 2020s? What will we start considering normal?

Is higher education a 'public good'?

That is, does all of society benefit from it, even those who are not using it? The phrase is a little like 'public interest', in that its strict definition gives way to something that it intuitively ought to mean. It sounds like it should mean 'good for the public'. Technically, a 'public good' must be non-excludable (it is impossible to exclude freeloaders from enjoying the good) and non-rivalrous (extra people consuming the good don't diminish its value). Almost nothing is totally non-excludable, apart from air and military protection. That's why the right is so obsessed with defence. It is the only thing they can see the point of spending public money on, because it's the only realm where everybody will benefit, no matter what (and also you get to kill enemies). Plenty of things have elements of private good, and elements of public good. Take healthcare, as an example of excludability; it would be possible to exclude me from visiting a tuberculosis sanatorium if I couldn't pay, but you cannot stop me benefiting from a city in which very few people have TB. Likewise, a lot of things are non-rivalrous up to a certain capacity: roads, the Internet, education. You can all use them at once, and then, wham – if there are too many of you, none of you can.

Higher education is a very typical public good: it is excludable, but has non-excludable elements; it can become rivalrous, but has a long slope where it is not. Everybody gains from it, whether in tax receipts or in a more productive economy, whether in boosted exports or the sheer vivacity and sophistication of a country in which everybody is very highly educated. Naturally, though, it's also a private good. You will earn more if you have a degree than if you don't, by and large. Why should I pay, so that someone else can earn more? That's the only question politics has been asking for nearly 20 years. That's what happens when you see higher education as nothing more than a monetary investment recoupable against future wages.

Ron Dearing, introducing the report that buried the idea of a free, publicly funded university system, quoted John Masefield's 1946 address to the University of Sheffield:

> It is a place where those who hate ignorance may strive to know, where those who perceive truth may

strive to make others see; where seekers and learners alike, banded together in the search for knowledge, will honour thought in all its finer ways, will welcome thinkers in distress or in exile, will uphold ever the dignity of thought and learning and will exact standards in these things.

He apparently saw no contradiction between the ideas he espoused and the policy suggestions he made.

Germany has just deemed the fee experiment a failure and made all tertiary education free. Lower Saxony was the last to go, after a free education movement that began in 1999. Germany has similar student numbers to ours. Across Scandinavia higher education is free; in most of Central Europe fees are under €1,000 a year; and almost nowhere are they more than €3,000. Either we're this booming economy, doing so much better than the eurozone, in which case why can't we afford similar public services? Or we're a flailing economy that can't afford education, in which case why cast Europe as the economic millstone?

Who are you calling unskilled, exactly?
As universities were being recast as skill-dispensers, the work that does not require a degree was being reframed as 'low-skilled': a huge raft of jobs, across the colossal sectors of retail, construction, care and hospitality, were deemed all of a sudden to require

no skill; and thus the low-wage economy was born, with between 5 million on low pay and 13 million in low-skilled jobs (low pay has a specific definition, which not all low-skilled workers meet, but they're probably not earning very much more).

All these jobs actually require a huge amount of skill: care-work demands not just the soft skills of empathy, compassion and insight, but the so-called harder skills of nursing. It takes organisational, problem-solving and often managerial skills, usually driving too. Pay and skill have pulled apart, and in order not to recognise or talk about it, we now say 'low skill' as a synonym for 'low pay' and assume that one low-paid person is as interchangeable as their zero-hours contracts suggest. Labour-force experts talk about the hourglass economy – jobs at the bottom, jobs at the top, nothing in the middle – and we all accept that. In fact, if you described it in terms of skills, it would be more like a flowerpot, with a slightly larger tier of jobs as skills increased. The low-paid do not deserve their poverty wages. What are we actually looking at here? A sudden proliferation of extremely easy jobs that a gormless teenager could do? Or the determined ratcheting-down of wages, which has then been post-rationalised by denigrating the people doing the jobs?

There's an educational solution to that, though of course it won't work unless it comes accompanied by an industrial solution, some rebalancing of wages and profit, some rejection of predatory corporate behaviour. The reason it's hard to negotiate collectively for the skills in these jobs is that they do not have qualifications attached to them, there is no regulatory framework, no licence to practice, no guild. There's no established trajectory, agreed by employers and unions, delivered by colleges, whereby somebody becomes a Proper Bricklayer or a Proper Concierge. The politicians of the last 30 years have shown insufficient interest in the kinds of jobs, the kinds of training, the kind of education that they cannot imagine their own children doing – lecturers grimly call FE colleges 'where other people's children go' – and the result is not a lack of skill, but a lack of credentials. The entire low-paid sector is like the Scarecrow in *The Wizard of Oz*: the problem isn't that the low-paid haven't got brains; it's that they don't have diplomas. The existence of that as a plot device makes me think this scam has been going on for longer than 30 years.

There are things that need to change about the paradigm: we need to change the trust we put in teachers, the faith we put in money, the results we value, the purpose of learning – the whole lot. But the shift I'd like to see most of all is to a government that, instead of regarding its people as a cost who need to be persuaded of rough realities, sees us all as assets – its main assets; no, scratch that – its only assets. Give or take some unusable amount of shale gas, this is the only wealth of a nation: the minds of its people, and what we will discover. An education system that started there, on that principle, would look completely different.

Did an immigrant steal your job?

A relative of mine whom I secretly suspect of having voted for UKIP in the European elections says, whenever we talk about politics, 'It's the people of the East Riding I feel sorry for.' Then she looks at her lap, not in embarrassment, or evasively, but more as a bull would look down, just before it charged you.

I've never taken up the challenge of her argument because I absolutely hate having one of those English arguments in which one person is waiting for the other person to call them racist, so that they can storm off dramatically. All the moves are so predetermined, it's like having an argument scripted by a daytime-TV soap. Drama's opposite.

The squeeze on incomes in the East Riding of Yorkshire is tight and unforgiving, and in that mix, somewhere, are some strong young people, who may be the figments of my relative's imagination but probably do exist, who would love a job picking carrots, but can't get one. Instead they face all these daily humiliations: being told to report to a super-market for their 'work experience', constantly monstered by a political culture that equates poverty with immorality. Imagine those people. Sometimes, on their way to be harassed by some Work Programme provider or other, they see busloads of Bulgarians on their way to pick carrots. Maybe they see them in the pub at the weekends, flush with cash; or maybe our young people can't themselves afford to go to the pub and just sit at home, imagining a pub full of Bulgarians. Get them on the subject of Bulgarians, and they probably sound pretty racist. Anything sounds racist when you stick 'fucking' in front of it. Yet what sane person doesn't feel sorry for the people of the East Riding? Who doesn't feel like a compatriot to those people, bound by something more specific and localised than just general human empathy?

English people won't do it

Agriculture deliberately hires foreigners, en masse, over local people. Even Europeans from the A8 countries – Poland, Latvia, et cetera – aren't cheap enough for the farming industry, which for decades had a special permit to employ people from even cheaper A2 countries (Bulgaria and Romania). The numbers were small – capped at 20,000. At the start of 2014 the Seasonal Agriculture Workers Scheme (SAWS) was abandoned altogether, when the A2 countries attained full freedom of movement.

In August 2013 I followed the newly minted Green Party leader, Natalie Bennett, round a soft-fruit growers' trade show in Kent, and she had a briefing with two men from the National Farmers' Union – famously one of only two unions in the country that are the opposite of left-wing (its last socialist leader was Sir Simon Gourlay in the late 1980s; the other union is Prospect).

Guy Poskitt is the carrot-man of the East Riding; he explained that they recruited immigrant labour for harvesting. 'And why is that?' Bennett asked, politely. The two men exchanged a look that I recognised from the bus-drivers who used to take my mother (and, unhappily, sometimes also my sister and me) to Greenham Common in the Eighties: 'Careful . . . she's irrational and dangerously wrong, but don't challenge her, because she might start crying or show you her armpits. Say a soft, platitudinous thing, while looking straight ahead.' I have spent my adult life avoiding this look. I don't want to be the hysteric. I desperately seek approval, from soft-fruit growers as much as anybody else. 'Well,' Poskitt said quietly, looking not at her but straight ahead, 'English people won't do it.'

Some reasons why you might refuse a job like this: you have to live onsite, because the work's labour-intensive, but you don't get paid for extra hours, because the Agricultural Wages Board has set an overtime price; and farmers would rather have more workers, paid the lower rate, than fewer workers, working harder, for a higher rate.[1] These are generalised points observed by the Migration Advisory Committee (MAC). I know nothing more about Poskitt's business in particular, for reasons I'll elaborate on shortly. The work is temporary, so you wouldn't emerge with a transferable skill. If you had any part-time work elsewhere, you'd lose it. It would not be great if there were people who liked to see you every day, like children. Physically, it's hard, but not dangerous.

So everybody, from the carrot-magnate to the MAC, agrees that 'UK workers generally are not prepared to supply their labour to this sector'.[2] But you only need to look at an oil rig to see that this isn't true: British people, like other people, will do any kind of work, so long as it's paid properly. Alternatively, you can import labour from a country where labour is cheaper or, to put it in the language that apparently you need an economic degree to understand, 'exploit global labour market imbalances'. SAWS was only ever the official tip of the cheap-labour iceberg. Huge swathes of agriculture in the east, from Cambridgeshire to Lincolnshire, rely on cheaper EU labour, whether provided by individuals or gang-masters, Poland or Croatia.

Misinformation swirls: a figure often cited is that Wisbech is now one-third populated by Eastern Europeans, immigration having swelled it from a town of 20,000 to one of 30,000. This simply isn't borne out by the census data, which has the entire local authority of Fenland home to 95,000, of whom

86,000 are UK-born – only 5,000 are 'other white', of which Eastern European would only be a subset (probably the main subset).[3] So there's overstatement, sure; but that doesn't mean that a large proportion of the working-age population isn't Eastern European. Everybody – from local UKIP candidates to charities working with the migrants – agrees that the new labour is treated badly, the work is insecure, the hours unpredictable, the workers scammed by employers and landlords. Everybody agrees that this makes it harder for UK-born workers to get jobs.

Anyway, back to the trade show in Kent: 'Oh,' said Bennett to Poskitt. He looked at his friend, who grew blueberries, and she looked at me, possibly (or possibly not) thinking what I was thinking, viz: 'You mean, "English people won't do it for the chickenfeed money I need to pay them, in order to stay profitable".' This has become an incredibly difficult thing to say: on what grounds are you privileging the people of East Riding or Wisbech over the people of Bulgaria or Lithuania? Well, you're not: you're defending your right to fair wages, irrespective of whether there's someone, somewhere in the world, who will do that job for less. But, in its simplest terms, it sounds a bit English Defence League. This creates a vacuum, where the people arguing for pay have been silenced for sounding xenophobic. Nature, abhorring a vacuum, fills it with people who will only speak about profit.

By that, I emphatically do not mean that Guy Poskitt is someone who will only think of profit: the farmers aren't making any money out of it, either. The supermarkets are making the money. The same globe that provides Bulgarians for less than Brits will provide you with a foreign carrot for less than a carrot from the East Riding. Follow the money – the farmers, even the largest of them, who will do anything to defend their business, aren't making huge margins. The supermarkets shaft their suppliers and make huge profits, which they distribute to their shareholders and executives. Poskitt, however, wouldn't be drawn on how much he is paid by the supermarket he supplies, because 'I have a good relationship with my customers.' Only dairy farmers are open about how badly they're treated by the supermarkets, being past the point of caring; but it is well known that the relationship between supermarkets and suppliers is neo-feudal[4] – the supermarkets say what they want, at what price, and the suppliers deliver it or go bust.

Was it, in fact, a supermarket that stole your job?

The assumption is that supermarkets hold suppliers to low prices, suppliers make it work with cheap labour, and we – the customers – win. In fact, prices never reflect reductions in cost. Simon Gourlay gave me this example: 'We've now seen wheat, which was £180 to £200 pounds a ton when I was farming, go down to just over £100 a ton. There's no way that even the most efficient UK farmer can produce wheat at £100 a ton. It's governed by the world market [or, rather, the futures market – see Finance]. It doesn't make any difference to the price of bread in the supermarket.' Obviously; otherwise bread would cost less than it did 20 years ago. What you're looking at instead is a simulacrum of value: supermarkets clustering around a price point they've decided to present as a bargain, then sticking a big yellow sticker on it, saying 'Bargain'. The same people who think it's good if Starbucks avoids tax (see Tax) because it makes our coffee cheaper also think that, if supermarkets paid more to their suppliers, our groceries would be more expensive. This assumes the supermarkets are passing all their savings on to us, which they are not. The funny thing is that supermarkets don't even have to threaten price rises. It has become 'common sense' that, if they were to behave more decently towards suppliers or staff, prices would rise; and if you even go near a conversation with higher prices in it, everybody freaks out. That's a low-wage economy for you.

What would help the people of the East Riding? A properly enforced living wage; worker-centred unionisation in agriculture, so that unattractive work was remunerated accordingly; more equality between farming and retail; less-predatory supermarkets, which would probably mean a mix of shops (some mutual, some co-operatives), which would then mean less emphasis on shareholders; lower pay among top executives: that's to start with. Leaving the EU? That's not going to do it. But limitless incoming cheap labour erodes the principles that build fair wages from about ten different directions. Politicians keep talking about averages: what matters are principles.

MPs live in fear of sounding 'anti-business', even when identifiable business behaviour is impoverishing their constituents. Essentially, no one wants to sound like the hysteric. Nobody wants to get the bus-driver look. But what if the bus-driver is wrong? What if the norms of the mainstream are only serving a tiny number of people?

In the absence of any systemic answers, liberal politicians hide behind sentimental assertion: 'Immigrants have been great for this country' and 'My dad fled the Nazis/Idi Amin, and I'll never forget what he said about the welcome he received.' It's true – all countries are built on the passion and resilience of the people who live in them. But it's started to make me feel a bit nauseous, because, like a lot of sentimentality, it's a deliberate misunderstanding of what the conversation is really about. Plus, since it is generally given by the middle classes, it is taken as an indication of middle-class people having no idea or curiosity about how people live who are not like them.

Why do working-class communities feel threatened by immigration when middle-class ones don't? Why, when those who are against immigration say they're not racist, should you believe them? Why is anti-immigration sentiment pegged not to the number of immigrants, but to the state of the local economy?[5]

The simple explanation is that it's the working classes who get shoved off the last rung of the ladder, when migrant labour comes in and is cheaper. If you're middle-class, it's not your home that's under threat; it's not your livelihood. This doesn't stack up, though. Middle-class migrants do come in; if a German person took my job, maybe I'd get another job rather than be out of work completely, but I'd still mind. As for housing, we're all angry that housing has become unaffordable, even those of us with a house. But migrants are very rarely housed, either, unless they're asylum-seekers put into squalid hostel accommodation by G4S.[6]

Through the prism of citizenship, though, it makes much more sense: our politics has citizenship as a very conditional state, one that you have to earn.[7] Rights are presented as the reward for the proper execution of responsibilities. Part of being responsible is earning enough money. People who aren't economically active, or who are active but don't have enough to show for it, are characterised as a drain on the state, rather than as part of the state. Disability is tainted with the constant suspicion that it's faked. Anyone in receipt of benefits (except pensions) is routinely portrayed as the cause of the nation's decline, and never as a source of its pride. This is an incredibly unpleasant, precarious way to live – repudiated by your own nation, disowned. It breaks an important bond, whereby we trust our country to see each of us as something important and precious, irreplaceable. A country that doesn't treat you like that, but weighs you and measures you, then castigates you for not being valuable enough, is going to swap you over in a heartbeat for someone cheaper or less encumbered or stronger. So of course you hate immigration: not because you don't like foreigners, but because you've just been punched in the face by the place that holds your heart.

Any political discourse that demonises its poor, in consequence, is going to find itself with a massive anti-immigrant nationalist movement. The answer isn't to halt immigration; it's to stop demonising the poor. Rolling your eyes at the voters of Wisbech, calling them bigots, then pandering to the bigotry you think they embody, with stupid new rules about migrants on benefits: that's still demonising. All of mainstream politics needs to open its heart to what's really being said, by UKIP and its voters, and by the people who feel sorry for the people of the East Riding. Why don't you see us all as assets? What kind of a nation doesn't cherish its own people?

Work from the bottom

Large industrial cleaning companies favour South American migrant labour because not only is it cheap, but it's often here illegally. That puts paid to their statutory sick pay and any other crazy requests they might make. Care-workers are actively recruited, again, due to 'chronic difficulties' in recruiting and retaining UK nationals[8] who are prepared to do the work. Conditions in this sector are appalling (see Poverty). There is no shortage of British people who care; there is a shortage of British people who can afford to be exploited like this.

This industry recruits from the Philippines, Zimbabwe, India and Nigeria, and this partly reflects post-colonial relations. Translated: you would have to have some crazy sentimental attachment to the UK to come over for this job, and also be someone who'd struggle to get a visa any other way.

The NHS is a huge recruiter of labour from abroad, and this is often given as a pro-immigrant argument: that, without migrant labour, we'd lose 40 per cent of our medics and auxiliary staff overnight.[9] This might be the most stupid of all the arguments. These recruitment drives are always the result of government failure. Well, not always – in 1948 we needed nurses in huge numbers and had never had a centralised nurse-training system. Since then, we've employed nurses centrally and trained them centrally, and if there's a gap between supply and demand, it's because there's been a training shortage. So, in the mid-1990s, training places were cut to save money, and when Labour brought in their targets in the 2000s they needed a lot of nurses, fast. Then they recruited mostly from outside the EU (because EU countries employed their own trained nurses); now they recruit mainly from within it (because Europe has gone bust). We are not looking at a successful policy: this is a failure. Broadly speaking, the British 18-year-olds who should have been trained as nurses in 1995 are now 38-year-olds doing worse-paid, less-skilled jobs instead. The NHS's staffing bill is much higher because a lot of this recruitment is brokered through agencies. Howard Catton, head of policy and international affairs at the Royal College of Nursing, observed: '£3.5 billion was spent on agency staff in 2013. I had someone say, when finance directors ask the foundation trust to sign off the agency costs, they have to pass the smelling salts as well.'

I interviewed two Spanish nurses recently, as it happens, doing some solar-power activism. They brought to this country everything you could ever ask for: skills, passion, politics, a new perspective, different experiences, youth and vigour. Migration is wonderful because people are. But don't dress it up for something that it isn't: a deliberated policy, reflecting widely held enthusiasm for a multinational workforce. It is just happenstance that other nations are able to help, in the desperate scramble to plug the gaps left by bad policy.

And finally, in this not-remotely-exhaustive survey of which industries get staff from where, Pret a Manger has been accused in the past of only giving you a job if you're not from the UK.[10] The Federation of Small Businesses gave this slightly mealy-mouthed but basically straight account of what's going on: 'A lot of our members do say that there is a work ethos advantage with foreign staff, but there are no figures to bear that out. They say that those from abroad have more willingness to work from the bottom and show dedication.' 'Work from the bottom' is the key phrase in all that – it is a synonym for 'eat shit'. The likelihood is that an unskilled foreign workforce is more biddable and less demanding than a British one: you're a stranger in a strange land; you don't march in and immediately start enforcing your statutory rights.

Has an immigrant stolen two of your jobs?

Polish people come in for totally contradictory criticism: they work too hard and ordinary mortals can't compete, yet at the same time they are lazy and claim too many benefits. There is more here than mental muddle: while there is basically zero evidence of benefit tourism,[11] the state of the UK economy is such that, if you remain here, have children and stay in a low-pay sector, you will inevitably end up, at the very least, on Housing Benefit, Child Benefit and in-work tax credits. This isn't because you are trawling Europe for the most generous welfare system. This is because it was your misfortune to land in a country that has allowed its housing market to become absurd. So there actually isn't a contradiction in accusing Polish people of both working too hard and claiming benefits: the conversation that urgently needs to be had is how is it possible to work too hard and still need benefits? This strikes at the centre of the meritocracy myth: if hard work doesn't make you self-sufficient, then maybe self-sufficiency isn't the badge of honour it's made out to be. Maybe self-sufficiency is just another accident of birth.

Pick your own insult

The urge to ridicule UKIP is hard to shake, since their internal contradictions are so glaring – some of their councillors sound like borderline Nazi eugenicists, suggesting compulsory abortions for foetuses with Down's syndrome. Others sound like bucolic socialists, set on restoring rural Britain to its glory by ejecting Europe and corporatism, which monolithic enemies are taken as interchangeable. How either of those notions squares with the other, or with the kingpin – a former stockbroker, married to a German, who doesn't like Romanians – is unfathomable. Yet I have come to wonder how useful it is to attack UKIP at its weakest points.

For instance: the South-west is weird. It has surging UKIP support, but very few actual immigrants. Indeed there is one set of data for East Devon in which the number of estimated foreigners – 4,000 – is the exact midpoint of their confidence interval.[12] In other words, it might have 4,000, or it might have 8,000 or it might have none. UKIP support is at its strongest in areas with the fewest incomers. Anti-UKIPers always have a lot of fun with that, because their candidates bang on about local jobs for local people when there is no evidence that anybody else wants their jobs.

However, UKIP's offer is much larger than 'We will get rid of immigration.' Its offer is: 'We will transcend the faceless smart-arsery of Westminster, which we all know doesn't care about your community.' So, when you go in like just another smart-arse, you might think you've taken them down, and you have; simultaneously you've made their point for them, about what kind of person you are.

This comes somewhere close to the fundamental problem of politics, the thing that has turned it into an irrelevant, impotent, trivial sideshow, despised by the squires of the South-west, despaired of by the activists of London, mistrusted by the unemployed of the East. The rules of debate are martial: you go for the weakest point, because that way you get a rout. As a military strategy, that works well (I actually have no clue about military strategy; this is just what I've heard), but as a debate about ideas, it more or less guarantees that you will devote your energy to petty – or at least peripheral – elements, while leaving people's minds about the strong, central tenets basically unchanged.

Numbers are important. Everyone needs accurate figures. There is no governance in the world that improves by knowing less. So it's helpful to discover that immigrants are 60 per cent less likely to claim benefits and tend to be better educated, yet less well paid, than their British counterparts.[13] However, as debating points, none of those work. If you want to make someone who fears immigration feel stupid, then go right ahead. But if you want to persuade that person to stop fearing immigration, stop talking about people as though they're more worthwhile when they don't claim benefits than when they do.

For Christ's sake, what's wrong with everyone? Almost nobody in the world will live their whole life benefit-free. I claimed benefit when I was on maternity leave, and right now I'm paying someone else's benefits with my taxes; and some other time I'll probably claim benefit again, when I get some disease and I'm too ill to work; and then, when I hit 65 or 70, it'll be benefits, benefits, benefits all the way to the grave, and I'll still be the same person, who made this country and was made by it. Foreign or British, we are not just units of economic sale, to be evaluated by whether we're net contributors or net recipients. To present foreigners like that is simply to reinforce the anxieties of people who are on benefits and who think you look down upon them for it.

Between 1995 and 2011 foreign-born nationals contributed £8.8 billion more than they gained. What does that even mean: 'gained'? It means 'had a baby, sent it to school when the time came; sprained an ankle, went to the doctor'. It means 'lived a full life in the bloodstream of this country'. This isn't a criticism of the research, so much as the political narrative. There's something awfully wrong with the way we talk about society; the blood cells are treated as parasites, and the parasites are treated as bone marrow.

That isn't very much, is it, £8.8 billion over 16 years? That's £550 million a year. It is a fact that immigration boosts GDP; it doesn't squeeze jobs, it creates jobs. Every immigrant coming into the country creates a need for more services, more goods, more housing, more restaurants, and that makes the country more prosperous.[14] Everyone concedes, however, that immigration doesn't profit those at the bottom. Indeed, this is quantified: for every 1 per cent rise in the share of migrants, average wages in the low-skilled and unskilled sectors drop by 0.5 per cent.[15] What does that mean in the care industry, which comprises 20 per cent foreign-born workers? It means that your pay is terrible. I don't blame immigrants, many of whom have been expressly recruited to work for low wages; I blame private-equity companies for predatory behaviour (see Poverty and Finance), and I blame councils for outsourcing their elder-care so unimaginatively in the first place (see Privatisation). But if you're going to say, 'Immigrants are great because they boost GDP', while making no reparation to those whose income is eroded, well, at some point they're going to reply, 'Stuff your half a billion quid a year, which I don't see any of. I'd rather be paid a living wage.'

What to do when a fourteenth-century serf steals your job

This story is not one amorphous band of foreigners versus one homogenous band of us. Migrants are stratified by money and power. Everyone always pretends that it's about the skills they have, but it isn't: students have a much higher status than asylum-seekers, but asylum-seekers are very often highly qualified, whereas most students, by definition, don't yet have a degree. A large amount of Eastern European labour is skilled, working here in low-skilled occupations because employers are only interested in them for the power imbalances that make them cheap.

The first law against labour being allowed to travel was passed in 1349.[16] The problem wasn't international; with heavy reliance on horses, another county seemed like another country. It was directly after a plague, and serfdom was coming to an end. Previous to this, poverty was an anointed state, and people could go to heaven just by touching the poor in a nice way; afterwards, you could be arrested even for looking poor. The economic imperative was plain: when labour is in short supply, labourers can jack up prices, but they don't have any leverage if they can't move. The Ordinance of Labourers therefore combined restriction of movement with regulation of wages.

This sounds very pre-free market, the enforcement of employer-supremacy by law; it was, after all, the fourteenth century. But what we're looking at here is the gradation of people's freedom to move, according to their wealth and power. The very idea of it being criminal for people to move about was enshrined in the concept of vagrancy: it was a crime of status. You couldn't be a rich vagrant.

That power dynamic still exists, and that will still be the result of restricting people's freedom to move: the poorer you are, the less freedom you will have. Tony Blair and Rupert Murdoch will be truly international, welcome anywhere, at home wherever they go; ultimate freedom will be ultimate wealth, and everybody's freedom diminishes the further they are from money. Those who are against immigration speak as if wages were a fixed pot, to be distributed in a bare-knuckle fight between the native and the newcomer. Of course they do: because the real story of wages involves a bare-knuckle fight between the worker and the employer, and that – from a profit point of view – is going to be really inconvenient. Before you fight for restrictions that will apply to you too, consider: nobody ever improved their bargaining position by tying their own hands.

The EU was devised to make people's lives better. It's there so that you can go to France if you're really good at textiles, or someone from Croatia can come here and be a psychoanalyst. It's there to multiply our possibilities, to crack wide open our horizons. It's there so that we can feel part of the trade agreement that was created to end centuries of pointless fighting, rather than feel that we're at the mercy of it. Very tight border controls, usually accompanied by very tight capital controls, stifle both economic activity and personal freedom. The poorer nation of the equation comes off worse, but you only have to look at East and West Germany to see that the rich one doesn't generally benefit.

It's hard to see how freedom of trade could even work without freedom of movement; but let's say that it could. We'd have created a situation in which investment could roam freely, while people couldn't. What would be the point of that?

If we're going to have freedom of movement, we need unionisation, collective wage negotiation and a coordinated rejection of workplace 'flexibility' if (when) all it means is an explosion of zero-hours contracts and all the insecurity that goes with them. But we need those things anyway.

Housing shortages and unaffordable housing are always going to generate anxiety about space and population. In fact there have never been more rooms in the country, per head of population. The problem is that they aren't evenly distributed, and the lack of a baseline – a coherent political rejection of squalor as an acceptable outcome for anybody – makes everyone anxious. Proper, socially owned housing, built to high environmental standards so that it doesn't bankrupt people to heat it; planned and executed according to some realistic estimate of how many people will need it and what their wages are likely to be; conceived with an image of what a dignified, fulfilling life would look like, rather than trying to cram people into the smallest imaginable spaces – we need those things too, otherwise competition in the private rental market will always intensify. But we need those things anyway.

When we make better policy for ourselves, anxiety about immigration will evaporate.

'We asked for workers. We got people instead.' Max Frisch

Here's the thing: there are countries in which they say explicitly what our policy has often said tacitly. If you are low-skilled, you are welcome, but only to do low-skilled labour. From the mass immigration demanded by the textiles industry in the 1960s, through the SAWS scheme where you can only pick carrots; from farm workers of the British colonies in the 1840s, through to domestic workers in Hong Kong and Singapore today, this is the pattern: a constant demand for labour in sectors where pay is low and there is a capital interest in keeping it down. In South Asia these people are mainly women, and in Singapore they are forcibly pregnancy-tested every six months and deported if the test is positive.[17] This is no good – it's no good for the existing population, since it holds wages down at the bottom. And it's no good for the maids, who are effectively treated as a serf class. Whatever you think about pregnancy, there are almost no acceptable reasons to deny it to another human being.

In any discussion about immigrants, there is a

choice: either you make the case for them as people, bringing all the vividness, originality, difference and inconvenience that whole people bring. Or you classify them as servants, who aren't part of the crop, and who are just there to grow the crop. That's Singapore's way, and apart from what it does to their low-skilled native population, it is immoral. It's interesting how many slow-motion economic crashes could have been avoided if someone had made a moral call in the first place. But our way – our peculiar British coyness – is to pretend to welcome migrants as equals, while making no plans for them to behave as anything other than units of labour.

If migration has an effect beyond wages and housing – say there's pressure on doctors, or housing – that effect has to be dealt with. Any government that can't afford more school places, or more doctors' surgeries, has fatally undermined its own constant refrain that the movement of people increases prosperity, but has also undermined the only contract under which immigration is acceptable.

Not me – no way has an immigrant stolen my job

The most middle-class thing on earth (apart from hummus, and being able to read with the telly on) is that you never object to immigration. You will never hear a middle-class person complaining that an Australian or a French person has stolen their job, even though it must technically be true – with three-quarters of Antipodean labour highly skilled,[18] and London the sixth-largest French city (per head of population) – that some middle-class British person is without the job he or she wanted, even hypothetically. Come on, Natalie Bennett is from Australia; maybe I wanted to be leader of the Green party.

The middle classes are taken as the backbone of the nation, and that position of civic importance is so secure that we don't need to guard it jealously. Indeed, it is precisely with a generous, open-minded attitude that we demonstrate to everyone how secure is our membership of the backbone class. Yet, in the past two years, a few of those in the highly skilled/highly educated bracket have had an insight into what it's like to be taken down a rung of a citizenship they previously thought was a club and not a ladder.

In 2012 the rules around spousal visas were changed, so you had to be earning £18,600 to marry someone and then bestow citizenship upon them. This was calculated as the minimum you'd have to earn to be 'benefit-free'.

The right to a family life is enshrined by the Human Rights Act of 1998 (Article 8); spousal rights were conferred half a century before that. The right to citizenship by marriage was enacted in 1948. Suddenly, and with very little fanfare, a new criterion for full citizenship had been introduced

– you were a proper citizen only if you weren't in receipt of any benefits. This attaches conditionality to about one-fifth of all British citizens, and, as swiftly became clear, to many in higher income brackets as well. Couples returning from abroad, in which one was a British citizen and the other a non-EU national, usually had to leave a job to come back, so they couldn't prove they'd be earning anything at all. In that moment the injustice of what had just happened finally penetrated: how can it be possible to circumscribe the rights of British citizens on the basis of their wealth? Even if the whole nation voted for it (by no means had it, for it wasn't in anyone's manifesto), how could that be viable constitutionally?

Citizenship, like the right to vote, cannot be means-tested; otherwise it has no meaning, it's just one class fluffing up another. Spousal rights have been in more or less constant legal challenge ever since, and I'm sure the ruling will be overturned at some point.[19] It was stupid and was not properly consulted and has cost a lot of money in legal challenges, and it's a classic example of why the first thing you want – before you've even established its ideological credentials – is a government that is good at governing. And yet the ruling has served a purpose: a group of people whose citizenship nobody would normally dare to question – affluent, enterprising, educated people – suddenly know how it feels to be de-citizenised.

If that sounds like a diversion – well, it is a tiny

bit; but it leads back to the only important argument: no immigration policy is possible without a foundation of solidarity. Before anyone new becomes British, we must state clearly: everybody British is equally British. Nobody's citizenship weighs more than anybody else's.

Swarmed by billionaires

Recently I have started to notice extremely rich people (call them the super-rich) complaining about foreigners who are richer than them (call them the super-duper-rich). It's always in private or incognito. An anonymous Notting Hill resident, a banker's wife,[20] wrote in *The Times* recently, 'The Russians have completely distorted the nanny-market.' A mother I was interviewing (also anonymously), whose son didn't get into the private school she wanted, said: 'Walk into those examination rooms and it looks like fucking Beijing.' People I went to school with, sending their daughters to the same school, say (quite quietly, I've noticed), 'It's not the same any more. It's full of aspirational Chinese.' Another anonymous interviewee described his modest house in Holland Park: 'It was just a normal two-up, two-down, before the Saudi Arabians moved in and everything went crazy.'

Rich migrants get into the country in two ways: by the Entrepreneur visa and the Investor visa. The first has some requirements relating to the conduct of real business; for the second, you have to put

£2 million into government bonds (it tends to be bonds) or invest it in UK companies. You then earn interest on the bonds, and you sell them when you leave: in effect, we're paying these people to live here. They're like the handsome couple that restaurants put in the window-seats to prove that the food is good. Their neighbours complain vocally about the 'new shitocracy', as another Holland Park resident described it, living next door to a Lebanese arms-dealer. The autochthonous residents of Notting Hill are no better disposed towards immigrants than the people of Wisbech. I am pretty sure they like them less; I am pretty sure they are less-nice people; 'arms-dealer' might be a wild guess, but to have amassed huge wealth, in a corrupt or oppressive regime, one would generally have had to collude with its values.

In 2013 560 Investor visas were granted, with a total of 1,000 dependants. 'The idea that this is going to distort the housing market,' said Carlos Vargas-Silva from the Migration Observatory, 'people are dreaming, if they think that.' However, it's possible – because places at major public schools are quite sparse – that rich people are being ousted by foreigners from some institutions they think of as their birthright. It's even possible that they've been priced out of their stuccoed houses, even if that effect is localised to one or two postcodes and is not discernible across the whole housing market. What's fairly plain, though, is that the perception isn't matched by reality, any more than it is in East Devon.

They're not really talking about square yards or public-school places. Nobody really thinks we're being swarmed by a handful of billionaires. They're saying something vaguer, but more reasonable: 'Is it just me, or are we turning into one of those countries where everything is for sale? And how am I supposed to stay at the top, in this broiling cesspit?' While I have no desire to see the upper classes fixed in place, in perpetuity, knocking them off their perch with a handful of oligarchs is not going to do anything to build the society that I'm interested in.

When the top 0.1 per cent have started complaining about immigration from the top 0.01 per cent, something comes into focus: wealth cannot be the organising principle of social hierarchy. Nobody – not even the fractionally less wealthy – can cope with it. If you feel some particular belonging, based on place (the philosopher Julian Baggini calls it 'heft', after the way sheep understand their territory[21]), then you want that place to feel the same way about you. Everybody wants to feel that they bring more to their society than the money they represent, and nobody wants to feel that they're living in a place where roots don't matter – only cash. Questions spin out from that: what do roots mean anyway? How does one acknowledge or express an allegiance that is deeper than money, but that isn't based on race or class? Does that allegiance even exist? But first, if you conclude that place matters, does that mean you have to be insular? Or can you be both nationalist and internationalist?

Porter, a foreign student has stolen my university place

Foreign students don't displace British students. Indeed, until tuition fees arrived, they were openly used to cross-subsidise us, providing a massive income stream for British universities. Not only does this count as an export, but everything the immigrant buys while at university – even a sandwich – counts as export income. International students contributed £6.3 billion in living expenses and £3.9 billion in tuition fees to the UK economy in 2011–12.[22] The Department for Business, Innovation & Skills (BIS) estimated that 'education exports' were worth £17.5 billion the year before (set against a total export of services of £97.3 billion).[23]

EU and non-EU countries (mainly China, India, Nigeria and the US) combined send nearly half a million students a year.[24] It's a huge number. It fluctuates, but currently stands at around one-fifth of the student body. There is no serious political party that objects to this, and nobody ever says British students are being 'swamped', as politicians have started to describe the general population.[25] Indeed, all of the language around EU migration is of civilisation being overturned by savage nature – we're 'swamped' or 'swarmed', our green and cultivated land reverting to its infertile bog state,

214

because of foreign people who are implied by the metaphor to be brown, but are mainly white. Not students, though; students are also civilised (cough, 'rich'). Even UKIP, while it says that 'priority must be given to UK students', doesn't object in principle.

It's illogical, really – one-fifth of the student body is in London, so if you want to talk about pressure on housing, you cannot fixate on EU migrants and ignore students. But it's really hard to be consistent, if you won't state clearly what your value judgements are based on, and who is included in your vision of nationhood.

Anyway, at the moment education is just a market success story; we produce a good thing, then sell it internationally. We represent 13 per cent of the global market, which is really something, given our size. The popularity of the policy relies on the market working: if standards stay high, degrees are still worth it, and UK students can still afford them. I foresee a hitch in this plan when British students realise what that debt-overhang really means (see Education), or when someone manages to privatise the loan book. But even when it works, it still isn't internationalism.

Government reports about higher education are all about finding new markets to sell into: building partnerships with other governments to garner more of their students. If you were thinking seriously about education-driven migration, with the good of your own citizens in mind, you'd want to fix those opportunities for us. Only about 20,000 UK students go abroad for their degree – they probably think they can't afford it, even though it's much cheaper, especially if you study in Germany. They probably think there's a language barrier, even though many courses are taught in English. If I were in government in the UK, I would be building relationships with the nations that send students here – assurances of mutual support for our respective citizens. I would be trying to create the genuine cross-pollination of intellectual endeavour, the real whole-globe freedom this should represent, rather than seeing foreigners as cash-cows and British students as the expensive sprawl of a piece of failed policy (see Education). In other words, what looks like a completely different set of migrants, governed by completely different policies, is in fact characterised by the same precepts that govern EU migration: foreigners are bagged up and weighed for the money or labour they bring; British people are either the recipients of that money and labour or irrelevant troglodytes.

Has that refugee stolen our respiratory disease?

So how does it work, when you bring nothing with you? How does the government treat you then? We have certain principles. We signed up to them in 1951,[26] when refugee status was enshrined in international law; and then again in 1967, when it was extended to include people who were displaced by circumstances other than the Second World War.

Nobody had a gun to our heads. We signed up to them proudly – we were glad to be people who had lived through a war and whose humanity had remained inviolate.

We could secede from it, if we were no longer interested in being in this club; if we no longer cared what we were, and what the rest of the world thought of us. But while we're signed up, these are the rules: if people come to you in fear for their lives, and they are genuine, you take them in. The spirit, if not the letter, of the law commands: 'And try not to be a dick about it.' Refugees arrive here in very small numbers: the European average of asylum-seeker applications is 0.91 per thousand of the population;[27] in the UK, it is 0.47. In 2013 it was 23,000, or roughly equal to the number of temporary carrot-pickers.

The UK Border Agency tries to make things as hard as possible by simple incompetence, maintaining a backlog of over 30,000 – more than a year's worth of cases. While they're applying, people are trapped in limbo, unable to work, housed in wretched accommodation by companies making hundreds of millions of pounds[28] out of the government contracts, then failing at them, then declaring they were impossible to begin with.

If, as an asylum-seeker, you dare to complain while you await the verdict, you discover a surprising side to the nation of fair play and the rule of law: the corridors where those things don't exist. I did a series of interviews with an asylum-seeker called

Chawada Matiwala, who lived in a G4S-run hostel in Stockton-on-Tees. The rooms were fetid, mouldy and titchy. She was only just getting enough to eat. The funny thing was that she had a first-class degree in social sciences from Zimbabwe. We talked about what asylum-seeker provision ought to look like: how you should undertake a humanitarian duty in a humane spirit; and how, when you outsource it to the private sector, they fleece the Home Office and walk all over the refugee. She had examples from Zimbabwe, Nigeria, Greece, France and the UK; a very broad, yet detailed perspective on the system that was crushing her and giving her baby, Khloe, respiratory diseases.

Matiwala also gave evidence to a Parliamentary Inquiry,[29] and the week after that started getting static from the Border Agency: letters requiring an answer by a date that preceded the postmark; demands for documents they already had, to be sent by Recorded Delivery, which she couldn't afford (her benefits were being paid onto a pre-loaded Azure card; don't get me started on that). The week after the interview ran,[30] she was threatened with eviction, which was overcome by various protests, mainly the work of John Grayson, from the South Yorkshire Migration and Asylum Action Group. A couple of months later we won an award for the piece, and Chawada was going to come to London so that we could collect it together. But she'd disappeared, and I never spoke to her again.

In the 25 per cent likely event that an asylum

claim is accepted, things get worse before they get better.[31] Your meagre support (as a pending case) is withdrawn, but very often your biometric residence permit doesn't come through in time, so you are suddenly expected to get a job and open a bank account with no documents, then rent a private flat with no deposit and no guarantor. People wait so long for refugee status and rejoice so hard at it; then, when it arrives, it comes accompanied by so many more Kafka-esque hurdles that this is the point, ironically, when people start having nervous breakdowns.

If you aren't accepted, you'll be put in a detention centre pending deportation, a policy that was hugely expanded from 2001. It's run for profit by the usual companies: G4S, Serco, Clearel. 'Nothing in my 30 years' experience of being a children's doctor prepared me for Yarl's Wood,' Professor Sir Al Aynsley-Green[32] wrote in 2010, describing 'sexually harmful behaviour' against children in the centre, tiny children left in the sole care of suicidal mothers, awful suffering – not inflicted by brutal regimes, but by our own agents, grabbing kids on their way to school, locking them up for months, leaving them sitting in cells in their polyester ties and grey Asda trousers, worrying that they never said goodbye to their friends. He saw children clinging to parents in fear of any newcomer; traumatised regression; bed-wetting; selective mutism; nurses from Serco writing 'jolly' and 'happy' in the notes of children who hadn't eaten in five days, and who were in shock or maybe on hunger strike. Is there anyone on earth who thinks it saves money, makes 'sound economic sense', to treat people like this? It doesn't. Millions are poured into the business of locking up families who, almost everyone agrees, 'would find it very difficult to abscond' from any accommodation, locked or not.[33] Millions are poured into an exercise that is basically vindictive, punishing those who dare to ask for help, to the limits of the state's power. I knew all this, and I knew we all knew it. I wasn't even going to mention it, to be honest.

Then, on 28th October 2014, it was revealed that funding had been cut for the coastguard services. The Foreign Office minister Lady Anelay gave a written statement to the House of Lords: 'We do not support planned search and rescue operations in the Mediterranean.' She added that the government believed there was 'an unintended "pull factor", encouraging more migrants to attempt the dangerous sea crossing and thereby leading to more tragic and unnecessary deaths'.

More than 2,200 people died in the space of just four months in 2014 trying to get across this sea. They are fleeing soldiers in the ISIS caliphate who want to behead them, and President Assad's chemical weapons. They are trying to escape civil strife in Afghanistan, oppression in Eritrea, starvation in Somalia. The idea that anyone would undertake this journey because they'd heard good things about the British coastguard service, or would be put off escaping near-certain death because they read (in Hansard) that safety facilities had dropped off – this is repugnant; but, before that, totally stupid. This move will not stop the flight of refugees. It will just ensure that more of them die. It makes sense, though, doesn't it? They have nothing; they are worth nothing; let them drown.

The mistake all along has been to accept the battlefield of immigration as a fight between the Treasury (reason) and the Home Office (emotion – specifically, patriotism); a clash between economic reality and nostalgia; between metropolitans and foreigners on one side, and hicks and racists on the other. The Treasury always wins, then throws a bone to the Home Office by letting it be as cruel as it likes to the people that a Treasury would never be interested in.

These oppositions are all fiction. The real issue beneath every question is: do people have an intrinsic value, or is everyone's value quantifiable by what they give and what they get? Even more fundamentally: is this policy driven by people? Or is it driven by profit?

Borders are a good thing. A world without borders – a world of free entry and exit – is a world without democratic government. You might find the National Security Agency and Google getting together to stitch together some governance, but representative government? Where all decisions are made by our proxies, where the institutions belong to us and exist to serve us? This stuff is bordered. I am not dismissing the possibility that, some time in the future, we will discover a way to be represented at a global level. But, right now, the real energy for a borderless world comes from the airports and banks. Partly they think it sounds modern, and mainly they think it will hold down wages and dilute the ability of states to enforce regulation. And they're right. Borders are not there to limit your horizons, but to give form, meaning and expression to your democratic identity.

To be able to breathe

Since you have that democratic identity, use it to create the society you want. What is Britain, to you? Fair play, the rule of law, freedom of speech, blah-blah – I never heard a set of principles that might just as well be claimed for any other nation. But every place that I look at burns with Britishness – from a chocolate-box Hampshire high street with a bronze of some warrior guy at the end, to the disaster shopping strip in the post-industrial North, two separate Greggs and a closed-down Jamie's Kitchen, charity shops and bookies and payday-loan companies. All of the places tell a subtly different part of the same story; all full of people I understand, who understand me. Brick Lane is as British as Buckingham Palace. The nationalism is not ethnic, but it is civic. We care about one another as more than strangers. If a community has been left behind by the dogma of GDP, then society has to go back for it. There is no vision for the future of Britain that does not include the East Riding, or East Devon, or Wisbech, or Ramsgate.

There are two stories of patriotism. One is indistinguishable from nostalgia, village greens and cricket and tea; Henry VIII, Cromwell, Churchill; triumph through obedience, understanding the world by knowing your place. That will never accommodate migration because it yearns for the past. Immigrants will always be the future. There will never be 600,000 Polish people in *Downton Abbey*, or any Filipino care-workers in a poem by John Betjeman.

The other patriotism is really compatriotism, solidarity based on place – shared institutions, shared understandings, shared decisions, shared looks over the tops of free newspapers, shared weaknesses, shared strengths, shared jokes: whatever it costs, share it. Crucially, a shared future.

These two senses of nation often coexist, except on immigration. Because compatriotism can accommodate newcomers. Not for the money they bring, and not at any price; rather, because the whole point is to create a society – a living, vital organism – whose borders need to be porous, or it won't be able to breathe.

The answers to immigration don't lie at a country's borders, but at its heart: are workers being undercut by people from poorer countries and, if so, what kind of a state allows that? Is there enough housing? Are there enough services? If not, why not? How can a state become so unambitious that the conditions its people live in are no longer its concern? Are asylum-seekers being used as an emblem of Home Office toughness, pointlessly victimised for show? This is our society; we don't just want it to be not-evil. We're not Google. We want to build something we're proud of.

But never think that people who reject immigration are saying an unimportant or uninformed thing. They're saying the most important thing a citizen of anywhere can say: I belong here. Why are you making me feel so precarious?

Who broke the bank?

Austerity: when the billionaires in business tell the millionaires in politics that the rest of us are too greedy.

On a stranger's T-shirt; I didn't get his name

What is this austerity? What are the principles that say it should work? Austerity evokes the homely simplicity of a Victoria sponge, the spare elegance of Danish furniture. Your government spent too much; now they have to spend less. Then, when they have got our house in order, we can loosen our belts a little, so long as we continue to live within our means. But how does it work in practice?

It doesn't. Nations aren't households. If you want to liken government debt to a household's spending, you have to imagine this family, as described by the economist Warren Mosler, explaining fiat money:

The concept of fiat money can be illuminated by a simple model: assume a world of a parent and several children. One day the parent announces that the children may earn business cards by completing various household chores. At this point the children won't care a bit about accumulating their parent's business cards because the cards are virtually worthless. But when the parent also announces that any child who wants to eat and live in the house must pay the parent, say, 200 business cards each month, the cards are instantly given value and chores begin to get done. Value has been given to the business cards by requiring them to be used to fulfil a tax obligation. Taxes function to create the demand for state expenditures of fiat money, not to raise revenue per se.[1]

If the parent reduces the number of business cards they'll pay for chores, then the weakest children of the household would eventually have to be evicted. That's what austerity would look like, in a household. Never mind that you are supposed to love your kid; it's an act of vandalism upon your own economy. Keynes called it 'the paradox of thrift': the more you save, the poorer you get.

To transpose this to a government: whatever we spend, the Treasury ultimately gets back; if I buy something off you, they will get it back in sales tax or in your income tax, or in your Capital Gains tax (if it's something big, like a house); or perhaps you will spend it by paying someone else, and it will come back in their income tax. The only money that doesn't come back to the Treasury is money that's saved, or money that's spent on foreign-made things, which will obviously go to that country's Treasury instead. The worst-case scenario, from a Treasury perspective, is money that is saved in a tax haven; the money itself disappears from the pool of wealth and isn't even taxed before it goes.

So if you want austerity to work, it needs to be inflicted upon people who, otherwise, would save that money or tax-haven it; or, at the very least, spend it on imports. All of us spend money on foreign goods, so that would work on anyone with money to spend. Only the upper-middle classes save much, and only the upper-up make any real use of aggressive tax avoidance.

If it were me, I would look at closing the relief on higher-rate taxpayers' pension contributions. Rich people will save that money anyway. Nobody wants to live in penury in old age, least of all people who have a choice. That would save £25 billion a year, equal to all the (optimistically forecast) savings of the Welfare Reform Act over an entire parliament (five years). There are pretty solid reasons to believe, however, that any act of austerity is likely to prolong or cause recessions, and the best thing to do about a spike in debt is simply to create the conditions in which people feel confident enough to save less. This is why fiscal contractions – periods of significant reduction in government spending – are so incredibly rare in peacetime developed economies.[2] There have only been a handful of episodes of successful fiscal consolidation, across the OECD, in the past 40 years. One was Greece at the end of the 1990s; those numbers turned out to be bullshit, to get into the eurozone. Two were in Sweden, one in Denmark, one in Canada; all of those were based on export markets to booming neighbours.

But imagine you're in a hurry, for political reasons. There are other ways to claw back benefits from the top tier – you could suspend Gift Aid. That's another £1 billion.[3] People squeal about it because it's lost from charities, but you're meant to be in a period of austerity, right? So you say, 'Our priority is to be able to afford our duties, nationally and internationally, as laid out in our manifesto. The altruistic intentions of our individual citizens must come second to that duty.' You could just suspend the charitable status of public schools, and it would be something.

The richer people are, the easier it is to impose austerity upon them without incurring the thrift paradox. To return to the household analogy, the rich person is a kid who has built up a surplus of business cards; so you can reduce what you pay him without destroying your family.

Some habits of the Austerions

Austerity in practice, however, has concentrated not on the rich, but on the extremely poor. So we've lost the Independent Living Fund, which goes to disabled people (saving: £320 million). Benefit sanctions are not explicitly designed to save money, but they've probably saved a bit. We've had the 'bedroom tax', which wrings very small amounts of money out of poor households (projected saving: £460 million; the real saving is likely to be two-thirds of that). Local Housing Allowance has been cut (intended saving: £750 million).[4] Pension contracts have been reneged upon for firefighters, and nurses have been sacked. There has been a public-sector pay freeze so severe that midwives went on strike for the first time in 133 years.

The first thing you notice is the trifling amounts of money: none of this will make any significant difference to expenditure. The public-sector pay freeze overwhelmingly affects the spending power of those in the middle and below. The number of Housing Benefit claimants has gone slightly down, because the eligibility criteria have changed, but the amount spent has gone up, because rents have increased. Making life harder for tenants doesn't actually fix a broken housing market. Who knew?[5] The closure of the Independent Living Fund is particularly self-defeating because most people used it to employ a carer to take them to work. So now you have a disabled person who can't work, a carer with no job, no tax receipts from either of them, a huge loss of human dignity and self-esteem, high-achieving people facing a new life of sitting on an incontinence pad all day, waiting for their 15-minute care-visit – to save an amount that might, in another department (see Housing) be lost down the back of the sofa.

The second thing you notice is that the people being hit are exactly the people who probably do not save, who probably do not spend a huge amount on foreign stuff, who almost certainly weren't using tax havens – whose money, when they had it, went straight back into the active UK economy. The best thing about poor people, economically speaking, is that they spend what they've got. So when you remove what might sound like trivial amounts – 775,000 people lost an average of £9 a week from the changes to Local Housing Allowance – that is money that doesn't get spent on a cup of tea or a bus fare. It is money that the Treasury has only saved in theory, because it has lost it in the process. There are more obvious ways in which trying to save ends up costing more: removing people's benefits, for instance, costs a lot in crime and malnutrition.[6]

That is what's so frustrating about the austerity narrative: not the pompous, sleeves-rolled-up, 'it takes a proper toff to clear up a mess like this' posturing, although I must admit that turns my stomach. It's the fact that, directed at the poorest in society, austerity simply will not work. And they know it won't work. So it's time to consider the possibility that this government, along with governments across Europe – the 'Austerions' as they're known – aren't being honest about their intentions. They're not trying to shrink the debt. They're trying to shrink the state.[7]

**All together now: we're just cleaning up the
mess left by the last lot**

It is an undisputed fact that a mess has been left.
Government debt is very high relative to GDP. I don't
really agree that the people who should pay the
price for austerity are the people who caused the
debt. It's a bit vindictive for my tastes. You can't run
an economy as a form of punishment. If you want
to hold people to account, then do so through the
proper channels – put them in prison, if you like –
and not with the levers of tax and spending. And yet
. . . we still want to know whose fault it is, right?
We're only human.

So, this government refers to the last lot's mess,
and they frequently refer to benefits dependency,
the something-for-nothing culture and generations
of worklessness. The inference is that there's something rotten that made the system malfunction,
some laziness emanating from its core. The smart
MPs never directly relate these two statements – the
mess on the one hand, and the feckless poor on the
other. This is because they are unrelated. If you were
to state openly, 'The last government broke the
economy by giving too much money to poor people',
rebuttal would be swift: actually, net general
government debt was pretty manageable between
1997 and 2008. At its highest it was just over 30 per
cent of GDP, and at its lowest in the low twenties.
For four years in the early Noughties the government
was running a surplus. This is all perfectly prudent.
There is nothing wrong with running modest deficits

in government: you'd have a problem if you were borrowing to cover your pensions bill, but borrowing to fund investment – in state-owned housing, say, or higher education – is what productive capitalism is all about.

Debt went over 40 per cent of GDP in 2008 because of the financial crash. It climbed to nearly 80 per cent in 2014, for the same reason. It is expected to top 80 per cent of GDP in 2017 because of the initial £977 billion committed in loans and guarantees,[8] to keep the cash machines running, and the £375 billion[9] given directly to banks as quantitative easing (QE), trying to stabilise the economy and the resulting recession. The financial sector lost this money making bets they weren't good for, and we are now paying for it. You can have sensible arguments about whether or not the bail-outs were a good idea. I question the certainty that bank failure would have led to a much worse recession than the one we're living through – I think maybe it would have just been worse for different people. There's been some modelling done on the counterfactual: what if no bail-outs had occurred?[10] It concludes that the depression would have been far deeper. But there are what-ifs that the model doesn't accommodate: what if that depression had made us look more seriously at the banking system, and had thereby prevented the next crash? What if the depression had been more profound, but the losses were distributed differently? I don't want to take a cheap shot, but this modelling is done by the same people – in this case, the same company, Moody's – who claimed to understand the possible risks that brought down the system in the first place, and who gold-plated investments that were actually rotten: we've got to stop taking it as read that the people with the giant computers have all the answers. They have very solid answers to the questions they pose, but they are only intermittently asking the right questions.

There was even some talk back in 2008 about bailing out the banks being a good thing – as the major shareholders, didn't we now own these institutions? This ownership has never been tested, nor any benefit reaped. By the beginning of 2014 RBS had lost all of its £46 billion bail-out in six years of loss-making.[11]

In short: there is room for debate as to whether the bail-outs had to happen, and there was some legitimate optimism that they might turn out to have been a positive move. But the cause of the debt crisis was the financial crash. This is settled fact.

However, the relentlessness of the messaging – the mess left by the last government, and the benefit culture – has created something that is more of an atmosphere than an actual idea. The last lot gave away too much money to poor people. And that's why we have no money.

Why did no one mend the roof while the sun shone? asked David Cameron in the Commons in 2008. The sun, in this analogy, was economic growth, but since so much of it was driven by a financial sector that had gone insane, I don't know if you could see it so much as sun shining as a malevolent heat-source mistaken for the sun, which was actually setting fire to the roof.

There's a kernel of truth in it: if you can govern for 13 years and end up with no clue about what's going on, in a massive sector for which you are ultimately responsible, then of course that's a failure. The fact that it was global can't turn it into your success. In order to meaningfully blame the Labour government for it, its successors would have to show that they understood how that responsibility chain worked, and – way more important – show that they were doing things differently.

Banks went bust because they were overexposed to one another's debts, and the debts were all junk. The debts were junk because things that were likely to be repaid had been parcelled up with mortgages that were never going to be repaid. By the time it became clear that the junk *was* junk, there was no way of separating it from the elements that were not junk. The parcelling – collateralised debt obligation (CDO) – came accompanied by documentation that, had anybody bothered to print it out, would have run to one million pages. There was no oversight. Why did the credit-ratings agencies give the CDOs a triple-A rating when they didn't know what was in them? Because bankers told them they were solid. Why did the banks themselves not worry about the fact that they didn't know what was in these investments? Because, even before all the bail-outs,

234

there was a discernible sense of impunity. The economist Prem Sikka reminds us that in 1997 the Department of Trade and Industry investigation into insider dealing found, among senior executives generally: 'a cynical disregard of laws and regulations . . . cavalier misuse of company monies . . . contempt for truth and common honesty. All these in a part of the City [of London] which was thought respectable.' However, 'blaming economic crises on "greed" is like blaming plane crashes on gravity', the free-market enthusiast Thomas Sowell said. Greed always exists. It takes a particular social environment for it to become the dominating trait.

There was a new normal, which New Labour presided over: non-existent oversight, regulators relying too heavily on the banks themselves, and a political class that blushed pink with delight whenever the financial sector invited it to a party. Taking excessive risks is fine; but you have to be using your own money. Talk to bankers now and it is amazing how many of them think the answer is a return to the nineteenth-century model of limitless personal responsibility: serious gamblers need to have something to lose as well as something to gain. If someone hands you a million-page analysis, and you could lose your house and have to pull your children out of private school if it went wrong, you'd say: 'Go and put this into four pages.'

Moral hazard is the danger that, when the consequences are meaningless and all the money is someone else's, people make imprudent decisions.

But that phrase is the only time you hear the word 'moral' applied to markets. If there's one thing modern life has demonstrated pretty conclusively, it's that markets are social spaces: a collection of people, like any other. Today's understanding is that society is moral and the market is amoral. So the market works to make us all rich, and society uses our innate kindness to tame it, and that way we end up in equilibrium. This is wrong. In the end, when you strip out the drama and the animal spirits and the stampedes, and the sheer excitement of it, markets are just people selling things to other people. The seller has to be able to say what the thing is, and to justify the price of it. Otherwise why bother with a thing at all – why not just punch the buyer in the head and steal his money? The buyer has to have all the available information about the thing; otherwise, again, it's not a purchase, it's a sting operation. If the buyer can't afford the thing and still wants to buy it, that must be the seller's concern. The seller either takes the money with the risk of default or doesn't take the money. The idea that you can suspend decency in such a space, and everything will still work, is a bit like taking an Uzi to a cocktail party. It might be okay if only one person did it. If five people did it, that would not be okay.

Even if bankers believed the CDOs they were selling were legitimate; even if they thought the dodgy element of each financial instrument was totally insulated by the low-risk stuff; even if, knowing the paperwork was impenetrable, they were all utterly confident that someone somewhere understood it – even if you make all these assumptions of stand-upness (and I think those assumptions are fantasy), you are still left with the subprime mortgages themselves, those dishonest contracts that destroyed confidence and, with it, the global economy.

Nothing holds water

For a subprime mortgage, you took a client on a low income and sold them a property which they could just about afford when the interest rate was low and the repayment rate was heavily discounted. A couple of years in, the repayments would go up. People often say the lenders banked on ever-increasing house prices, but that doesn't hold water; the way these deals were cut, sooner or later the borrowers would have been priced out of their repayments, whatever the value of the house. So one has to assume that the lenders knew these loans would fail: they were just banking on the value of the house having gone up by the time it was repossessed.

A debt that you know can't be repaid; a house that you expect to repossess – these are not real things. You're not selling what you claim to be selling, which is what the whole business is supposed to be all about.

Meanwhile, in the UK, mortgage lenders were also extremely nonchalant about the extension of credit to people on very low wages. The self-cert, the 125 per cent, the interest-only, the 32-year term: these mortgages would (and will) only work in the event that the housing bubble stays aloft for decades. It's a pretty unlikely proposition, but not as manifestly daft as the extension of unsecured credit lines. Nutty credit cards with £9,000 limits were sent, unsolicited, to students doing degrees in tourism. This pattern was repeated across the developed world, so that household debt dwarfed government debt by 2007: it reached more than 160 per cent of GDP in Italy, the UK and the US. Sweden, where incomes were higher, followed the same pattern, but not to the same extent (household debt reached just over 140 per cent of GDP, compared to a government debt that was half that).[12] None of this caused the crisis, which was all a repercussion of the CDO debacle. But that doesn't mean it won't cause its own crisis down the line, and the root cause will be the same: banks making irresponsible loans to people who take them because they're not earning enough to keep afloat any other way.

Two consenting adults

People say to me, 'It was the banks.' I say, 'Hang on, the banks had to lend to someone.' People feel in a sense that someone else is responsible for the decisions they made. Of course, if banks don't offer credit, people can't take it. [But] there were two consenting adults in all these transactions, a borrower and a lender . . . Some people are unwilling to accept responsibility for the consequences of their own choices.

Philip Hammond, then Defence Secretary,
May 2012

It has that surly brass neck of the driver who knocked you over trying to sue you for denting their car. You have the borrower, terminally short of money, taking an unrealistic risk on a loan because they're offered it. And you have the lender or trader, offering loans that are unrealistically risky, or financial instruments that aren't going to work, or buying and selling things for more than they're worth, because they can. Are they morally equivalent? Not really; desperation is a mitigating circumstance. And I think we can broadly agree that having financial expertise – even if you persistently ignore it – makes you the more culpable in a giant financial cock-up. Are the consequences proportional for both? No, here it's all wildly out. The low- and medium-paid are going to be suffering the consequences of this shrunk state for years, while the top 1 per cent has already, if it's honest, forgotten the whole thing.[13] So even if you peel the crisis right back to its bare components – a borrower and a lender, two consenting adults – the consequences were worst for the group that was the least guilty. That looks like injustice, and it is.

But both groups (indeed, let's face it, all of us) just adhered to the norms we saw around us. Much of what you'll read about this era, directly before the crash, describes us as classic boom-people: heady, heedless, high-rolling, inattentive. This is why people talk about the ocean, rather than the fish: do you blame the participants or the environment?

The ocean that created the behaviour was inequality intertwined with financialisation. At the bottom, and this is almost too obvious to say: in order to take on unmanageable debt, you need more than the shyster who's prepared to lend to you; you also need to need the money. We talk a lot about why debt is normal now, and for whom. It's normal for students because of student fees. Separate from the extension of government-sponsored debt, banks extend huge credit lines to students because they know student loans don't meet real student costs, and they know the student will then be tied to them for life (or until they become rich). Debt is normal for the low-waged, because of their low wages. It's normal for the median-waged, because their wages aren't great, either, and housing is too expensive. It's normal because it has been reframed as 'credit', and all the sting has gone out of the word – indeed, it sounds like something positive.

Clearly, though, if your wages are quite sufficient, you won't indebt yourself just to keep up with the Joneses. You won't buy things just to fill the unbidden limit on your credit card. You're not an idiot. People are still mainly borrowing in order to live somewhere, which was never on my list of sheep-like consumption. The Citizens Advice Bureau reported that the crisis areas were council-tax arrears and water debts, which are the clearest signs of debt caused by poverty. More than altering the behaviour of the people living on them, low wages create weak demand and a low rate of savings.

Why does inequality also cause rash behaviour at the top? Why does excessive wealth lead to market volatility? Huge corporate surpluses and massive personal riches do not seem to get ploughed back into the productive economy. Instead, as Stewart Lansley put it, 'a tsunami of hot money raced around the world at speed in search of faster and faster returns, creating the bubbles – in property, commodities and business – that eventually brought the British and global economies to their knees'.[14]

It's a little bit worse than it looks

I never took even a fleeting interest in this until I heard a 'financial innovator' give a talk. Until then I had actively avoided wondering out loud about bankers, whose behaviour always seemed to be a combination of the amoral and the incomprehensible. Who wants to be that angry person, who doesn't know quite as much as the insiders? God, not me. I would rather avert my eyes and work towards some functioning economy that is separate from the world of high finance, in much the same way as I buy clothes in Zara and don't engage with haute couture. However, finance and fashion have a number of crucial differences, not least that we don't all have to pay for the errors of fashion, nor do we find our ability to be clothed fatally compromised by its flights of fancy.

The financial innovator was Bruce Davis – he invented Zopa, the peer-to-peer lending company; and, later, Abundance, for crowd-sourced renewables. You'll meet him again in Environment. He said, not off-handedly, but as if it were so obvious that he didn't dwell on it: there's a practical problem with overpaying your financial sector. If individual bankers are earning two million quid a year, fledgling businesses no longer warrant their attention. How long does it take to get to the New Forest and look at a wind-farm? For almost any activity that needs wellies you'd write off the whole day, or £8,000. But that's the real economy – the factory in Newcastle that makes a component, the solar project in Nottinghamshire, the microbrewery in Kent. Selling real things to real people, producing energy, inventing beer: these are the processes that keep regions alive, that break up big electricity oligopolies, that inject life into the market, that create jobs. That's productive capitalism – you have capital, someone else has an idea, you buy the idea, they get the money. If it all goes well, life is improved; and if it doesn't, you lose your capital. But it was only money.

Finance is no longer interested in this activity: investment banks only want to inflate asset bubbles; retail banks are only interested in a particular asset bubble, the housing market – 85 per cent of high-street bank lending is to the existing residential market, not even to new development. This is a pattern across the developed world. 'Once there is an excessive amount of debt in the system created by the private side, we don't know how to get rid of it,' said Lord Adair Turner, former chairman of the Financial Services Authority, sounding disconcertingly nonplussed. 'We simply know how to shift it around the economy. So we can shift it from private to public, we can shift it from country to country, but we don't know how to get rid of it.' Hmm . . . bummer.

The casino side is comparatively straightforward – they're not interested in the productive economy because they have too much money. This leaves us with two problems: who will invest in real things when the investment sector won't; and what they're investing in instead. Davis, answering the first question, is out to persuade ordinary people to have a radical rethink, cut out the banks altogether and start lending directly to projects they believe in. Innovators, think-preneurs, people who wear cycling tops even when they've not been cycling: they're not all designing packaging. Some of them are doing something useful.

However, while the rest of us wait for them to build us a new model so great that it makes the old one obsolete, the second question is still hanging: what is investment invested in?

As they say about humans and chimps: our aims don't need to be at odds for us to ruin their lives;

our aims merely need to be different. Then all their needs come in second to ours, because we control the environment. Finance isn't actively hostile to the productive economy; it just screws it up, for reasons no more sinister than that it isn't interested.

For instance: what happens when someone buys an option? It's the right to buy (a 'call' option) or sell (a 'put' option) something at a particular price, at a fixed point in the future. The money you pay, which varies according to the volatility of the market and the term of the option (but let's call it 10 per cent), is the premium; the win is potentially very large (if you make an acute prediction about a volatile market – the price of oil, say), while your premium is fixed. So the obvious next question is: if you can win big, but only lose small, who stands to lose big? What does this do to the real economy? 'Oh,' people always say, as if you've asked something mildly interesting, but very abstruse and unimportant, like how to say 'rhododendron' in Latin, 'I don't know what it does to the real economy.'

This is the line on futures and options – derivatives generally, which is to say, a financial contract whose value derives from underlying market prices. They're not supposed to make any difference to real life: they are to life what betting is to horse-racing. They don't alter the outcome, they just make it more interesting to watch. The physical spot price of the commodity is the horse-race itself; the futures and options are just bets.

However, in real real life there is no central body,

no worldwide Wizard of Oz, determining what the spot price of wheat should be.[15] The only market making a visible, coordinated adjudication of the wheat price is the futures market, so that becomes the benchmark against which the real price is determined. If you want to put it in horse-racing terms, you have to imagine that none of the horses have riders and don't even know which way to run until the bookies tell them, which they do in a random, senseless order.

Everybody knows the large concentrations of capital aren't interested in the real economy; indeed, there isn't enough productive activity in the world for this to be invested in. The money is created by banks in order to speculate on bets created by other banks. This shadow economy is worth ten times ($750 trillion) world GDP ($75 trillion).[16] The UK's position is terrible. We have a £1.5 trillion GDP, household wealth (at the end of 2012) around £7.3 trillion and three major banks alone[17] with derivatives portfolios whose face-values are nearly £100 trillion. Seriously! Good luck bailing those out. Here, the complication lifts to leave a very simple picture: their bets are worth more than any of us have.

The rise of gangster capitalism
If derivatives traders don't care what happens to the underlying commodities, at least they're not engaged in active sabotage. In late 2014 we had a front-row view of a classic private-equity deal,

resulting in the demise of Phones 4U, taking with it 5,600 jobs. BC Partners bought Phones 4U in 2011 (the company had already been stripped for parts by a previous private-equity deal in 2006). They 'then' borrowed £205 million from City lenders, then paid themselves a 'special dividend' of £223 million. This gave them a profit of £18 million and left Phones 4U with debt on its balance sheet equivalent to four times its earnings. The idea behind a deal like this is that the private-equity company will improve the prospects of the company so much with their superior efficiency (by driving down wages) that its stock will go up. So if it works, it's because wages have been driven down. And if it doesn't work, the company goes bust, the employees lose their jobs, the bondholders lose their money and the private-equity firm still walks away with its profit. Ask yourself whether you can afford this kind of capitalism: can your high street afford it? Can your compatriots afford it? Can any of us afford it?

This is why a vast deal like the purchase of Heinz in June 2013 by 3G Capital and Berkshire Hathaway for $23.2 billion always results in factory closures and job losses a few months in. To the uninitiated, we see a huge sum of money on a price tag; think, 'That's great – the company must be thriving, to be worth so much; let's wish its new owners well, with their successful purchase.' In reality that massive cost was just flipped onto the business itself, whereupon the new owners immediately started talking about the urgent redundancies it would take to 'pay down the debt'. The phrase chokes me with anger. It doesn't mean 'pay back'. It means 'keep the debt just about manageable with an instalment plan'. They get a tax break on the debt repayments, so they're never intending to clear it. The debt is merely to be held static, used as a reason why employees have to stay on the minimum wage, forgo their career progression and their workplace benefits or get fired. The people who cut the deal walk away with $20 million – or £18 million, as in the case of BC Partners and Phones 4U.

The truth of it is that there's not a lot of fat on a mobile-phone sales company – or, for that matter, a string of old people's homes (see the private-equity takeovers in Poverty). They haven't, historically, got rock-solid employee protection and established pathways to promotion, with higher salaries attached. So often, when you scratch around to 'pay down' this new £200 million debt, you can't, and then you go bust.

That is the 'caring' side of modern investments – private-equity companies pride themselves on being responsible investors, people with the truest interest in the companies they buy. It could take one of these deals five or even ten years before it had achieved its objectives. However, what you see at the end of a leveraged buyout is not a company in a long-term loving relationship with its private-equity step-parent, but a bankruptcy or a Manchester United – suffocating under debts incurred by its buyout family, the Glazers, its own board replaced by members of that family, its business model turned into perpetual pay-down; its land sold, the profits to the family, that land leased back, the costs to the club.

Private-equity investors nevertheless look really solid compared to shareholders, whose current average investment is held for only three or four months.[18] The wages/profits conflict has been going on since the beginning of industry. Anybody sensible who does the work believes that the split of productivity should reflect effort and therefore go mainly to them; anybody capitalist who supplies the capital tends to think that's the important bit, and the split should go mainly to them. However, these people traditionally had something in common, which was the company itself. Everyone had skin in the game: the workers their livelihoods, the stockholders their money and reputations. That is what's been lost, in three-month profit cycles, shares held for less than half a year, CEOs rewarded only for shareholder maximisation, investors and managers in cahoots to screw the cost of doing the business as low as it can possibly go. Previously this struggle was held in balance by shared interest; workers and shareholders were neighbours along the same river, sharing a coast. Now they are in open opposition. Never mind that one side is getting steadily weaker, as its share of productivity gets less, and all the language starts to ossify around businesses as 'job creators', while employees are completely written off as creators of value. Nobody is taking care of business in this model. They are too busy fighting. It's like watching parents trying to raise a family when what they should be doing is getting a divorce.

How radical do you want to be?

Before even the welfare state, the first casualty of this crisis was sophistication; the ability to distinguish between 'more equality' and 'total equality', between 'better regulation' and 'total state control of everything'. Politics has become polarised; fights have got mean and dirty. Arguments have a weird absolutism: if you criticise any aspect of the system – even the bits that were clearly never intended – then you are arguing against capitalism. Ergo, you're arguing against freedom. Why don't you bugger off and go and live in North Korea?

The Green Party's economist, now also an MEP, Molly Scott Cato, told me about the international law of 'odious debt'. It was March 2013, and Cyprus had just been unmasked as a 'gimp state for Russian gangsta finance', in the surprising phrase of a columnist on the *Financial Times*.[19] It looked for a short time as though we were in for something quite violent or seismic, or maybe both. Then, in classic eurozone fashion, they kicked the grenade down the road. It'll probably explode next week instead.

A debt is 'odious' when it is incurred by a regime that is not acting in the national interest. It sounds a ridiculous thing to bring up, like the seventeenth-century law that you're allowed to shoot a Welsh person so long as he's standing in Wales and you're standing in England. But this is the legal instrument that America used when it invaded Iraq, as a justification for taking over the oil rights and not honouring the debts left by Saddam Hussein. In Spain, Portugal and Ireland groups are making the case that state debt incurred by policies that nobody voted for, to save banks whose activities had never been made plain, should be written off. Not (only) for moral reasons, but in accordance with international law. 'That's the radical answer,' Scott Cato says, 'to challenge where the debt comes from. Have a Citizen's Audit.' (How do you like the sound of that, radicals? 'What do we want?' 'A Citizen's Audit!' 'When do we want it?' 'To cover the tax period 31st March 2003 to 5th April 2007.') I put that idea, the same week, to the superstar economist – the George Clooney of progressive economists – Ha-Joon Chang. He was exceedingly cautious. 'Debt cancellation is sometimes necessary when the economy is tangled up and getting suffocated. The issue is which debts to cancel and under what terms. When people hear those words in black-and-white terms, they think: oh my God, those people are communists . . . I'm not in favour of revolution; I'm in favour of gradual changes. But that doesn't mean that my goal isn't radical. I want this system to be completely rewired, but to get there, you may have to deploy rhetoric that may not look strong enough to you, but will appeal more to more people.'

I am astonished by how radical the banks will be,

in defence of their own interests – in 2008 they tore up, for ever and overnight, the principles of free markets, of the 'self-healing market'. They took whatever public funds they could lay their hands on, to avoid any hit to their wealth. Meanwhile, outside these institutions we are scared even to question the validity of this debt, in case people think we're communists. It's totally reasonable. I'm not a communist. I would hate to live on a giant farm and wear collarless grey clothes. But we have to find a way to meet their radicalism with some far-reaching demands of our own. In order to look upon this as a success, we have to show that it won't happen again. The argument that bail-outs provide stability cannot be used twice. If there is a next time, I like to think that we will find a spine from somewhere and refuse to pay again; but, even if we don't, the chances are that we won't be able to afford it.

What would sorting out this mess properly be like?

The separation of high-street and casino banking has been touted for six years. If regular retail banking weren't related to speculative banking, HSBC could do what it liked with its derivatives portfolios. 'Too big to fail' would be a thing of the past. This was the whole point of separating the retail and casino elements in the first place, a move taken – not at all coincidentally – right after the 1929 crash.

However, the problem is both deeper and simpler than the retail/casino split allows.

Prem Sikka remarks, in his paper 'Banking in the Public Interest', that banking must have a social purpose. It cannot be a force for delinquency, in which we are left following the tracks of its mischief, discovering scams five or ten years after they started (the mis-sold PPI insurance, the Libor-fixing). It cannot exist outside the boundaries of honesty and fair play. I keep picking at the scab of this remark from a New York trader, Ezra Rapaport, about high-frequency trading: 'We're not seeking to improve the state of technology – we push the envelope to seek profit. The way I redeem it is seeing the benefit it has for my child and my wife.'[20] This is our world. This is our real economy, mopping up the mini-crashes, maxi-crashes and depressions created by people who think 'redemption' is something you can do for yourself, by grabbing everything you can. These are the people we currently have in charge. We will be suffering the consequences of this sociopathy for as long as it takes to stand up to it.

Sikka has other suggestions: one of the radical ideas is to restrict access for speculators to public courts. The complexity of these deals means that any litigation arising is monumentally expensive to the taxpayer. Perhaps even more important than cost is this – if they didn't have access to justice, beyond a given level of risk, they might have to behave in a more trustworthy fashion, or else merely desist.

Often people in finance are portrayed as only screwing 'real' people, or the 'real' economy, while respecting one another, the way regular criminals do. They have nothing like the loyalty, or even the coordination, of street crooks. Their policy is actually the 'greater fool' – that anything's a win so long as you can find a greater fool to punt it to. It seems rather philanthropic to go on providing justice to people who won't acknowledge it in their business dealings.

Then there's the Robin Hood tax or, to give it its full name, a tax on financial transactions. It builds in a huge disincentive to dodginess, and creates a massive international tax base that we can use to police the dodginess and maybe buy ourselves something pretty, like a hospital.

The link between regulators and industry insiders has to be broken. While we're here, tax codes cannot be written by accountancy firms who then give advice on how to avoid tax (see Tax). Political parties cannot take donations from firms to whom they then give NHS contracts (see Health). There should be no 'revolving door', where the civil servant who heads a public service then goes on to be consultant for G4S, as they bid for that contract (see Privatisation). Imagine going into a fledgling democracy, to help some people who've only just sloughed off a dictator. 'Not like that,' you'd say. 'That's bent.' I wonder how much casual corruption we simply accept because we don't think we live in the kind of society that would ever be corrupt.

Employees, borrowers and lenders should all have a say in how much senior executives get paid. The tax affairs of a bank should be transparent; if it has offshore holdings, it has to explain why. Banks cannot be audited by a company they pay. It's not a commissioned service, like having the loos cleaned. It's meant to have a regulatory function. It's meant to say things they might not like.

The least sexy of all is this final suggestion: 'The House of Commons Treasury Committee should hold an annual hearing into banking regulation to ensure that regulators are diligently and effectively performing their tasks.' How incredibly weird is that? We don't already ask how the regulators are getting along, whether they're diligent, whether they're effective.

Barclays was fined £38 million on 23rd September 2014.[21] A month after I started this paragraph it put aside £500 million[22] to pay for the investigation and, apparently, inevitable fines over Forex-rigging. I can't be bothered to explain what that is, because the pertinent point is this: those last fines didn't work. £26 million[23] at the start of the year, £290 million for Libor in 2012,[24] £198 million for sanction-breaking in 2010[25] – none of this makes a shade of difference to the conduct of this company. The comical thing about Financial Conduct Authority fines is that they all go back into a pool, which is then divided between the other banks. So if you're fined for some misdemeanour that you know all your peers were in on, you just have to wait:

soon enough you'll get your money back. And your peers always are in on it; that's the beauty. RBS (81 per cent public-owned) had to set aside £400 million for Forex-rigging fines, at the same time.[26]

Regulators, governments – all of us are making ourselves ridiculous, choosing a fine as a penalty: it will never be high enough to threaten their business, because then we'd just have to bail them out and make ourselves even more ridiculous. These are amounts they can just write off as the price of doing (unethical) business. Some bright lobbyist will one day try to persuade the Treasury that they should get a tax break on fines and, if George Osborne's still in charge, they probably will.

With this system we've turned banks into cyborgs, regulatory bullets pinging off them. If money is your highest value, and you have more of it than everybody who censures you, and their idea of a punishment is to charge you a sum without even realising how easily you can afford it, then I can see how this makes the world of rules look pretty pitiful, to the banking cadre. I don't think they were born bad.

The truly devilish part of it all is the casually urbane way in which anybody pointing this out gets slapped down; it's either gob-smackingly obvious, whatever your objection is (of course private capital doesn't have a social purpose; of course shareholders don't care about the company; of course banks rip you off!), or you could not possibly have the expertise to discuss it. It's like what's going on under the bonnet of a car: engines got more complicated, and people stopped looking; and now, if you do look, you get told off by the garage.

I don't really know how that £223 million 'special dividend' was paid, or when, or how the negotiation between BC Partners and the Phones 4U management went. I don't know the basis for the valuation of Heinz. I don't know whether the next bubble will come from derivatives or some other disaster altogether: a carbon bubble, a bond bubble, yet more thrashing from the mighty, wounded, idiot giant that is the eurozone. I do not know.

The onus should not be upon us to prove our credentials before asking a question. We are all paying for this. We pay for it with the low-wage economy; with the needless bankruptcies; with the unpaid corporation tax (see Tax); with the spendy football season tickets, if you're into that kind of thing; with the bail-outs of 2008; with that underlying feeling that nothing has really been resolved since. It is for finance to explain itself to us, not for us to prove that we deserve to know.

But doesn't the private sector just do everything better?

I find it helpful, when talking about national assets, to remind myself that we own them, and why. Before any discussion commences about whether or not we get a better deal or a better service when they're taken over by the private sector, why do they belong to us? Because we built them. With our tax, or our ancestors', or some combination of the two, we built them. I frequently feel as though that point is lost, in the political scrum to establish that – whatever subsequently went wrong – it was someone else's fault.

From everyone to a few

Conservatives love to sell national assets. It's just what they do. They wear thick cord and they hate shared ownership. Margaret Thatcher sold off water, trains, oil, gas, steel, the National Grid, phones, housing, airports, some bus routes. She sold whatever she could see, the better to effect 'the greatest shift of ownership and power away from the state to individuals and their families'.[1] This is pure rubbish. In 1979 we all owned our shared utilities, and 40 per cent of us also held shares in British companies. Now 12 per cent of us own shares, and the rest own nothing. The shift she created was from everyone to a few. Within those few, of course, a very few own almost all. There's something almost poetic about the Thatcherite vision: everything that came out of her mouth turned out to be not just wrong, but entirely wrong – the diametric opposite of the way things turned out.

New Labour, in this respect, were quasi-Conservative: they didn't sell-off assets, they got themselves into a hire-purchase agreement with the private sector, with the Private Finance Initiative (PFI), for everything they wanted to build. The terms were punishingly disadvantageous to them. It doesn't really make much sense, the PFI era. It's like inventing BrightHouse, then making yourself a customer of BrightHouse. They also sold human relationships (with outsourcing). I assumed they didn't sell off more raw material because there wasn't any left.

The Coalition proved that wrong: there was still Royal Mail and the NHS. Dur.

It's always a struggle to care about the privatisation of Royal Mail: everyone knew it would probably result in lower wages, because that is almost all anybody means by 'private-sector efficiency'. But it didn't seem to have the long echo into the future that, say, electricity had. Universal mass-delivery systems: who needs them really? Whatever it is, are you sure you can't email it?

This was just a failure of imagination, unfortunately. Few people foresaw how much a government really determined to redistribute wealth upwards could screw people over. The deal was done in October 2013. Vince Cable, the Business Secretary, who had promised never to sell off Royal Mail, was nervy and hurried. His banking advice, which he paid for handsomely (from Goldman Sachs, among others), suggested £3.30 a share. The stockbroker firm Panmure Gordon called this valuation more than £1 billion too low.[2] The nervy Cable held his nerve. On the day of the sale the share price climbed 38 per cent, which amounted to a cascade of money for the institutional investors whom Cable preferred. There were enough share bids from normal people to buy Royal Mail, but individuals were limited to £750 worth per person. Instead the shares were flogged to 'priority investors', mostly pension funds, on the gentleman's agreement that they would be a 'stable shareholder base' – that is, would keep hold of the shares for the early months while the price stabilised. Half of these shares had been sold within a few weeks. The taxpayer lost £750 million in 24 hours, and continues to lose. One of the big winners was Sir Peter Davies, a member of the management committee of Lansdowne Partners, which fund had made £36 million from the undervaluation by the following April. The choice of Lansdowne as a priority investor could have been historical affection between the Conservatives and the fund; its former Chief Executive, Sir Paul Ruddock, came by that 'Sir' in 2012, after a donation to the party of £500,000. Or it could have been a more general fondness; Davies's personal allegiance was established well before that, when he was George Osborne's best man in 1998. Or all these alliances could have been pure coincidence, given that sovereign wealth funds from Abu Dhabi, Norway, Singapore and Kuwait were also thought to have been invited (the process was not transparent). The salient point is this: there were many thousands of small British investors who applied for shares and were sent to the back of the queue in favour of so-called 'stable' investment houses, many of which cashed out as soon as they could.

The total undervaluation so far is £2.8 billion, which also includes the real-estate assets of Royal Mail, of which the National Audit Office concluded: 'We consider that the basis on which Royal Mail was sold did not fully recover the value of these sites.' £12.7 million, that advice from Goldman Sachs cost; it didn't even do as good a job as a guy from Foxtons.

For the national good
But none of that matters, right? When we transfer these huge utilities, the beneficiaries of that initial

windfall – whether they're plucky members of the public or the government of Singapore – don't actually matter, right? Because the service is so greatly improved to its average user, and the cost so reduced, that we are actively glad no longer to own it. Okay, no. Not ever, not in any sector, not from any angle. This is wrong. All our services are worse. They are worse than they were before, and they are worse than anybody else's in Europe. Industries that were too expensive for our own government to run are now often part-owned by other governments: the French, the Chinese, the Germans. Money is being made, but not by us, and ironically sometimes it is going into central treasuries, for the national good. But not our Treasury, and not for our good.

Our rail fares are comfortably the most expensive in Europe: £17 to travel 10 miles (£7 in Belgium); £96.50 to travel 100 miles (£29 in France); £125 to travel 200 miles (£35 in Italy).[3] The two most embarrassing conversations to have with a tourist are how much a Tube journey costs when you haven't got an Oyster card, and how much it cost them to get to Bristol. Just shaming. But these high costs do not mean the industry is profitable – far from it: direct public expenditure on rail is double what it was when privatisation occurred and is now £4 billion a year. This finds its way into shareholder dividends, so that between 1997 and 2012 on the West Coast Main Line, Virgin Trains paid out a total of £500 million in dividends and received a direct subsidy of £2.5 billion. The charges levied by the government, to the train companies, for using the track were £3.19 billion in 1994 and had gone down to £1.59 billion in 2012, which is effectively another subsidy. We've devised a system that can't survive without a £10 billion annual subsidy, and yet still charges passengers the uppermost fares that they can possibly afford. Infrastructure investment is negligible, except by Network Rail, which has to borrow to make that investment and now spends over half of its yearly budget servicing its own debt. Rolling stock is, on average, 18 years old, which is two years older than the average, pre-privatisation (and remember how much politicians used to rubbish the old trains, when they were softening us up for privatisation; maybe you don't remember, but it was a lot). The author of the most recent report on all this, Michael Moran, concluded:

At the dawn of privatisation we were promised not only a new business model, but also a new political model: one where backstairs manipulation of policy (for instance by Ministers) would be replaced by the transparency of open contractual competition and public regulation. Instead we have a mixture of crony capitalism, a world populated by well-paid lobbyists and well-networked insiders, and smoke and mirrors accounting which makes it impossible for normal citizens to penetrate what is going on.[4]

As we shall see, again and again, the genius of privatisation in all its forms is to make the provision of a service look so complicated, so daunting and so expensive that no ordinary, twenty-first-century state could ever dream of taking it on themselves. Except that they do: all over the developed world, states manage this.

The privatisation of water has resulted in our being hugely overcharged, owing to a financial arbitrage scam[5] that nets investors one billion quid a year, by one estimate,[6] and takes a tiny parcel of that billion pounds from each of our bills. The author James Meek has tracked the ownership of Thames Water, through the Australian investment bank Macquarie, to Abu Dhabi (whose sheiks' oil investment fund has a 10 per cent stake), on to Beijing (where the China Investment Corporation has 8.7 per cent), and so on.

What is the problem when your utilities are owned by other people's governments? Well, it's not a problem with foreigners per se. It's that they load the company with debt and don't invest in the infrastructure. So when Tewkesbury floods, it is because Severn Trent is paying its CEO £1.2 million a year, and £143 million to its shareholders. These figures are from 2007, the year of a flood that would have been averted by a £25 million pipeline. Pipelines are quite expensive; but then so are our water bills, which is how water companies are supposed to pay for them.[7] Floods are absolutely devastating, and can take five years out of a person's life and happiness. Politicians tend to make big promises during flooding about how money is no object, and I can see why they do, because it really strikes at the core of what it means to feel secure when you can't live in your own home and think it might be the fault of the Environment Agency. But in the end this is just more private-profit/public-risk. The government will always pay. The shareholders will always win.

> I do not see the government's task as being to try to plan the future shape of energy production and consumption. It is not even primarily to try to balance UK demand and supply for energy. Our task is rather to set a framework which will ensure that the market operates in the energy sector with a minimum of distortion and energy is produced and consumed efficiently.
>
> Nigel Lawson, 1982

All the same failures exist in the electricity sector that we can see with water and rail: the fabled competitiveness of the private sector never materialised, and our infrastructure is now under-invested and variously owned by the French government, two giant German companies, Warren Buffett and a J.P. Morgan investment fund. And others – heaps of others. The French government is actually quite a good employer, it turns out. So that's something. Our energy costs could be higher: they are higher in Germany. However, that is the result of massive investment in renewables, which means they now get nearly one-quarter of their electricity consumption from wind and solar power. We get 8.7 per cent from renewables. We get brownouts, they get the future. It's really annoying. This could be run so much better. But, most saliently, the task Nigel Lawson set himself was an idiotic one: energy production and consumption have to be planned, because when there isn't enough, or it is too expensive for people to use, that is everybody's problem.

PFIs – they call it 'one for the price of two'
When John Major first made a deal with the private sector for finance, in 1992, the Labour Party opposed it trenchantly. Harriet Harman called it privatisation through the back door, and Alistair Darling warned that it might look cheap up front, but would end up costing far more. Then, when the Labour Party got in, Alan Milburn gave an interview in which he said, 'It's PFI or bust.'[8] He had the wrong connective, of course: it was 'PFI and then bust' or 'PFI ergo bust'. Not realising this, the Labour Party had a bonanza. The casual bystander could be forgiven for thinking that Labour had simply made a mistake the first time, and it was a good deal after all.

In fact that bystander had wandered off hours or weeks before, because there is almost nothing more bewildering and boring than having a conversation about where you got the capital to build a hospital.

It's there, isn't it? You wanted it, didn't you? Well then.

In the traditional description for people who are only just interested, the problem with PFI projects is that they are 'off books' or 'off balance sheet' or (my personal favourite) 'incognito leverage'. Governments don't have to announce them as borrowing. Considering that, as of December 2013, there were PFI contracts worth £54.2 billion[9] – contracts that, over the course of their lives, will amount to £267 billion in government spending[10] – keeping them off books is a big deal. For scale, total net government debt is £1,483 billion. So it's like hiding around 3.5 per cent of your net government debt. That's not the hair-raising bit, not by a mile.

That was never the given reason for PFI: 'so we don't have to admit we've spent it'. Milburn's rationale was that private finance was the only source. There was no way a government could borrow this money on its own. This is a bizarre assertion: governments borrow money really cheaply internationally because they have guaranteed taxpayer revenue, so nobody worries about them paying it back (unless they join the eurozone). But at a micro-level, government departments have capital-spending limits; if you're not prepared to re-examine those limits (say, for instance, that you've made it an election pledge to stick to the last government's spending), then you could say that it was impossible for you to raise money.

Broadly, though, the point was the transfer of

risk. The private sector stumped up the cash, the government paid it back over time. A higher interest rate was paid, 'because it included a premium for assuming risks formerly underwritten by the taxpayer'.[11] The background was that, very often when governments tried to build things, they messed it up. Projects didn't come in on time. Budgets were doubled and tripled partway through. Governments managing their own projects always seemed to end up in a blackmail situation, where the cost of failure would be so high, politically, that they'd agree to anything. In theory, if a private company raised the money and managed the project, it would be their problem if things went wrong. The government would pay a fixed amount, a 'unitary charge' over a given period – 30 or 50 years – and that would cover repayment of the capital amount, plus payment for the fact that the company also serviced the hospital or the road, or whatever it was.

The price wasn't just set at a 'high rate': it was meant to be a very competitive tendering process, and companies would bid each other down. So that was the first thing that didn't work. The 'high bidding costs and lengthy tendering process' put all small and medium-sized bidders off,[12] leaving just a handful of – in one-third of cases, only two – very large companies bidding. The only reason the tendering process was so complicated was that the contracts were designed to be 'non-separable' – that is, the upfront money for the project was bound up with the contract for services relating to the project.

Things had to be non-separable to keep the whole lot off the books. So the accounting requirements, which were basically spin, changed the way the contracts were designed and thwarted the creation of a competitive environment.

If the tender process was going to be so long, it had to be worthwhile: the private sector was only interested in large projects, lots of land. Hospitals that needed a £30 million refit suddenly found that the only way to attract finance was to propose a £174 million new-build, so they had to roll in mental-health services as a sweetener; only then, sadly, they couldn't really afford it and had to make people redundant.[13] Some people (me, sort of) will remember how puzzling this all was: beautiful, gigantic new hospitals would open up, always accompanied by some misery-guts complaining about something: the miles-from-anywhere location or the loss of nurses or beds. The picture never really added up – did we have the money, or were we skint? – which was part of its genius.

There was also the lesser, but not irrelevant downside that small companies were driven off the turf: they couldn't shoulder a contract on their own, and they never got a decent subcontractor deal off the major players. So the very spending that ought to be earmarked for keeping local businesses alive – socially purposed projects to serve a community, paid for by that community – instead ended up closing a lot of them down.

Okay, so that was bad. Those winning the bids,

meanwhile, weren't leading experts in raising money or managing projects: the reason they were large enough to take the risk of bidding was that they were consortia, made up of the largest construction and service companies who would have been going for the work before PFI. The risk they were bearing was the risk that they themselves would fail to deliver. It's like insuring someone against the possibility that you urinate on their carpet. You know, you still might; but you could always not.

In fact, the analogy is not exact, because it turned out that things still could go wrong: which is when we discovered that the taxpayer bore the burden of the risk, after all. It turns out to be impossible for a private company to take responsibility for its own cock-ups. In 1996 the Home Office awarded a £76 million contract to Siemens to speed up asylum applications. By 1998 Siemens were floundering and needed another £120 million. By the middle of 1999 the backlog had increased in one year from 52,000 to 219,000. The contract was cancelled in 2001. A huge amount of money was lost in this process.[14] It is impossible to show, however, how much money was lost, because the National Audit Office only set the baseline after the contract was up and running. You could send them all the Freedom of Information requests you liked and they wouldn't be able to tell you this critical thing – was the contract value for money or was it not? – because value wasn't defined in the deal. Also in the mid-1990s, a benefits-card payment scheme was awarded to the company Pathway, in the hope of tackling benefit fraud. This theme is comically prominent in the Conservative worldview: never mind how many millions we're losing in these gargantuan deals with the private sector, as long as there isn't some single mother somewhere who's moved in her boyfriend without declaring it. The deal was signed in 1996. By 1999 it was plainly not going to work. By 2000 it had been cancelled, but the company still required payment. By the middle of 2000 the National Audit Office estimated that government savings would be one-quarter of what they were projected to be. The Post Office had spent £571 million 'acquiring an asset which does not at this stage yield sufficient income to justify the cost'. £127 million was wasted outright by the DSS, which was nearly half of its budget for Customer Accounting and Payments. The private company, meanwhile, via its parent company ICL, brokered (with the threat of interminable legal action) a new deal with the Post Office worth between £600 million and £1 billion. It was effectively a bail-out, before we all used the term.[15]

Scroll forward seven years to the financial crash, as finance started to dry up, and you see the government stepping in all over the place: schools, hospitals, the widening of the M25. The irony is that this coincided exactly with the first round of quantitative easing. So on the one hand, the government was pumping £375 billion into the economy, from March 2009[16] (they never let on how radical this was). On the other hand, PFI deals started to flounder and had to be bailed out in February 2009, at a cost of 'probably no more than £4 billion, absolute tops', according to Tim Pearson, spokesperson for the PFI industry.

Why couldn't those contracts have been broken? Then, the minute Company X was no longer up to the job, the project could have been taken back into public hands, using the billions of pounds that the state was actively looking for things to spend on.[17] This is what governments always used to do in a recession, when they wanted to get money into an economy that was seizing up: spend money on infrastructure that we could all use, that we would then all own. But the contracts can never be broken.

Why does G4S get paid, regardless of the outcome? How is it possible for Chris Grayling to have signed probation contracts that guarantee a decade of profits to companies, with a £300–400 million break-clause, whatever happens?[18] Because the contracts can never be broken. There are so many clichés about what the public sector is meant to be bad at: efficiency, competitiveness, incentives. The only consistent, unarguable evidence of weakness I've seen is this: it is absolutely bloody useless at negotiating with the private sector. It is almost as if it doesn't want to win.

I had a conversation in passing, in a bar, with a guy who worked on the other end of these deals and said that nobody writing the contracts had ever thought the risk was meaningfully transferred. This was in summer 2014, and we were talking about the late Nineties and the early Noughties. So I texted him later to see if he would go on-the-record off-the-record (that is, say it slowly enough that I could write it down, but still be anonymous). Got this back: 'That's not quite how I remember the conversation. We did note that there were a variety of different views on PFI, but the [bank] house view is that they represented good value for the British taxpayer.' Then, from a different number: 'My work phone could be seized at any time. Please do not call me again.' Tomas Carruthers, who now runs the Social Stock Exchange and was previously a stock-broker, laughed at this coyness: 'Anyone on the stock exchange could tell you how bad PFI was.' 'Seriously?' 'They were deals only a civil servant would sign.'

All the data is released by the Department for Business, Innovation & Skills: how much capital was spent on the project, how much will be paid back over the term of it. It doesn't tell you very much. The amount paid back – the unitary charge – is the amount initially borrowed plus the service charge, over the life of the project, and BIS doesn't tell us the service charge. The unitary charge makes no sense without more detail on the discounts (or lack thereof) on the debt repayment (more in a second). So I can look at this spreadsheet and see Sunningdale Park Property: capital amount, £12 million. Estimated unitary charge payment: £500.57 million. Geophysical Mining Data Project: capital amount,

£4 million. Unitary charge, £163.66 . . . yes, million. How is this even possible? How can a mid-Bedfordshire schools project cost £24 million, yet require unitary charges of £454 million? How can that be?[19] But in terms of evidence, I don't have the smoking gun. All I have is a heap of people who've been shot.

Two Scottish economists, Jim and Margaret Cuthbert, posit that a basic accounting error was made across the piece:

> Let us start with one example, a hospital project in England with a capital cost of just under £70 million. To finance the building the consortium borrowed over £60m from banks, at an interest rate of just over 6 per cent: the consortium itself provided almost £10m subordinate debt for the project, for which it received a more generous 15 per cent, and the consortium also put in an equity stake of £1,000 (no, we have not misread the decimal point: we genuinely mean one thousand pounds). The project shows the classic signs of inappropriate indexation, with the senior debt being paid off quickly, and hence senior debt charges declining rapidly – but with the whole unitary charge being indexed over the full 30-year life of the project at 3 per cent per annum. As a result, the projected returns to the consortium are eye-watering: the £1,000 equity input is projected to earn dividends totalling to more than £50m.[20]

The truly depressing thing about all this is trying to have a conversation with a politician about it, which I last tried on a panel with Stephen Williams, Liberal Democrat MP for Bristol West. He was making some asinine point about the national debt and how his tough decisions were paying it down, and I said, contrariwise, that the policies were having no impact on the debt, and were just causing needless hardship among people who had nothing to do with it. 'What about PFI?' he said. 'Your lot borrowed all that money, it was just off the books.' He mistook me for a Labour MP, or maybe a close advisor to Gordon Brown, which was fine, because he was flustered. But the fact – which he must know – is that PFI contracts are still being signed all the time. Nothing has been done to staunch this haemorrhage of public money. The political line is: 'This business, which we all agree is appalling, must continue because there's no way of doing it that is not appalling. PS: it was someone else's fault.' This is just pathetic. There comes a point at which we have a democratic duty to find better politicians.

Guddi Singh is a paediatric doctor who has taken a year's sabbatical to campaign for the NHS; she has started holding public meetings about PFI, just sounding out civil society to see if it has any ideas. The obvious place to start is with a legal challenge to the contracts themselves. It's interesting to see how broad the objection is to PFI: from corporate lawyers and banking insiders who can't see how this swindle was allowed, to policy wonks who object to the illegible accounting, to surgeons whose clinical budgets have been cut to fund unitary payments, to the unions who've done so much of the research, to the people who have to live with the inferior services that result. 'We need more than legal strategies,' Singh said. 'There is a way out of it, we just have to get on the same side. My overriding sense,' she added cheerfully, 'is how angry people are. It's not just "tax evaders are so annoying" anger. It's much more profound – "this scam is ruining my life".'

You need a bit of humanity

You take a duty that used to belong to the state and you hand it in a contract to a private company. That's outsourcing. There's very little systematic attempt to figure out how much the government spends every year: instead, academics give it a shot[21] and large management consultancies make estimates, for the benefit of their corporate clients. In fact we should know, as a democratic right, that £82 billion was spent over the course of the 2010–2015 parliament on outsourcing duties to the private sector, 42 per cent of it central government spending, 30 per cent local government and 13 per cent healthcare.[22] We should know that this is twice what was spent in the previous parliament. These contracts should be discussed openly by the politicians who sign them. They never are. In most sectors, there are four or five dominant companies; in some sectors, only two or three. Some corporations seem to be on the list for everything; one minute they're running electronic tagging, and then suddenly they are property experts. They are in court for seven different crimes, from fraud to unlawful killing, and yet they are offered more government work. They pay no corporation tax and yet are in receipt of £1 billion worth of government contracts.[23] Half the population feels that there is no accountability once these contracts have been signed,[24] and they're right; the mystery is what the other half think is going on. How does all this happen? Surely the whole point of outsourcing is that you find somebody who is actually good at something, and who wants to do it because they have a social purpose?

Nope: rule number one is that the whole business has to be crammed with stupid rules, the stupidest being 'Bidders must have prior experience of dealing with a contract this size.' This as good as guarantees that you won't get a company with a specialism, because the contracts are massive. You'll never find anyone with prior experience of doing a whole county's probation service when you've only just started outsourcing your probation service. What you get instead is a company with experience of running a whole county's asylum services. These are not the same skills, by the way: rehabilitating criminals and managing refugee applications; the only thing they have in common is that you need a bit of humanity to do them properly, which trait never crops up in any of the contracts.

Rule number two is that, however bad a company turns out to be, they must always be awarded fresh contracts, even after a government has promised to offer them nothing again, even after they have been convicted of fraud,[25] shown to be incompetent[26] and their members of staff have appeared in court for killing the people whom they had been contracted to care for.[27]

Rule number three is not a rule, it is just the way things are always done: services are contracted out to the cheapest provider, which generally means the largest provider. They can keep their bid low by subsidising it with their own capital reserves, then negotiate it upwards later. You can never find the details of how it was negotiated up, because it's all commercially confidential. All you know is that the smaller, more expensive providers – who might have paid their staff more – have been put out of business, and the contract has mushroomed in price anyway.

Rule number four is that, when a very few companies supply a huge number of services, they become vast: not only are they too big to fail, but they are too rich to sack. This may be the real reason behind the new breed of contracts, whereby companies get paid anyway, whatever happens. It has become unrealistic for governments to pretend they have any negotiating power. So why not just admit they're over a barrel in the contract phase?

Rule number five is that the state is always the backstop. You're the government. You cannot walk away from an old people's home. You cannot divest yourself of statutory responsibility for clearing away rubbish. Whoever's fault it is, you pay. Recently compensation awards have been made to the people whom G4S abused. The government, having already paid for the contract and paid again when it failed, still has to chip in on these claims. And rightly so; it was their stupid idea. G4S, while it accepted the payouts, never accepted liability. The subsequent lives of the young people in whose name the case was brought makes for really grim reading.

What these rules mean on the ground will differ from sector to sector, but it never means anything good.

Really interesting work developing carer-robots

We know what outsourcing looks like for care-workers (see Poverty), but there is also an effect on the cared-for. When pay is low, turnover is high; in some areas so high that you are almost certain to have a stranger giving you a bath at least once a week. People hate this. Call them weird, but they absolutely hate having a stranger come in, strip them naked, then give them a bath. Geoff Walker runs Sandwell Community Caring Trust, a social enterprise in the Midlands. His staff are suspiciously happy – I interviewed a couple of them and kept checking their pupils to see if they'd been spiked with E. Typical turnover in care-work is 30 per cent a year; his is 6 per cent. 'What we understood,' he said, 'very early on, was that if we wanted the people we cared for treated with dignity and respect, treated properly and made to feel good about themselves, we had to do the same for the people who cared for them. There is a real link between how we feel about ourselves and how we treat other people.'

It's just never going to work, the other way round: getting everyone's wages as low as they can possibly be, for profit; it is never going to yield a decent life for the millions of people in a carer/cared-for relationship. Adult social care is the example I always use, when I'm out on the town arguing about how, when people say 'private-sector efficiency', they really mean 'low wages'. There's about 15 minutes of debating how low the wages really, truly are and then, once it's understood that I'm right, we argue about what this situation will look like in the long term, and then someone says, 'In Japan they're doing really interesting work developing carer-robots.' That's when I know I've won. Seriously, why not just get a terminator-robot to shoot your elderly parent in the head?

Whose fault is it? The fault is that capitalism has been turned on its head. Wherever there's a guaranteed income stream, private-equity companies buy the business, load it with debt, take the profit. From then on, staff are always paid as little as possible, under the weight of the debt. I personally think this is all about commissioning: councils that don't want to take the care-homes back under their own control should only outsource to asset-locked social enterprises, and should not let private-equity deals anywhere near them. Unions, especially the GMB (which has gained about 100,000 members, mainly from the care sector), don't think this would make enough difference when a lot of the care is commissioned by private families. They're a bit more hardcore than me. I don't mean more politically radical, necessarily. I mean they once turned up outside a private-equity investor's local church with a camel. They might be right – perhaps it is time to bring in the camels.

But, in the meantime, why can't we make more demands of our local authorities, which are, after all, democratically elected? There is only one council in the country that has it written into the care-work contract that the pay rates should take travelling time into account.[28] Councils are signing contracts for their adult social care which they know, via arithmetic, don't add up to a minimum wage for the care-workers. The same state that allows these people to be underpaid then has to top up the wages, pay the Housing Benefit, pay a pupil premium for their children, and deal with the fallout from families where the parents are never around because they can't put food on the table in a 40-hour-week. And for what? To deliver a 20 or 30 per cent profit to shareholders. Ultimately the contracts aren't even cheaper: Geoff Walker can deliver these contracts on a social-purpose basis, without taking a profit, for the same cost. The government is spending all this money; they have power; they have mass. They could use it to make society better, to make wages fairer, to make care more human, to make people happier. At the moment they're just choosing not to.

Going opco-propco

Perhaps you're wondering why these private companies ever go bust, if they're designed so carefully to turn profit, at the expense of any other consideration. The short answer is 'It was never in their business plan not to go bust', and this is a salient feature of the new face of private investment. It used to be a source of shame for a company to go bust: now it's only humiliating if you're the one holding the shares when it all blows up.

The slightly longer answer is the 'opco-propco' deal: the company is split in two, with one part that operates the business, one that holds the property and assets, and then the operating company rents the building off the property company. The point is the amount of debt you can raise: you're a private-equity company buying a care-home chain for £1 billion. A bank would lend you 70 per cent for a buyout, so you'd have to find £300 million. But they'd lend you 90 per cent on a property portfolio, so you could load the propco with the value, borrow 90 per cent against it – wham, you've got a chain of care-homes, a guaranteed income stream and as much debt as you like. Two problems ensue: one immediate and obvious, the other subtler and pernicious.

Southern Cross is the textbook example: via a series of complicated buyouts and opco-propco deals, the American private-equity group Blackstone bought it (and finished with a profit of £1.1 billion, having sold the propco to the Qatar Investment Authority). The operating company was locked into 'upwards-only rent increases', and was suffocating: if a resident was paying £400 a week, £150 was going in rent. The staff, already ground down to the lowest possible wages, were having to bring in their own biscuits from home for the residents. The union couldn't make any headway; when Southern Cross said they were too broke to do anything differently, they were telling the truth. All the money was going on debt, to service the QIA. Even though it was stressful, it was a blessing when Southern Cross went bust; all the homes were eventually dispersed to different operators, debt-free. Now the GMB is trying to forge an alliance between the Local Government Association, the Department of Health and the Department for Communities and Local Government to fix a fee for residential care so that every care-home pays the living wage. But the unspoken element of that idea is that this business has to exclude these antisocial investors. The profits they skim off are simply unaffordable. Leveraging ruins industries: it could be the AA or Phones 4U or an old people's home. They are not saddled with debt for any productive purpose; it is purely so that someone who has done nothing but cut a deal can walk off with a huge sum of money. Then, somewhere down the line, the care-homes can no longer afford biscuits. If this were widely known and discussed, I am confident there is not one person in the country who would agree with it.

A horrible stain

There is also a darker side: when private-equity companies get involved with anything residential, as well as loading it with debt, they buy properties in the cheapest possible areas: South Yorkshire and Lancashire in the North, Kent in the South. In the children's home sector, 54 per cent of residential homes are run by private companies. Charities have been completely edged out of this, and now run only one-tenth of homes. Two of the three biggest private providers of foster placements are owned by private-equity firms. The irony is that foster-carers themselves are modestly paid, because of historical worries that, if you paid them enough that they could give up work (which they'll have to do anyway), you'll attract people who are only doing it for the money. So we're splitting hairs about whether the family should have £350 or £380 a week, while handing over the running of children's homes to people who don't even pretend to have an interest in children's welfare. They are only interested because they have identified a guaranteed income stream.

More than half of children in care have been placed out-of-area, often hundreds of miles away from their home borough, which means changing school, rarely (if ever) seeing their social worker, and being cut adrift from every adult they've ever known. The placing authority has no obligation to notify the local authority to which the child is sent. The justification sometimes given is that they have to be moved away from a gang, or some tenacious association. But Euan Holloway, from the Children's Society, says that only applies in 'a handful of cases'. Children's home provision has developed based on house prices. So London has 130 homes, for a population of 7.8 million, and two boroughs have no children's homes at all; Lancashire has 101 homes, for a population of 1.5 million.[29] When the Rochdale sexual-abuse scandal broke, it had 41 homes for a population of 200,000; only one child in any of them was originally from the borough. Stockport had 300 kids in children's homes, of whom only 28 were from the borough, and it was only because they have Ann Coffey – a really good constituency MP – that the situation even came to light.[30] The homes are sometimes 'one-on-one', but that doesn't mean one kid, living in one house, with one adult. It means rotational staff, so the child might go to sleep with one person in the house and wake up with someone completely different. Coffey said, 'Essex were paying something like £200,000 a year for this kind of placement in Rochdale.' The government warned local authorities to stop using out-of-area placements;[31] considering all the drivers were financial, and that same government was cutting local authority funds by an unprecedented amount, this warning was somewhere between a platitude and a punch in the face.

We're currently taking the most damaged children in the country, placing them miles away from any adult who cares about them and dumping them (that's the technical term) in the poorest boroughs. Right across public-sector outsourcing, from the Work Programme, where A4e were paid more for placing an unemployed person in work than the person in question was getting paid, to private-sector prisons, where hopelessly poor inmates had to pay for their own bedding, I never saw anything as crazy as this.

Society is currently racked by the conversation about child abuse in the North of England: 1,400 girls in Rotherham; undisclosed (but, many say, similar) numbers in Darlington, Sheffield, Rochdale and Stockport. It's an open secret that the way residential care is organised creates a sitting target for people who want to sexually exploit children. Ofsted figures published in 2012 revealed that children's homes in England – caring for 4,840 children, including 1,800 girls – had reported 631 suspected cases of young residents being sold for sex in the past five years.[32] Considering that children very often don't report sexual exploitation, don't even recognise what's going on and are frequently disbelieved when they do, 631 is unlikely to be an accurate estimate.

Political correctness is the problem, apparently:

this is what prevented the police and social services investigating charges of abuse, because they were mainly against Asian men. The interpretation is truly bizarre, because simultaneously Westminster was convulsed by accusations of a paedophile ring at the highest level of government in the 1970s. We're on the cusp of a scandal about child abuse in public schools: there are now 150 public schools with current or historical allegations against them. What do we know about child rapists – from Rotherham, from the Catholic Church, from the British public-school system? That they are predatory; that they will organise their entire lives around gaining unfettered access to children; that they prey on kids who are vulnerable, but I am not using that word in its modern sense of 'poor' or 'delinquent', but rather 'any kid whose parents are not around'. Is there a particular attitude of Asian men, that British children deserve to be sexually exploited? Possibly, but it is one that is shared by white Catholic men, the public-school educated, the public-school educators. It is a horrible stain on the species that this occurs at all, but I can tell you one way to make children in care safer, without having to resort to implausible racial explanations, and that is: stop running their care for profit. It is hard enough to protect children when you put them first, and impossible when you put them second.

Either this is all fine; or it's terrible, but there's nothing we can do about it. Or we figure out a better way. Those are the choices – society is the stake. The first two choices are bullshit. Everywhere in the world, councils, unions and regular people are taking back outsourced services. In America one-fifth of outsourced services have been taken back in-house (73 per cent citing poor quality of contractors, 51 per cent because the private sector was more expensive). By 2011 in Germany the majority of energy-distribution networks had been returned to public ownership, and they're working to bring back waste disposal, public transport, water, social care and social housing. The same year 96 per cent of Italians voted to keep water services public; similar campaigns to renationalise water are happening in Brazil, Uruguay, South Africa and Greece. Paris remunicipalised its water supply in 2010. Newcastle Council fought the privatisation of its IT services, and Islington Council brought many of its services in-house when it found that was the only way to honour its living-wage promise. Norway's Model Municipality movement has been reversing privatisation and competitive tendering since 2005.[33]

What all these movements understood was that it wasn't really about protecting pay and conditions for the people doing the jobs; it was about the fact that they knew what they were doing, and they cared about it, and they lived with its results. That's what public servants and people on the ground will always have over giant, faceless corporations: we actually care what happens. Giving a toss is our secret weapon.

Did we leave it too late to avert the environmental apocalypse?

What do I actually want? Seriously, nothing major. I want to leave the planet habitable, comfortably habitable and still beautiful, for my children, their children, other people's children – if mine don't have any, or even if they do . . . basically, for the entire future. I never want the world to end.

I want the ice-caps still to exist when I die, and I want to halt the loss of wildlife. I'm not going to yank your chain about the majestic, extinct Iberian lynx, but I do think creatures, plants, landscapes – the whole lot – have an inherent value besides what we take from it, in pelts or tusks or medicines or biodiversity.

I want the oceans to remain clement for fish of all sorts, even the ones I don't plan to eat. I don't want a bio-engineered global-warming solution, where some billionaire throws up a reflective disc into the atmosphere and that keeps us all safe, until it fails.

I don't need a hero, though many people in the field are heroically clever, and thank God for that.

I don't want to live under a protective dome, as we adapt to a hot planet. I don't want anybody to live like that. I don't want to be permanently beholden to a handful of fossil-fuel providers, telling us on the one hand that oil isn't running out, while on the other hand that it must always cost more this year than it did last year. I don't want to be faced with the brutality of the way I live, every time there's a spill or a war. I don't want to have to whistle really loudly and think about something else, whenever a report comes out from the Intergovernmental Panel on Climate Change (IPCC).

I don't want to put nature second to profit that almost nobody will ever see. I don't want nature even to be in a cost-benefit analysis, against some jerk who thinks he can own it.

All I want is for the world to be cooler, greener, safer, as beautiful as it is right now and to last for ever. It's really not so unreasonable. It's no more or less than we all want. So why does it feel so lonely? Why does even thinking about the environment make me feel so impotent and yet so guilty? If there's nothing I can do, how can it be my fault?

Originally, in the Eighties, environmentalism was set up as a question of personal responsibility: how much can you conserve? How much carbon can you offset in some other way? What pleasurable thing can you do without? Why are you so selfish?

This thinking hits all the wrong points, like notes

on a xylophone: scarcity, solitude, every man for himself in a dark and uncertain future, waves of distrust. It quells the only three feelings that a movement for change needs – cooperation, ambition and optimism. It must have taken me 30 years to figure out that you can't build momentum for anything unless you say that it'll be better than what we have now. Then it took me another decade to figure out that, with a green revolution, that could actually be true. Renewable energy doesn't have to be less fun than torching carbon; by definition it will be more fun, because it won't cost as much and it won't run out. Zero-carbon, food-neutral housing isn't worse: it's better. Green cars won't be slower: they'll be faster. When you build a better future, you don't defer your enjoyment of the present, you make that better as well. If I could live my life again, this is the one thing I'd do – go back in time and realise this sooner.

The first public scientific consensus that mankind was warming the planet came in the late Eighties, at a conference in Toronto. It was the result of work that had been in train since the Sixties and Seventies, James Lovelock's Daisyworld modelling, Franco-Soviet ice-core analysis. It was not the result of sustained persuasion by hippies. The fact that it reached the same conclusion – we are going to hell if we don't sort this out – is a coincidence.

There is no longer any contention around this issue. There are different analyses of how much warming we can take; how much of the earth would be uninhabitable and under which scenarios; how much warming we can avoid; the sometimes-subtle distinction between an adaptive strategy and making things worse; and whether or not the earth itself will die, or only humanity.

But the idea that science is locked in some internal struggle, unable to thrash out even the first principle of the threat we're facing: that's nonsense. 97 per cent of peer-reviewed scientific papers say that global warming is man-made.[1] IPCC scientists are 95 per cent certain: we are making the earth warmer with carbon emissions.[2] If we continue to use carbon until it's all run out, the world will become too warm to sustain human life. Consensus on that scale almost never happens in a field of active enquiry. Even those building agreement as to the roundness of the earth and the constellation of the stars had some fierce opponents, who only stopped fighting when they died.

A lot of people worry about what sceptics and deniers are doing to the debate; I don't think they're the problem. Yes, I get a chill of frustration when some articulate but fundamentally irrational man (it is always a man), educated beyond his intelligence (he always went to Christ Church) thanks to the many thousands of pounds dropped on the premium public-school tuition that never penetrated his skull, is given a platform on a public-service broadcaster (it is always the BBC) to dispute scientific evidence of which he has no understanding. Naturally I get frustrated. I'm only human. But I don't think those clowns are taken very seriously any more.

What's really derailing, delaying, fragmenting and otherwise sabotaging progress is the idea that it's all hopeless, and there's nothing much we can do. I would take a denier over a fatalist any day. People whose only objection to green energy is that it's not necessary will, if they have an open mind, embrace it in the end anyway, because it is cheaper, more elegant and, geopolitically, more stable. People who think that fossil fuels are killing us, but it's pointless trying to do anything because nobody else will, and it's probably too late, and in the end we're all fucked and maybe it's for the best, because we're inherently destructive: those are the really tough nuts to crack. I've been one of those nuts myself. Some days I still am one.

A cooling breeze
Bruce Davis (see Finance) created peer-to-peer lending, then went on to found the UK Crowdfunding Association.[3] Peer-to-peer is interesting because it breaks the stranglehold of banks. During the great boom years you would not have predicted that anything could challenge banks in the personal lending market – they were giving out credit cards like sweets, they seemed to have a limitless capacity to suck up risk. All it took, however, was for someone to have an idea. Obviously it was much more complicated than that, and the establishment (then the

Financial Services Authority, now the Financial Conduct Authority) threw up all kinds of barriers. But good ideas are, in the end, irresistible. That market is now worth £1.6 billion, and the only thing limiting it is itself; it tries to make sure people are credit-worthy before it lends to them. In that respect it's a lot like the old-fashioned banking system, before banks went mad.

So this has some radical messages, particularly what it says about creativity and its potential to change an apparently immutable reality. But it's not very radical in its visible results: most people on Zopa are still saving the money to put their kids through university or borrowing it to regrout their bathrooms.

Crowdfunding is similar in principle, in so far as it cuts out the traditional players and goes straight to individuals. Davis uses the phrase 'democratised finance' a lot, because that's another revolutionary element: the idea that you don't have to be a high net-worth individual to want to put some of your money into the future, for your own security and also to influence that future. He crowdfunds for renewables, but obviously, in principle, you could crowdfund for anything, so long as you could persuade enough people that it was worthwhile. The minimum investment in many of these projects is £5. Your return probably will not change your old age very much, but if we all did it, you can imagine how different 2050 would look.

In 2012 Davis had just started raising finance for

a wind-farm in St Briavels in Gloucestershire. It is a single turbine, run on one farmer's land. It lacks that eerie impressiveness of the massive Scottish and Welsh wind-farms, where the turbines stalk along heathery ridges, like invading aliens. It's not puny – you couldn't wrap two arms around it – but it's not going to answer the energy needs of the whole of Gloucestershire. Also, it looks a little bit lonely.

Consider, though, what it *does* answer. The local Green candidate, James Greenwood, was there at the turbine's launch – a well-intended gathering in a strip-lit parish hall, followed by a pint in a pub, which is just about the only environment where English people are ever normal with each other. 'That thing out there,' he started, feelingly: it was like the clipped, carefully unemotional turbo-speech at the end of a play about the First World War. 'That thing out there powers this village. You never have to worry again about another cubic metre of gas, coming from somewhere where you have to fight to get your hands on it, economically, militarily . . . How exciting is that?'

But what about when the wind's not blowing? That's what the naysayers always ask, isn't it, when they're trying to persuade you to just get back in your box and leave it to the experts? It's not always windy, is it, greeno? No. No, thank God, it is not.

Britain could be the Saudi Arabia of wind. Buffeted on every side, exposed on every peak, its camping holidays and barbecues hostage, always, to this peculiarity of its location. Every time I write about it, I try to cut and paste the figures from the last article, only to find that a new record has been set. In August 2014 wind-energy in the UK outstripped coal-energy on five separate occasions – on 17th August it hit a new daily record, meeting 22 per cent of the UK's energy needs. I'm describing the wind industry as it exists right now – after a full term of government frontbenchers actively opposing it (Owen Paterson, as Environment Minister, put his hostility to wind at the centre of most of his public speeches; he was also a climate-change denialist who wanted to scrap the Climate Change Act[4]). Imagine the state of this industry if it had some central support. Denmark very often has 100 per cent wind-power. In December 2013 it exceeded 100 per cent and had to export some energy, and turn some turbines off.

There are three goals to keep in mind: one, it is possible on a windy day to get all your energy from the limitless physical conditions, if only you're prepared to make a proper investment in infrastructure. Two, the lack of constancy isn't necessarily the problem that it's made out to be: a European supergrid, increasing connectivity between nations, could ultimately yield a situation in which, when there wasn't enough wind in Spain, they could import from Denmark. It's always windy somewhere. Three, this really could be a local answer to a local problem, spiralling into a national and international answer to a global problem. It can be as ambitious or as modest as you see fit. It can be a single turbine powering a solitary village for a quarter of time, or it can be an entire country running a surplus. You can go out right now and buy a stake in a wind-farm for a fiver. You don't have to wait for a Conservative Environment Minister to care about the environment; though, obviously, it would help if he did.

The benefits of wind are so obvious now[5] that not even people who make their opposition to it a political calling card have been able to stand in the way of major investment projects. However, in the UK greenlit wind-farms tend to be offshore, because that sidesteps local opposition from people who think they kill birds. Since offshore is much more expensive, this typically involves private investment, because it is an accepted fact in Anglo-American politics that governments can't build things that will make their country better, in case it interferes with the free market. Ironically, foreign governments still do build things – so 68 per cent of nuclear generation and 50 per cent of offshore wind, in the UK as of 2012,[6] was outsourced: not to the private sector, but to foreign governments. It's ridiculous; we have this abundant free energy source. We invented wind-power. And we have to stand by, while governments drag their feet to keep in with local Rotary Clubs, while all the expertise goes abroad, while allegiances and supergrids are built up elsewhere; and when we finally get to the point where it is agreed that we need to build the infra-structure, we can't even do that ourselves. It all has to be outsourced to a foreign state. Small-scale investments could be a game-changer, even if it just changes the game in your village. But what this also needs is a bit more collective anger: we could really be getting somewhere with this, and instead we're stuck in a hamster-wheel of defunct technical arguments and political position-taking that pretends to be 'pragmatic', but is really just pandering; other developed nations left all this behind in the 1990s and got on with things.

Enemy fire, friendly fire

> What might the new fire look like? The old fire was dug from below. The new fire flows from above. The old fire was scarce. The new fire is bountiful. The old fire was local. The new fire is everywhere. The old fire was transient. The new fire is permanent.
>
> Amory Lovins, *Reinventing Fire*

Energy, Amory Lovins means; he's in love with this metaphor. You get carried away with it and then end up having to translate him.

I encountered Mr Lovins when I was chairing an event for some green-energy fundraisers. Its main purpose was as a platform for Vivienne Westwood, who warbled on, rolling conspiracy theories into the crowd like boules into a box of frogs, so that everyone looked a bit surprised and embarrassed, but put up with it because she donated a load of money at the end. So a panel had been assembled around her, one of whom was Lovins, about whom I knew nothing except that he had set up the Rocky Mountain Institute (some kind of research body). My only impression I'd formed from an email trail, in which he said he had a 'hard finish' at 6 p.m. I had in mind a slickly suited, silvery-haired American, who would tell everyone how to sell environmentalism: a mixture of motivational self-talk (we can do it!) and psychology (don't tell people about a bad thing that might happen to the residents of Bangladesh; tell them what's about to happen to their own front garden). Listening to that stuff is enlightening, but it's like going to a sales conference. Even if you believe in what you're selling, it's a bit demeaning.

Lovins arrived wearing a brown bowl on his head. A Dutch solar campaigner went to hug him and he leant away from the embrace as if he had a protective magnetic field. He talked pretty fast, because of his hard finish. A lot of his sentences started with instructions like, 'Consider the two facts of automotive physics.' He was wearing the bowl on his head because it was made of an ultra-light carbon-fibre composite; he hit himself on the head a few times, to show how strong it was. It was a bit surreal. The point was massive; the point was a revolution.

Transportation is the biggest American consumer cost, after housing. They use 13 million barrels of oil a day on fuel, which costs them nearly $1 billion.

If they built vehicles differently and powered them electrically, that oil could go unburnt. $3.8 trillion could be saved every year (2010 prices). Convenience, safety and performance could all be boosted, not compromised. The accepted truth about driving is that heavy cars are safer than light ones. This, along with status anxiety, has driven the fashion for SUVs across the developed world, which has resulted in even more pointless oil consumption, at the precise moment in history when we're all supposed to have realised what that consumption means. American cars, over the past decade, have gained weight twice as fast as American people, which is pretty impressive, given how fast the people have gained weight. The thing is, that safety concern – it's not true: it was just a mistake in the interpretation of the data. It is size, not weight, which improves car safety.[7]

Two-thirds of fuel use is weight-driven; lighter cars can be greener, cheaper, faster and safer. They're more expensive to make, but you'd make that back on fuel, coupled with the fact that they don't deteriorate. Change to battery-powered electric cars and these benefits multiply. In the UK the numbers are different: we don't drive so much, the distances are smaller, we have fewer cars, we have better public transport, we tax petrol. If we were doing politics the old way, we'd say, 'Well, we're already a lot better than them; let's just aim slowly to become more like Scandinavia.'

We're stuck in a 'do the same thing, just a bit less'

thought process. Not only is it insufficiently ambitious, but it is inherently boring. If the US can reduce its automobile fuel use by 95 per cent, over the next three decades, then so can we. Do you want the future to look like *The Fifth Element*, or do you want it to look like *Mad Max*? I'm thinking specifically about their transport infrastructure here. In political terms, you wouldn't want the future to look like either of those films.

Lovins removed the bowl from his head and started talking about his house. He hasn't spent any money heating his house for two decades, but recently, as solar bricks have become more sophisticated, there's been a spot in his stairwell so warm that he can grow his own bananas. I didn't know then what the climate was in the Rocky Mountains; January temperatures range from -6 to 7 degrees centigrade. So the bananas were just a playful afterthought. The point is that solar doesn't just work a little bit. Solar power is amazing. Solar power, not by coincidence, turns out to be as awesome as the sun.

By early 2014 half a million homes in the UK generated their own energy, through solar power. That's two gigawatts of power, and a complete mindset change. Since utilities were privatised in the Eighties and Nineties, the market has been all about six big providers, large central power-stations, powerless consumers and governments that, if they're the good guys, whine at the providers to be a bit less greedy.

Solar cracks that wide open – what if you could generate all the power you use from your own roof? What if you could have a local energy project that made you self-sufficient as a community, or even left electricity over that you could sell back to the National Grid? What if your kids' school had a solar-powered roof? What if solar technology had improved so much that it was set to hit grid parity – which is to say, cost the same as coal – in 2020? This is just in the UK. It has already reached grid parity in Germany, Italy, Spain, Portugal, Australia and the US. The price of solar, over the past 25 years, has gone down by a comical 99 per cent. For the first time, in the US and China in particular, solar is competitive with other fuels on a purely cost basis; which is to say, completely forgetting carbon emissions and renewables targets. It is not better because it's greener. It is better and it is also greener.

Most of that price drop was down to solar generation getting more sophisticated. The expected next leap is a combination of improved battery storage and new smart tech to deal with peaks in demand. According to the IPCC, the 'technical potential for solar is the largest of the renewable sources by a large magnitude'.[8] The Wall Street brokers Sanford C. Bernstein use words like 'doom cycle' and 'terrorgraph' – not for the environment, but to describe the conventional-energy sector. What do you do if you're an old-fashioned fossil-fuel company? Up until now they've simply bad-mouthed solar, particularly behind-the-scenes, lobbying governments. But it's like telling people not to get a mobile phone because they're extremely heavy and crackly and they don't fit in your handbag. Eventually people will wake up to the fact that phones have moved on, and your argument hasn't.

The implications of solar for big energy companies are vast, and are already reflected in their credit ratings. The value of European energy companies has fallen by half since 2008. Their credit ratings have been cut from the majority at A2 or A3 to the majority now at Baa1 and Baa2.[9] This is pretty major. It's like being Germany one day and Thailand the next. The reason is this: old-fashioned power-stations rely for their profit on peaks of demand. Solar power sets out to erode these peaks. As soon as you can battery-store the power you generate, it doesn't matter what time of day you use it.

So the obvious next question is this: why, when solar has enjoyed progress unheard of in energy since the discovery of petroleum, haven't you heard more about it? Why haven't there been street parties? Why do mainstream commentators still suck their teeth when it's mentioned, and say things like 'I've heard those panels cost 20 grand, and it takes 20 years to make the money back'? Why, for that matter, haven't we all installed them? Finding the definitive answer to all this is like chasing deer: you might catch one and lose the 17 important ones. It's a bit techie. Does any person of normal temperament want to read about technical development, about the difference in cost between battery storage and liquid hydrogen? Do you really want to hear every time the solar cells go down in price? I don't know – maybe you do. I know I don't, any more that I'd have wanted to read about how a computer the size of a room became a laptop lighter than a hardback. Familiarity comes with use, and half a million users still aren't enough for that to get into the national bloodstream. Juliet Davenport, founder of Good Energy, which only deals in renewables, has this extremely sunny attitude and talks a lot about things that work. The Solar Schools project, for instance: 'What I like about the schools side is really that it comes back to this point of individuals being able to take control. You begin to take hearts and minds with you. The more people touch renewables, indirectly or directly, the more people accept that actually it does work.' Germany is the flagship example of this, in which so many people are accustomed to generating their own energy that towns are starting to take themselves off the national grid.[10]

But there are two big, intersecting hurdles of industry and politics, which even she will concede. 'It's so difficult to know what's going on behind closed doors, but I've heard the edges of conversations in which this new technology is being dismissed, and you're thinking, "Of course it can work. Of course it can deliver." That dismissal tactic is used quite often in terms of keeping everyone else away.' It's hard to overstate how much the Big Six stand to lose from these new developments. Not only customers; fossil fuels get more from the

British government in subsidies than renewables do. The UK is the fifth-largest funder of this industry in the world.[11] This simply wouldn't stand, if there was widespread recognition that other, cheaper, better, cleaner, altogether less deadly fuels were available.

Excluding draughts and other things you never wanted to talk about

The problem with demand reduction is that it sounds so incredibly boring. 38 per cent of our total greenhouse-gas emissions are just wasted energy, leaked from buildings. Before we have to reinvent any elements, before we have to electrify our cars, we can just improve the way we already live.

I met Ed Matthew, from the pressure group Energy Bill Revolution, while I was trying to avoid writing this book. Under what other circumstances would you go for a face-to-face conversation about saving energy?

Fuel poverty itself yanks my chain a little. You're considered fuel-poor if you're in a 'Low Income High Costs' (LIHC) bracket: that means, if your fuel bills are above average and if, after paying them, your remaining income puts you below the poverty line.[12] I think the measure is quite stupid, missing out a lot of people who are choosing between heating and eating, but who don't count as fuel-poor because their costs are only average – instead, they are boring old poor poor. I think they changed the measure to make the numbers go down and, sure enough, the numbers did; nevertheless, 10 per cent of people still count as fuel-poor.

Energy efficiency is measured A to G, and 35 per cent of people in a G house will be below the poverty line (in 2012 new-build standards were changed to a 1–6 star system[13]). Does that mean that nobody who had the money would ever put up with a G-band house, which is as draughty as a tent put up on Dartmoor, by someone reluctantly doing a Duke of Edinburgh challenge? Or does it mean that no amount of money would ever make a G-property warm enough, so that however rich you started, you'd always finish below the poverty line? Probably it means the first – by health-and-safety standards, both categories F and G are simply unfit for human habitation, yet 10 per cent of private rentals are in these bands.[14] A and B are impossible to achieve unless the house is a new-build – there were only 138,000 dwellings in this category in the whole country, at the last count, which means that nothing like all newly built homes are properly energy-efficient, which, by the way, is absolutely nuts. When David Cameron made his promise of 100,000 new homes at the conference of autumn 2014, he exempted them from the energy-efficiency standard. So this pitifully insufficient number of houses will be built, which people will then have to go back and retro-fit, if we don't want to carry on losing nearly 40 per cent of our carbon up our chimneys.

We know how much energy we have to save, and we know how to build houses so that we save it. And yet we don't do it. The construction industry is entirely geared towards holding on to undeveloped land until the last minute, building incredibly cheap stock and selling it as fast as possible (see Housing). We're burning all this energy so that politicians can make promises they don't understand, and the construction industry can make profits that their direct predecessors wouldn't have understood.

If category C is the highest a retro-fitted house could reach, you'd hope, wouldn't you, that the majority of UK homes would be in that category? In fact, the majority are in bands D and E. So you have F and G as the 'dangerously uninhabitable' bands; A and B as the 'hopelessly unattainable in current market conditions' bands; C as the one band in the middle that even a moderately ambitious and green government would be reaching for; and D and E, where most of us are. Information about energy efficiency – in your surveyor's report, or your local sorting office or similar – is all conveyed to the simple citizen in coloured bar-charts, which look like a government warning on how much salt you're supposed to eat, and which bore you to death. As soon as you delve more deeply into it, it fills you with rage. So you go straight from tedium to boiling anger, without any of those phases in between, like 'fascination' or 'sense of possibility'. This is why people don't talk about energy efficiency very often.

What also bugs me is that fuel poverty is always presented as an unfortunate constellation of factors that just happened to hit at the same time: it's unfortunate that energy prices went up at exactly the same time as wages went down, at exactly the point that people stopped being able to buy their own houses, or maintain them properly once they had. These are all features of the same problem: energy prices have gone up because there's no real competition in the energy market, just six big companies acting and charging with suspicious synchronicity, to the benefit of the shareholder and the detriment of the customer (see Privatisation); wages have gone down because, again, the proportion of money sucked out in profit, to the shareholder, is too great (see Poverty); landlords are under no pressure to maintain their properties because rents are rising faster than wages, and the relationship has become asymmetrical and beggars can't be choosers (see Housing).

People aren't struggling to pay for fuel by accident. When some people make a lot of money with very little effort, other people have to try extremely hard to keep their heads above water. If you're not prepared to say that, then you can shove your loft-lagging and your draught-excluding tape.

This is the attitude with which I approached the conversation with Ed Matthew; and I still think fuel poverty has to be seen in a wider context of general poverty and income distribution. But it is time to reimagine housing, so that we can at least imagine ourselves spending enough money for the right reasons.

At the moment £1.3 billion a year is raised by the Energy Companies Obligation (ECO), which is nominally a charge made to energy companies by the Treasury, but which in fact just gets put straight onto your bill. This is the 'green crap' that desperate political parties offer to scrap for you, when they're really up against it and can't think of anything else. Often they don't know exactly what it is they're offering to scrap – the deputy leader of UKIP, Paul Nuttall, said at their conference in 2014 that they would get rid of green taxes: pressed for the details of what a green tax might be, he said, 'carbon capture'. There is no carbon capture in the UK – not in real life. We've known how to do it since 2003, but we've done nothing. Indeed there are only two active Carbon Capture & Storage operations in the world, one in Canada and one in China. This is not an unfortunate, one-off mistake, although conference season that autumn was tragic to watch, like a shambolic dress rehearsal. But the kind of politician who thinks that pounds in a voter's pocket are more important than making a collective effort to save the world is almost always the kind of politician who doesn't know anything about anything.

Anyway, so we have this ECO and that money is supposed to go into insulation. There is also the Green Deal, which is a system of market-driven loans. Nobody is given anything for free; the loans aren't even that cheap, as the interest is around 7 per cent. You'd be better off just going to a bank, or putting the cost on your mortgage. It's supposed to be this great shining advert for the free market, creating a better, cleaner, less energy-intensive Britain, without the government having to get involved. Its results are absolutely pathetic – 2,000–3,000 homes have taken it up. They haven't even bothered to count them accurately, there are so few. Green Deal lenders actively avoid the fuel-poor, because the likelihood is that their homes aren't warm enough to begin with, so any improvements made to their energy efficiency they'll take in extra warmth, rather than money-saving. This will make it very unlikely that they'll be able to pay back the loan. 25 million homes have to be zero-carbon by 2050, and we're going at a rate of 2,000 (or 3,000!) every four years. I can't even be arsed to work out how long that would take, for rhetorical purposes. Too long. The eco-insulation is often done by cowboys, and leaves people with a huge black mould problem that they didn't have before. The market – I hate to bore on – is good at some things, but it is no good at delivering government policy.

Ed Matthew said that the ECO isn't enough; he wants money from the infrastructure budget, which is massive. He wants £5 billion over the life of the next parliament to spend on retro-fitting, and £10 billion to spend on new housing stock. It sounds like a lot, except that at the moment more than that has been earmarked for roads. Not potholes, not maintenance, not road safety or cycle paths or lollipop ladies: we have £16 billion to spend on new roads. We are teetering on the edge of a housing crisis, heading for an environmental disaster on which the whole world is agreed: and we spend our money on roads.

Houses are infrastructure; shelter in the first instance; energy-savers if they're built correctly, energy-producers if they're built better. These are the cornerstones of a liveable society, and if we're going to do better – make everything safer, cleaner, cheaper, less polluting, less harmful – then houses and the way we heat them are going to represent a huge amount of that, probably more than half. Houses are so much more important than how directly you can drive from one place to another. It baffles belief what our current priorities look like.

The non-eco house

It's time to consider what, exactly, is going on here: why a political class that is atrophied by cost-cutting can still find huge sums to do damaging, pointless things; why it is that they say they understand the housing crisis, or the challenge of climate change, and yet do the precise opposite to what is required. I am not a born conspiracy theorist, and I think there's a fair amount of regular human frailty, a lack of imagination – the inability to conceive of moving money from one place to another – coupled with a degree of cowardice.

When decisions are made that suit nobody that

you can imagine, you can be sure nevertheless that they suit somebody. That person, or rather that company, will have paid a PR person to change the narrative[15] (it's not money that could be used for housing, it's investment to promote economic growth); a different PR person, probably, to sort the media; another one again to have the Westminster launch of the think-tank report,[16] advocating something that is probably a little bit more radical than the key players require (this punches out some space and makes the end-suggestion sound reasonable). Before long, broad-based pro-business organisations like the CBI and the London Chamber of Commerce come to accept pro-road activism as part of the pro-business package. Rogue peers will start to come out with 'bold' ideas that reinforce that growth narrative – Lord Wolfson, for instance, has started to push for a motorway between Oxford and Cambridge. He called it the 'Brain Belt', which is ironic, considering what a stupid idea it is. It's actually not good for business to prioritise transport over living standards. Nobody benefits from wasted energy, or a population struggling to afford their basic housing and energy costs. But, in an adversarial political system, it is often more efficient to identify the people who are most similar to you and agree with them, rather than consider the issue in any detail.

The thing about lobbyists is not that they're evil, or even that they are that rich –they may be rich, and they may dangle lucrative future jobs in front of

MPs in return for cooperation, but I don't believe anybody's being bribed with brown envelopes wedged with cash. Lobbyists have one thing over the rest of us that money can't buy: they know what they want. They never give off a feeling of hopelessness, or a sense that what they want is too large, or too nebulous, or too unrealistic. They simply know what they want, and then they say it. We really need to be more like them. We want energy-neutral homes. I'm not anti-road; when money is no object and cars are 45 per cent lighter, better access to Stevenage will be no more than the nation deserves. But right now we need plentiful, carbon-neutral places to live in. Just ask for it. Keep on asking. It's our money. A lot of it is also our land.

In spring of 2014 the New Economics Foundation (NEF), a left-wing think-tank, started campaigning to close London City Airport. I didn't previously have anything against this little airport, but the case is robust: it's only useful to those in the banking sector, of whom the top tier get helicopters from the tops of their offices anyway. So we're keeping a large chunk of London,[17] with a two-kilometre crash zone, clear of useful development in order that 2.4 per cent of total London passenger demand can get to Frankfurt slightly faster than if they had to get the Tube to Heathrow. The land is still leased from the local authority, so could be brought back into public ownership with a compulsory purchase order.

Homelessness took a radical turn in this borough – Newham – at around the same time, when some evicted young mothers started the group Focus E15 (they'd been offered accommodation 100 miles away; 'They still want us to commute in and service them,' one of them, Jasmine Stone, said. 'But from how far?'). Why would any civilised society put up with massive swathes of prime real estate given over to the convenience of middle-ranking employees of the city's most destructive industry (see Finance), while the people doing normal jobs were blithely priced out, like relics? What rational city would ever do that?

Behind the scenes, NEF guessed that it couldn't be long before Boris Johnson came up with the same idea. Crossrail will be ready in five years, and the journeys across London will render the time advantage of City Airport negligible. It might even close itself down. In the hands of the Conservative mayor, however, you can be reasonably sure that the land would not be bought back by compulsory purchase order, but rather would go straight to developers, to build flats for investors in Dubai, who don't need to worry about how shonky or energy-inefficient they are, because they don't intend to live in them. This would do nothing for the people who grew up in Newham and can no longer afford to live there. As important as knowing what you want, and asking for it, is knowing what you want and asking for it first.

The plan on the table wasn't just to close the airport and buy back the land. The Green Cities Foundation interjected here with a proposal for four giant blocks, 2,500 units in each, a total of 10,000 homes. I often try to draw them, to get people to share my enthusiasm; it always looks as if I've drawn four giant penises and then, depending on the company, the conversation either comes to a sudden halt or some wise-arse decorates them with testicles and hair. Anyway, imagine four things that shape: they have solar bricks at the top and each has a different biosphere, so it can grow different food. The windows are made of solar glass, which, incidentally, had only just been invented at the point of this design (the prototypes get better all the time). Transparent solar panels might be the third point on the triangle for this energy form, along with the price reduction and potential for storage. If each of your windows could generate power without your even noticing, really, why wouldn't you?

Salad grows down the walls of the giant pods, and there is some deal with fish droppings that I didn't really commit myself to understanding. When Ashley Dobbs, the founder of Green Cities, said the buildings would be food-neutral, I didn't get the impression he was including any meat. But shops will still exist, after this revolution of sunshine and lettuce. What initially drew my eye was a giant blue pipe winding around each structure, like a water-slide. It was just an idea of the architect's; maybe people could cycle down giant pipes and get their bikes back up using a pulley system. It struck me for the first time how sought-after these buildings would be, across every income bracket.

Our dishevelled political culture is obsessed with trilemmas – you can have it cheap, you can have it de-carbonised or you can have it secure. You can build it for 'keyworkers' (poor people) or for 'young professionals' (42-year-olds) or for 'investors' (foreigners). People with vision recognise that you don't have to choose. You can build homes that everybody wants to live in, whether they're rich or poor. You can sell them to people who can afford them, or you can rent them affordably to people who can't. Considering that you'd otherwise be paying Housing Benefit to some private landlord, you cannot, as a local authority, lose. This plan was costed at £1 billion. There is scope for crowdfunding a project like this, so long as the council had the vision to buy back the land and the innovation to consider a partnership with a million people who had £100 each, rather than a PFI deal with two or three giant investors, in which it would inevitably come off worse (see Privatisation). Before any of that can happen, the demand has to be there, clear and constant.

Amory Lovins, Bruce Davis, Ed Matthew, Ashley Dobbs, Juliet Davenport, Jasmine Stone: they are not famous and probably never will be. Lovins, in fact, is quite famous in green circles, and has an ex-wife called Hunter who has a proper cult following. Generally, though, nobody calls them 'uber', and they're not mad genii. They are just people trying to find a workaround for a stuck politics. Every hurdle thrown up has somebody, somewhere, trying to figure out a way round it. It might be a Green or an inventor or an entrepreneur or an activist; it might be a member of a local political party; or it might be someone who has utterly had it with conventional politics, but hasn't given up on society. Human creativity is the one limitless resource that's going to save our bacon, here. Cheaper than wind, less of a footprint than solar, genuinely inexhaustible – when you see it, line up behind it. It can't do this without us.

We'll always have Paris (until December 2015)

> This deal at Copenhagen represents the lowest level of ambition you can imagine. It's nothing short of climate change scepticism in action. It locks countries into a cycle of poverty forever.
>
> Lumumba Di-Aping, chief negotiator for the
> G77 group of 130 developing countries,
> Copenhagen, 2009

There is a joke made by climate-science campaigners, they all do it: 'I'm actually 24,' a grizzly old grey-haired bear from Greenpeace or the IPCC will say, 'but I was in Copenhagen, and this is how I came out.'

192 nations went into the Copenhagen negotiations, hoping for a giant leap forward: developing nations in particular wanted at least to discuss how the planet might be kept to 1.5 degrees of warming,

rather than two degrees. We think of two degrees as a safe upper limit, but in fact it will still lead to some tragic loss of landscape and habitat, food shortages, water-wars and natural disasters. We've already locked in 0.8 degrees of warming. It seemed in 2009 as though a lower limit might be achievable, with the level of global consensus there was at that time. Copenhagen put paid to that.[18]

However, the main reason it was considered a failure is that it delivered no international deal at all. There was a last-minute agreement stitched together between the United States and the BASIC countries: Brazil, South Africa, India and China. Devastatingly, what you're looking at is clique behaviour – a teenager having a sleepover could have told you that, if the five cool countries go off and do their own thing, everyone else is going to be left with a really unpleasant taste in their mouths, and so it transpired.

People often blame underlying political conditions. The US President has enormous power, but no flexibility; if he budges at all, the Senate can veto it. This is a huge barrier, since a nation so powerful cannot help but set a benchmark for compromise and manoeuvre. If the US arrives with the undertaking not to compromise on anything or manoeuvre anywhere, everyone else feels like they're being taken for a mug. China, meanwhile, went into the deal suspicious of EU targets for global emission, believing – you could argue, fairly – that their growth was being stifled to make up for greenhouse-gas build-up that they'd had nothing to do with. 'Grow first, clean up later' was their motto, as it had been every other nation's when it was in the middle of an industrial revolution.

Directly after the accord in which nothing real was agreed, people scratched around for reasons and found them everywhere. The news cycle, the pressure groups, the default EU position never to go against America unless something extraordinary happened, like World War Three: all of these, and many other factors besides, were held up as plausible reasons for the hopeless missing of pitiful targets.

Nearly a year later, in November 2010, WikiLeaks began the great wave of leaked international diplomatic cables.[19] While there was a lot of fun in the mix (the Chinese Ambassador called the late Kim Jong-Il a 'flabby old chap', and Hillary Clinton wondered whether Argentina's president was taking anti-anxiety medication), arguably the most important revelation was that America and China, the world's largest polluters, had already stitched up a deal before they even got to Copenhagen.[20] The Kyoto agreement had bound all developed nations to greenhouse gas-reduction, while leaving developing nations to non-binding targets. America never ratified that agreement, so it effectively cast itself as a developing nation. That was never going to work for Copenhagen; so the US, and China, were either going to have to accept binding carbon limits or find some way to kibosh anything binding anyone. It is pretty plain that they decided on the latter. You can see why people emerged crying from these talks. It wasn't just sleep deprivation.

But – and this is a gigantic but – that does not mean the talks had no positive impact. Two degrees of warming was the first limit the world had ever convened upon: every time any international discussion about climate change occurs, this is what they work towards. If you think it's lame, imagine where they'd be without it.

China came out looking like the bad guy, which – coupled with its suffocating Beijing fog of 2013, together with a European market demand – set it on the path to be the renewables giant of the world. It achieved this in roughly five minutes, while Germany was still putting its pants on. By 2020 China is likely to be getting one-fifth of its usage from renewables. By 2015 it wants 100 gigawatts of wind capacity and 35 gigawatts of solar, to which end it spent $67 billion in 2012 alone.

Barack Obama, meanwhile, launched the Climate Action Plan, which is the most significant shift in the priority of environmentalism that any US president has ever made.[21] It's extremely intelligently framed, focusing on changes to fossil-fuel power-stations, their efficiency and emissions allowances. Even if a Republican president comes in and overturns the whole thing, these adaptations will be more expensive to undo than to maintain. Another of the articles is a commitment to 100 megawatts of renewable provision on federally assisted housing, coupled with energy efficiency – which is to say, treating housing as energy infrastructure, exactly what we should be doing in Britain.

Our Climate Change Act of 2008 was drafted in the shadow of Copenhagen – as astonishing as it sounds now, the person who shamed Gordon Brown into an 80 per cent emissions-reduction target by 2050 (Brown wanted 50 per cent) was David Cameron. What happened to this man, that he's gone from nothing less than a crusader to the kind of person who makes lukewarm promises to build cruddy housing that leaks energy? If you read him in a novel, you wouldn't believe him.

The Act was extremely influential in this country; yes, there are politicians now who want to scrap it, but it would take a brain-freeze of some magnitude to persuade the body of them – after the hottest six months the earth has experienced since records began in 1880[22] – to follow. Yes, it also looks like we might miss the carbon budget after this one (they're divided into four-year targets, with a mean taken over the four years); then it risks becoming like the Child Poverty Act, a poignant reminder of a time when politics had a stated intention of doing a pro-social thing, at least here and there. But we will hit the carbon budget of 2013–17, which is because of the Act, which is because of Copenhagen, and this is what Copenhagen did: it taught the globe how to negotiate with itself.

What it taught was that agreeing a target, then sitting down to see who could be fingered to deliver on it, doesn't work. Nations don't all huddle together and come up with a plan to solve the world's energy problems. Nations aren't up to it: they just don't have the humility and the trust. But what they can do is decide in advance what they're prepared to bring to the table, and that can be influenced (also in advance) by their perception of how they're viewed on the world stage (this is a particular deal for America and China), by the politics and voters of their own countries, by charities and scientists, by sustained argument. Having established this, participating nations are now asked to frame what they're prepared to offer well in advance of December (by March 2015) and for that to be transparent.

This is the time when organised public opinion can move the parameters of what's possible. This is when it will pay to be as consistent as a lobbyist, as noisy as a climate-change denier. I don't want to say this will be the political fight of our lives – there'll be another treaty five years on from this one. Nothing is ever final in international politics, or any other kind. Yet if we know one thing, it's that every year counts. If we know one other thing, it's that we are the first generation to understand how important this is, and the last that can do something about it. I know, I know; I think I lifted that (if not verbatim, then certainly in spirit) straight from Gordon Brown, just before the Denmark debacle. It could disappoint, Paris; and the more thought you give it beforehand, the more horribly disappointing it could be. But imagine if it didn't disappoint, and imagine if that was partly because of you.

What next, where now?

This is the part where I'm supposed to start with the practical suggestions: lobby for this; argue for that; campaign for some other thing; boycott them; give money to this charity; if you run out of road, check what they do in Denmark and fight for that. The very bit that's meant to brim with optimism and possibility is the bit that depresses the hell out of me.

Imagine I suggested something like a Basic Citizen's Income (and I believe in this, by the way): every citizen receives an unconditional income, from the state, that affords a decent, dignified, fulfilling life. People who didn't need it would have it taxed back from the rest of their income. Benefits, pensions, maternity leave, student maintenance loans, all these labyrinthine structures we put in place to stop each other starving would be rendered obsolete. Food banks would be instantly unnecessary. This, finally, would be a meaningful adaptation to the 'flexibility' that the modern business claims to need: as well as an upward pressure on wages, it would create a workforce that could weather the new insecurity with some power of its own. There would be no stigma, no high marginal tax rates. It would encourage risk, innovation, entrepreneurship. Classic self-interest arguments insist that this would discourage paid work and drag the nation back into the Dark Ages: like all self-interest arguments, this is only ever shown in a computer model based on the self-interested individual, and is never demonstrated in real life. One study in Manitoba, Canada, showed that the only people whose working hours decreased when an unconditional basic income was paid were new mothers and teenagers, who spent, respectively, a bit more time with tiny babies and on school work. Come on - we can manage that, right? We haven't gone so nuts with market wisdom that we can't conceive of those activities as having a value to the nation, even if one couldn't immediately count it.

You will rarely see 'unconditional basic income' mentioned without it being prefixed with the word 'radical'. The minute anybody calls anything radical, the conversation seizes up. People start imagining a dystopian future, where your life savings can be appropriated by the state, and meat has been replaced by synthesised protein. The genius of the right is that when they have a radical idea, they never say it – they just do it. 'Let us carefully observe those good qualities wherein our enemies excel us,' wrote Plutarch. 'Endeavour to excel them, by avoiding what is faulty, and imitating what is excellent.' The (hopefully, soon, or even already, ex-) Chancellor George Osborne is particularly good at presenting ideas that will change society forever as just more unavoidable business-as-usual. His vision for the future of Britain, outlined in the Autumn Statement of 2014, was one in which the state was shrunk to the size it had been in the 1930s and we could no longer afford fundamental things, like universal access to justice. When challenged on his radicalism, he called his critics 'hyperbolic'. It wasn't because he was dishonest: it was because, when you believe what he believes, his policies are merely common sense. Carefully observe him, if you can bear to. See how his inalienable truths turn radical ideas into obvious solutions. We have truths of our own.

In contrast to the Basic Citizen's Income, the living wage is an idea that mainstream politics is pretty comfortable with; apart from some dark mutterings about the threat of inflation, there is broad agreement that businesses would do well to pay people enough. However, this is pitifully cap-in-hand, a begging gesture to employers, made on the understanding that they hold all the cards. All it does is theoretically raise people to a level where they can subsist (and, without simultaneous action on housing costs, it still leaves the low-paid chronically vulnerable). It does not address key questions: why are jobs that require quite high skills now characterised as low-skilled? Where does it end? If a court interpreter is suddenly a minimum-wage job today, does that mean a criminal barrister will be on the minimum wage tomorrow? Introducing a new floor-price to a human being is not going to address this steady erosion; it is just too feeble.

You could have exactly the same conversation about housing: the radical solution is a mass programme of building by the state, to deal with the fact that the free market has failed. It has failed to produce decent living space for people who work like dogs and expect less and less, and it has failed to answer any of the environmental questions thrown up by the energy wasted by our housing stock. These failures are monumental. So, sure, the solutions have to be pretty monumental, too, and immediately we're into 'radical' territory.

Nothing ever looks realistic to the status quo, except more of the status quo: ideas that will be embraced by the political mainstream will only ever be superficially better than the ideas to which they already adhere. So if your mainstream is in a dark place – unimaginative, unambitious, captured by corporate interests, engaged in a fire-sale of state assets – the ideas it will allow in are going to be pretty sepulchral as well.

The Brazilian philosopher Roberto Mangabeira Unger did a lecture tour in London in 2013, in which he said: 'We have lost faith in any of the large available understandings of how structural change takes place in history, and as a result, we fall back on a bastardised conception of political realism, namely that a proposal is realistic to the extent that it approaches what already exists. This false view then aggravates [our] paralysis.' What hit me then was the word 'realistic' – it's the thing people say when they don't want change. It's the thing No-campaigners said to Yes-ers in the Scottish referendum. 'You are not being realistic.' 'It's a nice thought, but not realistic.' Pure political atrophy, in the circularity of that entitlement – 'Unfortunately, your hope for a better future turns out to be unrealistic.' 'Who decides what's realistic?' 'Me, because I'm in charge.' 'Why are you in charge?' 'Because I'm so realistic.'

Meaningful, hopeful change is not going to start with a shopping list of policy suggestions: it will start when we create a new normal.

There is no real disagreement that wages have stagnated and are too low. But there is a political fatalism that this is the modern way – that through some combination (which nobody ever clarifies) of China and computers, human effort simply isn't worth what it once was. This is absolute rubbish; wages are low because profit is high. Rather than ask what we can do to supplement low wages, ask why profit has to be so high. There is no way to run a successful economy when the bottom 80 per cent of it doesn't have any disposable income. Even if you're prepared to cope with people going hungry in the sixth-largest economy in the world, even if you're prepared for the private debt-bubble that plays into the hands of a rapacious financial sector, you are still left with the existential question: what's the point of causing, and then trying to solve, all these problems for ourselves, just to stimulate profit? What earthly reason is there for the whole nation to be straining every sinew for shareholder maximisation? What's the point of a system in which the class contributing the least effort gains the greatest reward?

The housing conversation, in conventional debate, is bizarre: it is broadly agreed that British people want to possess their own house. Then there is this embarrassing silence, while nobody admits that, for most people – most of our children – this will never happen if the system proceeds along its current lines. We will talk quite freely about landlords behaving in unfair ways (revenge evictions, unwarranted rent increases) but we will never have the conversation underneath that, where we admit that this is what a rentier economy looks like: one side has all the power, and the other side has none. We will talk about how it's a bad thing for children to grow up with mould on the walls and get respiratory disease, but we will not articulate what minimum standards should look like, for the people at the bottom of the pay-spine. The status quo relies upon these silences. If you accept that homelessness is wrong; if you concede that slums are wrong; if you admit that nobody deserves to live in squalor, whether that's in a bed-and-breakfast or a rotting shed, then you have to spell out the principle underneath that. Housing is a basic necessity and a human right. Our responsibility to one another – to extinguish squalor for this generation and the next – has not abated since William Beveridge first called it evil in 1942. Nothing's changed; your right to live in a place that doesn't make you ill remains more important than someone else's right to make a profit from your necessity.

In the House of Commons there's a committee room that for some reason seems to be earmarked for lefty meetings, so you find yourself in there a lot, if you believe in abortion and think politics is screwed. At the front is a painting called 'King Alfred Inciting the Saxons to Repel the Danes', and some wiseacre always (sometimes) says, 'If only he had failed. We might have the welfare state that we deserve.' And at first I thought it was funny because of its acknowledgement that we were all quite bored and had been studying the painting for 40 minutes (meetings are too long); then I finally realised: it was funny because we can never be the Danes, not unless we go back in time to AD876 and become them from the inside out. During the Scottish referendum elections the (I'm just going to go ahead and call him 'thinker') thinker Gerry Hassan repeatedly said that if we vote Yes, we don't just skip off and become Scandinavia. I thought at the time he meant that hard work and dirty fights await; it doesn't just happen. Only from a distance can I see what he was actually talking about: you become the social state that you all believe in. The Scandinavian welfare model – in which everyone has a right to social security, and they have invented the word 'flexicurity' – was not handed down from above, it came from the bloodstream. If we tried to copy their policies, it would be like trying to copy a cool person's hair.

I have a lot of arguments about charity, along the lines of 'Why don't you give everything away, if you care so much about society?' I waste a lot of time arguing the toss about this, but it's true. The easiest way to make these arguments is to be Jesus; to be infinitely generous; to care about all humanity an equal amount. I am not like this. I care more about my children than I do about yours, for instance. I don't even want the total sharing of all things, and I have no way of demonstrating my infinite generosity (because it is not infinite). Waiting for a saint appeals to a kind of left-wing purism, which has a lot in common with eco-purism (do nothing, unless you can do everything), but it's suffocating, and defeatist, and a waste of democracy: we are capable, with hearts that are only moderately pure, of building a system that works in a broadly fair way.

When the Deputy Prime Minister Nick Clegg, basically as a popularity exercise, secured free school meals for children in years Reception to Three, I got a windfall benefit of £800 a year. The lowest-paid equivalent family (that is, two working parents, two kids of five and seven) has lost £600 a year through a combination of changes to Child Benefit and Working Families Tax Credit (they already got free school meals). Their £600 has, apparently, gone straight to me. It makes me angry, in an urgent, denaturing way, like I've drunk five pints of Stella on an empty stomach. I understand the case for universal benefits – they are easier to administer, they end stigma – but in a policy environment of outrageous meanness, to take from the poorest and give to the rich. It's just a scummy way to run society: grind the poor to the very dust of their income, give money away as though it's suddenly of no issue to people who don't need it, then turn around – so innocent! – and say, 'I'm sorry, I didn't realise you didn't need it! Why don't you give it away then?' It's a straight misunderstanding. It has misunderstood the principles of social security. Often when you hear a story and it's so unjust that you feel yourself propelled to act, and you have spare money, or spare capacity so that you could raise money, you want to do that. That's fine, we can all do that as well: but charity doesn't build a good society. Kindness is no substitute for justice.

Consumer boycotts, likewise, offer a certain kind of relief; that spurt of anger – how is society to function, if companies have no pride in being part of it? – followed by revenge (well, see how Amazon like it, when I buy all my Christmas presents at Argos! Whose tax affairs, incidentally, I have not scrutinised). Individual acts will always be inconsequential. Realising my boycott had no consequence and that Starbucks still seems to be doing fine, I always feel demoralised, and also remember how much I used to like Starbucks. So, in the event, my individual act did have a consequence: it sucked away my optimism and made the way things are seem like the way things always have to be.

There is no point in acting alone: it isn't a useful complement to acting together – it is the diametric opposite. The solid, practical thing to do today is not Click on a Link to Complain about a Thing. It is not Invite Your Friends to Support a Policy. It is not Dig Deep into Your Pockets for a Cause. You need to participate, to be among people who believe what you believe. If you want to save the NHS, join the National Health Action Party. If you want to save the world, join the Green Party or Greenpeace, or join a transition network, or a renewables co-op, Brixton Energy or Community Energy Brum. If you want to lobby government, join Friends of the Earth. If you want to conserve, join the Wildlife Trusts. If you're worried about agriculture and business, join the Food Assembly. I once met someone with a plan to make Birmingham completely self-sustaining, in its food production, by 2030; she was an oncologist in her normal life and just did it as a hobby. She had everything figured out, apart from avocados. But that was in 2009, so she has probably made some major leaps with solar greenhouses by now (doubt-less in conjunction with her local renewables co-op).

If you care about equality, join the local Equality Trust; or, if there isn't one, start one. If you care about high finance, financialisation and the dubious policy of leaving money creation in the hands of psychopaths, join Positive Money. I couldn't believe it when I heard they had local branches, who meet on a regular basis and discuss what might be better ways of creating money as a pro-social instrument. How absurdly hopeful, to think that you and some people who live near you can sort out such a thing. But if not you, then who?

If you care about PFI, join People Versus PFI. If you care in a generalised way about money being sucked upwards at the expense of society, join the People's Assembly. If you care about politics, equality and the environment, join Compass. (It doesn't have to be Compass – that's just the one I happen to be in. It could be the New Economics Foundation.) If you care about housing, join Generation Rent or a local group, New Era 4 All or Focus E15 (those are local to me). If you care about tax evasion, join UK Uncut. If you care about everything, join Campaign Lab. If you care about corporate corruption, join the Modern Corporation Project. If you care about education, become a school governor. Join the Anti Academies Alliance. There's a view that true activists don't join groups, they just do it – anti-frackers, migrant-rights activists, road protestors. I've never stopped a road or climbed a tree, but I think the principles are the same. However they act, they don't act alone, and they don't delegate. 'There goes more to it than bidding it be done,' as an advisor said to Charles I, sometime before the King commenced fighting his own people and had his head cut off.

There is no point in acting alone, but to speak to one person who shares your values is like doing a haka. The world cracks open and victory becomes inevitable. I'm serious. Try it.

As I finish this, we're marching into an election in which established, 'normal' opinion runs on a spectrum from mediocre to fascist. I never thought we would be arguing about whether the children of migrants were really British, or whether disabled people really deserved support, yet here we are. We've got to the point where we cheer anyone who defends social security and doesn't blame foreigners (for very much), even if their next suggestion is about surrendering to the markets and managed decline. I'm not going to tell you how to vote: you know what you're going to do and probably feel as sullied by it as I do. But the truly wrong-headed, deflating thing is not the insufficiency of the mainstream; it's the idea of waiting for mainstream politicians to give us the answers. I think a lot of them are probably okay people, but if there's one thing my entire life has shown me, it's that leadership will not come from the centre. Politicians cannot make the weather. They can cope with the weather by means ranging from good to terrible. But only we can make the weather. Whatever it is we want, we can get: but we have to get it together.

NOTES

WHO AM I, TO THINK THINGS LIKE THIS?

1 www.tuc.org.uk/economic-issues/labour-market-and-economic-reports/only-one-every-forty-net-jobs-recession-full-time

2 Danny Dorling, *All That is Solid*, Penguin, 2014

3 Niall Cooper, Sarah Purcell, Ruth Jackson, *Below the Breadline: The Relentless Rise of Food Poverty in Britain*, Oxfam, 2014

4 www.prnewswire.co.uk/news-releases/experts-urge-parents-to-make-every-day-a-vitamin-d-day-as-uk-winter-arrives-279844662.html

DOES POVERTY STILL EXIST?

1 Keith Joseph, *Stranded on the Middle Ground*, Centre for Policy Studies, 1976

2   Michael Orton, *Something's Not Right*, Compass, 2015

3   High Pay Centre, *What Would the Neighbours Say?*, 2014

4   www.mirror.co.uk/news/uk-news/britain-largest-drop-wages-eu-4177421

5   Paul Gregg, Stephen Machin and Mariña Fernández-Salgado, *The Squeeze on Real Wages: and What It Might Take to End It*, National Institute Economic Review, February 2014

6   IFS, *Living Standards, Poverty and Inequality*, 2014

7   www.barnardos.org.uk/news/Poor_families_wave_goodbye_to_Bank_Holiday_beach_trip/latest-news.htm?ref=98360

8   Niall Cooper, Sarah Purcell, Ruth Jackson, *Below the Breadline: the Relentless Rise of Food Poverty in Britain*, Oxfam, June 2014

9   Stewart Lansley, *Inequality, the Crash and the Ongoing Crisis,* The Political Quarterly, October to December 2012

10 Ludwig Von Mises, *Inequality of Wealth and Incomes*, The Freeman, 1955

11 Magdalena Bernaciak, Rebecca Gumbrell-McCormick, Richard Hyman, *Trade Unions in Europe*, Friedrich Ebert Stiftung, 2014

12 Richard Wilkison and Kate Pickett, *The Importance of the Labour Movement in Tackling Inequality*, CLASS, 2014

13 Linda Tirado, *Hand to Mouth*, Virago, 2014

14 Office for National Statistics, *Analysis of Employee Contracts that do not Guarantee a Minimum Number of Hours*, 30 April 2014

15 ONS Labour Market Statistics, *Statistical Bulletin*, November 2014

16 www.dailymail.co.uk/news/article-2381787/ Buckingham-Palace-uses-controversial-zero-hours-contracts-summer-staff-employment-costs-down.html; www.ft.com/cms/s/0/ff75254e-9f89-11e2-b4b6-00144feabdc0.html#axzz3OrYenZq2

17 www.nytimes.com/2014/10/17/business/walmart-workers-seek-wage-bump.html

18 www.britannica.com/EBchecked/topic/559184/ Speenhamland-system

19 Matthew Whittaker, *Closer to the Edge*, Resolution Foundation, July 2013

20 Cuts in Social Care, *Unison Local Government Report*, February 2011

21 Ibid.

22 Gordon Brown's Budget Speech in Full, 2006 www.theguardian.com/uk/2006/mar/22/budget2006.budget

23 The 50th centile is the number below which fifty per cent of the population falls. It's also called the median

24 Equality Trust Wealth Tracker, May 2014: 'In the

last year the 100 richest people in Britain saw their wealth increase by £40.1 billion to a colossal £297.133 billion'

25 www.theguardian.com/politics/2014/nov/12/ pricewaterhousecoopers-tax-structures-politics-influence

26 www.unitetheunion.org/growing-our-union/ communitymembership/

HAS THE NHS HAD ITS DAY?

1 www.britishfuture.org/wp-content/ uploads/2013/01/State-of-the-Nation-2013.pdf

2 Sir William Beveridge, 'Social Insurance and Allied Services', HMSO, 1942

3 Henry Willink, *A National Health Service*, HMSO, 1944

4 HC Debate, – 1st May 1946, vol 422 cc159-313

5 Norman Fowler, *Minister's Decide: A Memoir of the Thatcher Years*, Chapman's, 1991

6 Conclusions of a Meeting of the Cabinet held at 10 Downing Street on Thursday 9 September 1982 at 10.30 am: 'Much could be done to reduce the size of the public sector by privatisation in areas such as health care, education and many local authority functions.'

7 Nicholas Mays, Anna Dixon, Lorelei Jones, *Understanding New Labour's Market Reforms of the English NHS*, The King's Fund, 2011

8   www.rcgp.org.uk/news/2014/february/34m-
    patients-will-fail-to-get-appointment-with-a-gp-
    in-2014.aspx

9   www.nhsforsale.info/uploads/images/contract%20
    alert%20report%20Apr-Apr%20final%20(1).pdf

10 www.theguardian.com/society/2014/nov/19/
    private-firms-nhs-contracts-circle-healthcare-
    bupa-virgin-care-care-uk

11 www.unitetheunion.org/news/tories-in-15-billion-
    nhs-sell-off-scandal/

12 socialinvestigations.blogspot.co.uk/2014/03/
    compilation-of-parliamentary-financial.html

13 Karen Davis, Kristof Stremikis, David Squires,
    Cathy Schoen, *Mirror Mirror On the Wall*, The
    Commonwealth Fund, 2014

14 www.healthdata.org/sites/default/files/files/
    country_profiles/GBD/ihme_gbd_country_report_
    united_kingdom.pdf

15 www.plosmedicine.org/article/info:doi/10.1371/
    journal.pmed.0050066

16 www.forbes.com/sites/toddhixon/2012/02/21/
    health-care-costs-the-art-of-the-practical/

17 James G Kahn et al, *The Cost of Health Insurance
    Administration in California: Estimates for Insurers,
    Physicians and Hospitals*, Health Affairs, 2005

18 www.economist.com/news/united-states/
    21603078-why-thieves-love-americas-health-care-
    system-272-billion-swindle

19   www.nybooks.com/blogs/nyrblog/2013/apr/02/
     new-american-sadism/

20   www.time.com/198/bitter-pill-why-medical-bills-
     are-killing-us/

21   Elizabeth Warren, Teresa Sullivan, Melissa Jacoby,
     Medical problems and Bankruptcy Filings,
     Norton's Bankruptcy Adviser, May 2000

22   www.reuters.com/article/2009/06/04/us-
     healthcare-bankruptcy-idUSTRE5530Y020090604

23   Nicholas Mays, Anna Dixon, Lorelei Jones, *Under-
     standing New Labour's Market Reforms of the
     English NHS*, King's Fund

24   Zack Cooper et al, *Does Hospital Competition Save
     Lives?* http://www.lse.ac.uk/LSEHealthAndSocial
     Care/pdf/Workingpapers/WP16.pdf

25   You can read the full version, Allyson Pollock's
     critique and Zack Cooper's response, here: the
     Lancet, issue 9809, 2011, volume 378

26   www.telegraph.co.uk/health/health
     news/10939063/Third-baby-death-linked-to-
     contaminated-hospital-drip.html

27   www.slideshare.net/bentoth/the-jubilee-line-of-
     health-inequality

28   www.dannydorling.org/wp-content/files/
     dannydorling_publication_id3089.pdf

HAVE YOU EVER WONDERED WHY YOU CAN'T AFFORD A HOUSE?

1   illustreets.co.uk/blog/maps-and-apps/london-house-prices-evolution-over-13-years/

2   Danny Dorling, *All That is Solid*, Penguin, 2014

3   www.oecd.org/eco/outlook/focusonhouseprices.htm

4   www.telegraph.co.uk/finance/newsbysector/constructionandproperty/11060993/Mapped-where-your-money-goes-furthest-in-Britains-housing-market.html

5   www.bbc.co.uk/news/business-28648704

6   www.dailymail.co.uk/news/article-2071421/Saving-deposit-home-31-years-1993-took-eight.html

7   www.theguardian.com/business/2013/jun/04/george-osborne-help-to-buy-moronic

8   www.ons.gov.uk/ons/rel/mro/news-release/non-financial-balance-sheets-2011/uk-worth-7-3-trillion.html

9   James Meek, *Private Island, Why Britain Now Belongs to Someone Else*, Verso, 2014

10 House of Commons Library, 'Extending home ownership – Government initiatives', 8 April 2014

11 www.ft.com/cms/s/0/605cdea2-fb69-11e2-a641-00144feabdc0.html?siteedition=uk#axzz2bSxxb2J6

12 www.gov.uk/government/uploads/system/uploads/

attachment_data/file/335751/EHS_Households_
Report_2012-13.pdf

13   england.shelter.org.uk/get_advice/your_housing_
     situation/private_renting

14   www.theguardian.com/money/2010/jun/10/
     landlord-regulation-proposals-scrapped

15   www.wriglesworth.com/news/25-wriglesworth-
     news/314-buy-to-let-reaches-18-years-and-comes-
     of-age?Itemid=107

16   www.lslps.co.uk/documents/buy_to_let_index_
     jul13.pdf

17   www.gov.uk/government/uploads/system/uploads/
     attachment_data/file/284648/English_Housing_
     Survey_Headline_Report_2012-13.pdf

18   Shelter, Policy Library, Social Housing 2009

19   A Freedom of Information request by the Labour
     party showed that 96% of people affected by the
     tax had nowhere smaller to move to: www.labour.
     org.uk/96041-into-3688-wont-go

20   www.independent.co.uk/life-style/health-and-
     families/health-news/the-bedroom-tax-on-
     bereavement-grieving-families-to-face-spareroom-
     benefit-cut-within-three-months-9047658.html

21   www.insidehousing.co.uk/regulation/bedroom-
     tax/ids-bedroom-tax-has-saved-taxpayer-
     830m/7007273.article?adfesuccess=1

22   www.riverside.org.uk/pdf/Testing%20DWP%20
     Assessment%20of%20Impact%20of%20SRS%20

Size%20Criterion%20on%20HB%20Costs%20
University%20of%20York.pdf

23 ONS, *Young Adults Living With Parents*, 2013

24 Andy Hull and Graeme Cook, IPPR, 2012

25 Danny Dorling, *All That is Solid*

26 sw.stat-xplore.dwp.gov.uk/webapi/jsf/
dataCatalogueExplorer.xhtml

27 Laura Gardiner, *Housing Pinched: Understanding
Which Households Spend the Most on Housing*,
Resolution Foundation, August 2014

28 David Clapham et al, *Housing Options and
Solutions for Young People in 2020*, Joseph
Rowntree Foundation, 2012

29 www.kpmg.com/uk/en/issuesandinsights/
articlespublications/pages/building-the-homes-
we-need–programme-2015.aspx

ARE TAXES FOR THE LITTLE PEOPLE?

1 I actually have nothing against Lakeland as a shop.
Only the catalogue

2 When you make a massive cock-up like this, they
put an investigation team on you. Which in practice,
means a lady from Merthyr Tydfil ringing you up
and going 'Can you tell me whether you did this
deliberately or by accident?' And you go, 'By accident,
by accident!' And she goes, 'I'm satisfied that you did
it by accident.' Which I did find kind of amusing, even
though, as I say, it really was an accident

3   In fairness, this wasn't because we were all stupid. Wages didn't begin to stagnate until 2003 in the UK

4   David Byrne and Sally Ruane, *The UK Tax Burden: Can Labour Be Called the Party of Fairness?* 2008

5   Simon Duffy, *A Fair Income: Tax Benefit Reform in an Era of Personalisation*, 2011

6   Richard Murphy, *Closing the European Tax Gap*

7   My working definition of rich is the top 1%, which is households on more than £368k pa. Conservatives prefer the top 10%, because it makes inequality look less bad. But the top 1% is so much richer than even the one per cent below them that they are, now, the story of wealth. And how that situation came about would bear some analysis, but not now, and not by me.

Obviously, if I went with the top 10% I would have to call them 'us' not 'them', since I earn £120,000 a year. But that would be fine; this isn't intended as an attack on the characters of rich people, based on my fake membership of a non-existent 'middle-class' that is bang in the middle of the income curve. Bad situations come about when the power balance is messed up, not because some classes are inherently evil

8   www.bloomberg.com/apps/news?pid= newsarchive&sid=awahZj_qyZDs

9   webarchive.nationalarchives.gov.uk/ 20111005150656/http://www.hmrc.gov.uk/ stats/mtg-2011.pdf HMRC only started calculating

the tax gap this decade, after pressure from Richard Murphy, who coined the phrase and made the first calculations. He now estimates the gap to be between £70billion and £120billion: www.taxresearch.org.uk/Documents/PCS TaxGap.pdf file:///Users/Zoe/Downloads/5528_tax_justice_report_lores_1.pdf

10 www.stokesentinel.co.uk/Help-starving-kids/story-21314618-detail/story.html
    The depressing thing is that when you say 'Stoke Bin-Kids', a lot of people know what you mean

11 Prem Sikka has shown many times that the average length for holding a share has gone from five years in the mid-60s to two years in the mid-80s to three months in 2008. theconversation.com/empowering-shareholders-wont-revolutionise-corporate-culture-4938

12 www.equalitytrust.org.uk/resources/our-publications/course-correction-pre-distributive-case-50p-top-income-tax-rate

13 Here is a list of tax avoidance schemes that were banned in July 2014: www.gov.uk/government/uploads/system/uploads/attachment_data/file/326655/Reviewed_Tax_Avoidance_Scheme_Ref__Numbers_July_2014.pdf 1200 schemes in total, with 10,000 company members and 33,000 individuals, one of whom was Andrew 'Plebgate' Mitchell, who reacted dismissively to the revelation.

14 Nicholas Shaxson, *Treasure Islands*, Bodley Head, 2011

15 www.finfacts.ie/irishfinancenews/article_1025198. shtml

16 www.starbucks.co.uk/blog/starbucks-commitment-to-the-uk/1240

17 www.igmchicago.org/igm-economic-experts-panel/poll-results?SurveyID=SV_2irlrss5UC27YXi

WAS YOUR EDUCATION BOG-STANDARD?

1 Jon Rabash, George Leckie, Jennifer Jenkins, Rebecca Pillinger, *School, Family, Neighbourhood: Which is Most Important to a Child's Education?*, Significance, 2010

2 Stephen Gorard, Rita Hordosy, Nadia Siddiqui, *How Stable Are School Effects, Assessed by a Value Added Technique?*, International Education Studies, 2013

3 Christopher Lubienski and Sarah Lubienski, *School Sector and Academic Achievement*, American Educational Research Journal, 2006

4 Chang-Tai Hsieh and Miguel Urquiola, *When Schools Compete, How Do They Compete?* National Bureau of Economic Research, 2003

5 www.oecd.org/pisa/pisaproducts/pisainfocus/48482894.pdf

6 www.isc.co.uk/educational-news/2014/07-July/2014-07-28#article9

7   cdn.yougov.com/cumulus_uploads/
    document/3xah64ycrs/YG-Archive-NUT-parents-
    survey-180313.pdf

8   physicsfocus.org/lies-damned-lies-ofsteds-
    pseudostatistics/

9   www.theguardian.com/education/2013/apr/15/
    margaret-thatcher-education-legacy-gove

10 schoolsweek.co.uk/secondary-opens-with-17-
    pupils/

11 www.gov.uk/government/uploads/system/uploads/
    attachment_data/file/301146/Investigation_report_
    Silver_Birch_Academy_Trust.pdf

12 www.dailymail.co.uk/news/article-2799380/170-
    000-year-superhead-blew-4-500-new-desk-1-700-
    fridge.html

13 www.theguardian.com/education/2014/nov/13/
    nearly-half-academy-trusts-related-party-
    transactions

14 Robert Barrington and Nick Maxwell, *Corruption
    in UK Local Government: the Mounting Risks*,
    Transparency International, 2013

15 Hilariously weak Written Statement made by: The
    Minister of State for Schools (Mr David Laws) on
    25 Nov 2014

16 Jane Wills, David M Watson, Jim O'Connell, Clyde
    Chitty, Jamie Audsley, *Citizen Schools: Learning To
    Rebuild Democracy*, IPPR, 2013

17 Tony Blair at the Labour Party Conference, Septem-
    ber 1999

DID AN IMMIGRANT STEAL YOUR JOB?

1 MAC, *Migrant Seasonal Workers*, May 2013

2 Ibid.

3 www.nomisweb.co.uk/census/2011/DC2101EW/
   view/1946157207?rows=c_ethpuk11&cols=c_age

4 Joanna Blythman, *Shopped*, Harper Perennial, 2010

5 mainlymacro.blogspot.co.uk/2014/10/uk-
   immigration-and-social-attitudes.html

6 www.insidehousing.co.uk/care/g4s-has-10-days-
   left-to-rehouse-349-people/6524444.article

7 Bridget Anderson, *Us and Them: The Dangerous
   Politics of Immigration Control*, Oxford University
   Press, 2013

8 Commission for Social Care Inspection, 2005

9 Stephanie Snow and Emma Jones, 'Immigration
   and the National Health Service', History and
   Policy Magazine, March 2011

10 *Evening Standard*, Joshi Herrmann, 23 January
   2012

11 www.theguardian.com/commentisfree/2013/
   oct/14/benefit-tourism-facts-european-
   commission-report

12 www.migrationobservatory.ox.ac.uk/top-ten/5-
   local-area-statistics

13 Christian Dustmann, Tommaso Frattini and
   Caroline Halls, *Assessing the Fiscal Costs and
   Benefits of A8 Migration*, UCL, 2009

14 www.theguardian.com/uk-news/2014/oct/19/ immigration-policy-ukip-restrictions-european-union

15 Stephen Nickell and Jumana Salaheen, *The Impact of Immigration on Occupational Wages: Evidence from Britain*, Federal Reserve Bank of Boston, 2008

16 Bridget Anderson, *Us and Them: The Dangerous Politics of Immigration Control*

17 Danny Dorling, *Unequal Health, the Scandal of Our Times*, Policy Press, 2013

18 MAC, *Migrants in Low Skilled Work*, 2014

19 www.appgmigration.org.uk/sites/default/files/ APPG-Migration_Family_Migration_Two_Years_ On.pdf

20 'Banker's Wife Lifts the Lid on London's Elite', *The Times*, October 12, 2014

21 Julian Baggini, *Welcome to Everytown*, Granta, 2008

22 HM Government, *International Education – Global Growth and Prosperity*, 2013

23 ONS, *Europe Remains the Dominant Market for UK Export and Import of Services*, 2013

24 UK Council for International Student Affairs, International Student Statistics, 2014

25 www.theguardian.com/uk-news/2014/oct/28/ david-blunkett-praises-michael-fallon-swamped-migrants

26 UNHCR, *Convention and Protocol Relating to the Status of Refugees*, 1951

27 Dr Scott Blinder, *Migration Observatory: Asylum*, July 2014

28 Three companies were in receipt of asylum housing contracts from the UK Border Agency worth £1.7billion: G4S, Serco, Clearel. www.publications.parliament.uk/pa/cm201314/cmselect/cmhaff/71/71vw32008_HC71_01_VIRT_HomeAffairs_ASY-57.htm

29 www.childrenssociety.org.uk/sites/default/files/tcs/asylum_support_inquiry_report_final.pdf

30 www.theguardian.com/theguardian/2012/dec/14/asylum-seekers-contractors-mothers-housing?INTCMP=SRCH

31 Lisa Doyle, *28 Days Later, The Experiences of New Refugees in the UK*, Refugee Council, 2014

32 Professor Sir Al Aynsley-Green, *The Arrest and Detention of Children Subject to Immigration Control*, 11 Million, 2010

33 www.parliament.the-stationery-office.co.uk/pa/cm200809/cmselect/cmhaff/970/09091604.htm

WHO BROKE THE BANK?

1 Warren Mosler, *Soft Currency Economics*, MMT, 1995

2 Michael Mendelson, *The UK in 2011 is not Canada in 1996*, Caledon Institute, 2011

3   moneyweek.com/merryns-blog/abolish-tax-relief-on-charitable-giving-58416/

4   Commons Library Standard Note, 'Measures to Reduce Housing Benefit Expenditure', 11 October 2013

5   Everybody knew

6   Crisis Policy Briefing, *Housing Benefits Cuts*, 2013 www.jrf.org.uk/sites/files/jrf/conditional-benefit-systems-full.pdf

7   David Cameron keeps claiming to be 'paying down the debt'. The UK Statistics Authority keeps correcting him, most recently in the letter from Andrew Dilnot to Chris Leslie MP, dated 3 October 2014. It makes no odds at all; from the Prime Minister's perspective, if 100% of people heard it, and 50% heard the correction, that's 50% of people who still believe it. It's not very Prime Ministerial

8   www.ons.gov.uk/ons/dcp171778_344397.pdf

9   www.bankofengland.co.uk/education/Documents/targettwopointzero/t2p0_qe_supplement.pdf

10 Alan S Blinder and Mark Zandi, *How The Great Recession Was Brought to an End*, Moody's Analytics, July 2010

11 www.telegraph.co.uk/finance/newsbysector/banksandfinance/10664372/RBS-has-lost-all-the-46bn-pumped-in-by-the-taxpayer.html

12 Wolfgang Streeck, *The Delayed Crisis of Democratic Capitalism*, Verso, 2014

13 www.tuc.org.uk/economic-issues/corporate-
governance/city-bonus-pool-twice-big-its-
corporation-tax-bill

14 Stewart Lansley, *Inequality, the Crash and the Ongoing Crisis*, Political Quarterly, 2012

15 Brett Scott, *The Heretics' Guide to Global Finance*, Pluto Press, 2013

16 www.bis.org/press/p131107.html

17 Prem Sikka, *Banking in the Public Interest*, CLASS, 2014

18 Andrew Haldane, 'Control rights (and wrongs)', Wincott Annual Memorial Lecture, London 2011

19 ftalphaville.ft.com/2013/03/22/1435062/cyprus-
just-pop-the-red-pill-please/

20 www.theguardian.com/business/2014/jun/07/
inside-murky-world-high-frequency-trading

21 www.fca.org.uk/news/barclays-fined-38-million-
for-putting-16-5-billion-of-client-assets-at-risk

22 www.barclays.com/content/dam/barclayspublic/
docs/InvestorRelations/ResultAnnouncements/
2014Q3IMS/BarclayplcQ32014IMS.pdf

23 fca.org.uk/news/barclays-fined-26m-for-failings-
surrounding-the-london-gold-fixing

24 www.ft.com/cms/s/0/2a4479f8-c030-11e1-9867-
00144feabdc0.html#axzz3LUlM13Vu

25 www.protiviti.co.uk/en-US/Documents/Resource-
Guides/Guide-to-US-AML-Requirements-
5thEdition-Protiviti.pdf

26 www.theguardian.com/business/2014/oct/31/
royal-bank-of-scotland-rbs-sets-aside-400m-forex-
rigging-fines

BUT DOESN'T THE PRIVATE SECTOR JUST DO EVERYTHING BETTER?

1 James Meek, *Private Island*, Verso, 2014. This is a
brilliant book about privatisation, by the way. If
utilities are your main thing, go and read his and
then come back and finish this.

2 www.nao.org.uk/wp-content/uploads/2014/04/
The-privatisation-of-royal-mail.pdf

3 www.telegraph.co.uk/news/uknews/road-and-rail-
transport/11043893/Rail-fare-hike-Britain-vs-rest-
of-Europe.html

4 Michael Moran, *The Great Train Robbery: Rail
Privatisation and After,* Centre for Research in
Socio-Cultural Change, 2013

5 James Meek, *Private Island*, Verso, 2014

6 Dieter Helm, *Tradable RABs and the Split Cost of
Capital*, OFGEM, 2008

7 James Meek, *Private Island*

8 www.theguardian.com/politics/2001/jun/05/
election2001.politicalcolumnists2

9   HM Treasury, 'Private Finance Initiative Projects: Summary Data', 2013

10 www.theguardian.com/politics/datablog/2010/nov/19/pfi-public-finance

11 Allyson Pollock and David Price, *Public Risk for Private Gain?* Unison, July 2004. Pollock has been knee deep in this data since the mid-nineties. You can hear her academic prose getting more and more elegantly exasperated in every report. It would be funny, if you didn't have to live here

12 National Audit Office, 'Improving the PFI Tendering process', HC (2006–07) 149, pp12–15, 8 March 2007

13 'There is considerable evidence that very large schemes are more attractive to the private sector.' Wallsgrave Hospitals NHS Trust: Full Business Case, August 1996

14 National Audit Office: 'The Immigration and Nationality Director's Casework Programme', HC 277, March 1999

15 National Audit Office: 'The cancellation of the Benefits Payment Card Project', HC 857, August 2000

All case studies from *Public Risk for Private Gain?* Allyson Pollock and David Price, Unison, July 2004

16 www.bankofengland.co.uk/education/Documents/resources/postcards/qecomp.pdf

17 Josh Ryan Collins, Tony Greenham, Giovanni Bernardo, Richard Werner, *Strategic Quantitative Easing*, New Economics Foundation, 2013

18 www.theguardian.com/politics/2014/sep/11/
    poison-pill-probation-contracts-moj-serco-g4s

19 docs.google.com/spreadsheet/ccc?key=
    0AtE8tc3zky-CLdFVBNWFGbGdCeVd
    1YWhkcDRFRFLTaHc&hl=en#gid=3

20 Jim and Margaret Cuthbert, *Lifting the Lid on PFI*,
    Scottish Left Review, 2012

21 *The Size of the UK Outsourcing Market*, Oxford
    Economics, 2011

22 ISG, EMEA Outsourcing Index, July 2014

23 National Audit Office, *The Role of Four Contractors
    in the Delivery of Public Services*, November 2013

24 www.populus.co.uk/wp-content/uploads/2014/09/
    Populus_IfG-Government-Policy-Polling_Data-
    Tables.pdf

25 G4S and the Tagging Scandal: www.bbc.co.uk/
    news/uk-26541375

26 G4S and the Olympic Fiasco: www.telegraph.co.uk/
    finance/newsbysector/supportservices/10070425/
    Timeline-how-G4Ss-bungled-Olympics-security-
    contract-unfolded.html

27 Still G4S: www.mirror.co.uk/news/uk-news/jimmy-
    mubenga-death-deportee-cried-4566461

28 EHCR, *Close to Home, An Inquiry into Older People
    and Human Rights in Home Care*, 2012

29 Ofsted: *Children's Social Care Providers and
    Places*, November 2014

30 Quoting an unpublished interview with Ann Coffey MP; broader context in *Who Cares? Cross Boundary Looked After Children*, Lancashire County Council, 2011

31 www.gov.uk/government/news/councils-told-to-stop-housing-vulnerable-children-miles-away-from-home

32 www.publications.parliament.uk/pa/cm201314/cmselect/cmhaff/68/68we11.htm#footnote_6

33 Hilary Wainwright, *The Tragedy of the Private, the Potential of the Public*, Public Services International and the Transnational Institute 2014

DID WE LEAVE IT TOO LATE TO AVERT THE ENVIRONMENTAL APOCALYPSE?

1 www.theguardian.com/environment/2013/may/16/climate-research-nearly-unanimous-humans-causes

2 www.ipcc.ch/report/ar5/

3 Obviously, in collaboration with a ton of other people. I edit them out for brevity

4 www.theguardian.com/environment/2014/oct/13/owen-paterson-proposal-to-scrap-climate-change-act-is-bonkers

5 www.lse.ac.uk/GranthamInstitute/wp-content/uploads/2014/03/PB-onshore-wind-energy-UK.pdf

6 Reg Platt, *A New Approach to Electricity Markets*, IPPR, 2014

7   Michael Van Auken and John Zellner, *Updated Analysis of the Effect of Passenger Vehicle Size and Weight on Safety*, Dynamic Research Inc, 2011

8   IPCC Mitigation of Climate Change, Working Group III

9   Reg Platt, *A New Approach to Electricity Markets*, IPPR, 2014

10 *Jühnde*, Wildpoldsried, Feldheim: Berliners voted on it in 2013 but bottled it

11 Shelagh Whitley, *Time to Change the Game: Fossil Fuels and Subsidy*, Overseas Development Institute, 2013

12 www.gov.uk/government/statistics/annual-fuel-poverty-statistics-report-2014

13 www.gov.uk/government/policies/improving-the-energy-efficiency-of-buildings-and-using-planning-to-protect-the-environment/supporting-pages/code-for-sustainable-homes

14 www.gov.uk/government/collections/english-housing-survey

15 Tamasin Cave and Andy Rowell, *A Quiet Word: Lobbying, Cronyism and Broken Politics in Britain*, Random House, 2014

16 *Which Road Ahead?* Government or Market, Institute of Economic Affairs, 2012; *A New Road Ahead*, Institute of Directors, 2014; *Bold Thinking; Roads Report*, CBI, 2012; The Right Road to Reform, RAC Foundation, 2014; The Road

to Growth, Localis, 2013; *Building Confidence in Infrastructure*, Reform, 2012; *State of the Nation Infrastructure*, ICE, 2014. I'm only stopping because the point is made, not because this is a full list. Oh no

17 Elizabeth Cox and Helen Kersley, *Royal Docks Revival*, New Economics Foundation, 2014

18 Framework Convention on Climate Change: Copenhagen Accord, 2009

19 www.theguardian.com/world/2010/nov/29/wikileaks-embassy-cables-key-points

20 www.spiegel.de/international/world/copenhagen-climate-cables-the-us-and-china-joined-forces-against-europe-a-733630.html

21 White House: 'Fact Sheet, President Obama's Climate Action Plan', 2013

22 data.giss.nasa.gov/gistemp/tabledata_v3/GLB.Ts+dSST.txt

Acknowledgements

I owe Paul Myerscough and Ben Rowell such a debt of gratitude that the easiest thing would be never to see them again. Thanks also to Neal Lawson, Bruce Davis, Aditya Chakrabortty, Tom Clark, Tim Lusher, Danny Dorling, Becky Gardiner, Dawn Foster, Marie O'Riordan, Julia Walsh, Polly Russell, Rochelle Monte, John McMullan, David Graeber, Neil Foster, Carys Afoko, Allyson Pollock, Laura Gardiner, Darren Brook, Fran Boait, Helen Kersley, Tony Greenham, Richard Murphy, Chris Hewett, Anna Thomas, Jo Brand, Lisa Nandy, Kath Viner, Duncan Exley, Charlotte Moore, Bill Kerry, Robert Sharples, Warwick Mansell, Laura McInerney, Ralph Berry, John Roberts, Celia Richardson, Carlos Vargas-Silva, Rob McNeil, Bridget Anderson, Su Maddock, Hilary Wainwright, Chawada Matiwala, Alex Little, Linda Burnip, Simon Duffy, Stewart Lansley, Molly Scott Cato, Ha-Joon Chang, Guddi Singh, Euan Holloway, Ann Coffey, Ed Matthew,

Juliet Davenport, Ashley Dobbs, Jasmine Stone, Alastair Harper, Aidan Pettitt, Stuart Wilson and Alex Hilton. Both Sophie Lambert and Emma Mitchell deserve something much more than thanks, more like homage. These people don't help me at all, but I'd find it very difficult to do anything without them: Stacey Williams, Chris Jepps, Thurston Jepps and Harper Jepps.